The Introduction to Greek and Roman History Series

The Introduction to Greek and Roman History Series

Featuring

Golden Laurels, Silver Seas: A Concise Survey of Greek History from the Bronze Age to the End of the Hellenistic Period

and

The Wolves of Mars: An Introductory History of Rome from the Rise of the Monarchy to the Fall of the Western Empire

Aeon History

uxori liberisque

and

fratri parentibusque

Contents

Golden Laurels, Silver Seas

*A Concise Survey of Greek
History from the Bronze Age to the
End of the Hellenistic Period*

Aeon History

Introduction

As the sun sinks behind the distant hills of Greece, you gaze across the bustling city of Athens. Leaning against a gigantic column of the Propylaea, the Acropolis' mighty gate, you imagine yourself standing there nearly 2,500 years ago. What had it looked like, unobscured by the veil of history?

Long ago, the groves of cypress, pine, and fir were thicker, filling the valley between the grey hills. Bracketed by outflung land, the Saronic Gulf's blue-grey waters lapped the shore, bringing ships from all over the world. Behind you, the Acropolis rose in the height of its glory with painted statues, garlanded pillars, and walkways thronged with philosophers and scholars. The whole world came to Greece.

Even today, you can almost feel their presence. The weight of the years has taken its toll on the Acropolis and other ancient Greek structures, but many columns still stand as a testament to the ancient Greeks who laid the foundations for Europe, and the modern world. Here, the first form of democracy arose, western philosophy began to inquire, and the residents helped draw political lines that would impact Europe and the Middle East for millennia.

Athens: The Birthplace of Western Culture

Ancient Greece. The name conjures up many images—philosophers, statues, crumbling stone monuments, and distant wars. Life in Ancient Greece was very different from what we are used to today. It was politically fragmented, with over 1,500 city-states dotting the mountainous landscape. Each of these city-states, called a *polis* by its inhabitants, had its own government and way of life, creating a diverse cultural landscape (National Geographic Society, 2022).

Athens, one of the larger *poleis*, was home to roughly 300,000 people during its height in the 5th century BCE. Compared to modern-day urban areas like Tokyo, Beijing, or Mexico City, that might not seem like a lot of people, but in ancient times, Athens was a major hub (Williams, 2008). Like Memphis, Babylon, and Rome, Athens was ground zero for major changes in the ancient world.

Some of these changes had long-term impacts on how we interact with each other today. The Greek alphabet evolved over time, was adapted, and finally used in most European languages. Using their language, ancient Greeks transformed academic knowledge, creating libraries, defining fields of study, and formulating theories that would be remembered for centuries.

Within this society, the fathers of philosophy, medicine, and history helped to create the frameworks of knowledge through which we still view the world. These scholars also preserved ancient tales, researched medicine, and synthesized common knowledge, which they spread to all corners of the ancient world.

Studying Ancient Greece, therefore, shows us where many of our fundamental presuppositions come from. Moreover, it allows us to understand how those ideas developed. We can learn why philosophical and political theories evolved, what life was like before the Golden Age of the Greek Empire, and how those changes still impact our world. In studying the decline of Ancient Greece, we can also gain perspective on the dynamics of nation and culture-building and what leads to the fragmentation of great empires.

Ancient Greece has a lot to teach us. Through the stories of its early history, the rise of its empire, and its eventual decline, we can learn about the people who transformed the world—both yesterday and today.

Voices of the Past

Biology. Geology. Mythology. Theology. All of these words are based on Ancient Greek. Their ending, "logy," comes from the Greek word "logos," which is related to ideas around reason, order, logic, and the power of words.

Interestingly, this word is linked to "lego," the Greek verb for "I speak" (*Logo-*, 2017). For the Ancient Greeks, the importance of one's voice was directly linked to the exercise of reason and logic. From these concepts arose a culture that transformed the world with new ideas of how to govern, organize society, and engage with culture.

Fast forward to the 21st century. In a world that views voting, personal property, and safety from predation as natural rights, Ancient Greece might feel like a whole other world. It's all too easy to lose the vitality and energy of the culture that *invented* the ideas we take for granted in a mountain of dates and names. History can become stale. In worst-case scenarios, it simply ends up a vehicle for our own perceptions and ideologies.

However, by exploring and experiencing the life and times of the Ancient Greeks with an open mind, we discover a complex, chaotic, and colorful world. But the Greeks talked about their experiences. They employed the power of the *logos*, revealed their hopes and dreams, and shared the challenges of their lives. Now, we can benefit from their wisdom.

Navigating Greek History

History helps us understand ourselves, gain perspective on our experiences, and find common ground with the people around us. Unfortunately, many present it as a slog. You probably know some important dates and names from school, but you might wonder, what's the point?

Golden Laurels, Silver Seas provides a concise, engaging, and accessible overview of Ancient Greece's history. Yet, it tries to balance these qualities with a comprehensive approach, covering all the most important elements of ancient Greek culture. Therefore, we believe it is a valuable resource for anyone interested in this fascinating period of history.

In this book, you will:

- discover engaging narratives told in chronological order with cultural insights, historical context, and important details.

- gain a comprehensive understanding of Ancient Greece's history, culture, politics, and contributions to the world.

- get to know the famous figures of Ancient Greece, from Homer to Herodotus, from Socrates to Aristotle, from Alexander the Great to Pericles.

- enjoy engaging and dramatic accounts of significant events like the Trojan War, the Battle of Thermopylae, and the death of Socrates.

- save time and effort by accessing all the important information about Ancient Greece in a concise, easy-to-read format.

We sincerely hope that *Golden Laurels, Silver Seas* will provide you with a comprehensive, easy-to-read introduction to Ancient Greece. Non-specialist readers of all levels should find it accessible, whether they are seasoned history buffs, or young newcomers to the heroic stories of Athens, Sparta, and many other Greek tales from the past.

Note: All translations from ancient sources are by Aeon History.

Part 1: Prehistory to the Bronze Age Collapse

Chapter 1: The Early Aegean

Across the silver sea and under blue skies filled with thin white clouds, a ship rollicks from one white-capped wave to another. The world seems a vast emptiness, dotted only by small rocky islands covered in gorse, grass, cypress, and pine. The ship pays no heed. They are moving northward to where the distant grey-green humps of the mountains beckon.

The men and women in this ship are from Crete, the largest of the Greek islands. They have come searching for new land. Dark-haired, dark-eyed, and gorgeously dressed in vibrant clothing, the Minoans (as we call them) represent the most advanced civilization in the region from the late 3rd to the early 2nd millennium BCE. Their remaining sculptures suggest that the women often wore floor-length gowns that fell in sectioned pleats, while their tops swooped to their waistline with plunging V-necks, revealing their breasts. The men, kilted and lightly armored, also wore cloaks and plumed helms.

During a time when civilizations hunkered down along the edges of mighty rivers, the Minoans were one of the few peoples to risk the intemperate seas. Their ships carried their culture throughout the Aegean and beyond. They produced artistic frescoes, elegant gold jewelry, finely crafted pottery, labyrinthine palaces, and enjoyed lively sports. Trade, religion, politics, and agriculture flourished under their care. The mysterious early civilizations of Crete and Greece laid the foundation for the future of Europe, and the rest of the world.

The Greek Landscape

Between North Africa and Europe, the Mediterranean Sea stretches. Toward the east, it meets the shores of modern-day Egypt, Israel, Syria, Lebanon, and Turkey. In that corner of the Mediterranean, to the northwest of Turkey, the Mediterranean Sea opens into a smaller sea that spreads between Greece and Turkey. This is the Aegean, dotted with the beautiful islands of Santorini, Rhodes, Chios, and Naxos.

General groupings can help to visualize island locations a bit easier. The Ionian Islands sit in the Ionian Sea, to the west of mainland Greece. The Aegean Sea is home to the Saronic, the Sporades, the Cyclades, and the Dodecanese island groups.

The Saronic Islands are wedged between Athens and the east coast of the Peloponnese. The Sporades hug the eastern coast of mainland Greece north of Euboea. The Cyclades are particularly important for early Greek culture and dwell in the center of the Aegean to the north of Crete. Finally, the Dodecanese Islands stretch southeast toward modern Turkey, culminating in Rhodes, the largest of the group.

Looking more closely at the Greek mainland, we see that it is a peninsula: to the east, the Aegean Sea;

to the south, the Mediterranean; to the west, the Ionian.

Down the middle of this peninsula runs the massive Pindus Mountain range, the lower reaches of the larger Dinaric Alps of the Balkans. Other mountain ranges are found in the northeast of Greece, such as the Voras Mountains. The Peloponnese Peninsula also has its own Taygetus Mountain range. The tallest of the mountains, Mount Olympus, reaches an elevation of just under 9,500 feet. Remote and majestic, Mount Olympus became connected with the realm of the gods (Ancient Greece Geography: Landscape & Map, 2023).

At lower altitudes, however, Greece remains firmly in the realm of men. The slopes, hills, and sheltered plains allow for olive trees, forests, and green land suitable for farming and herding. In the south of Greece, its clement Mediterranean weather means that winters are not very cold (rather, they are rainy), while the summers are hot and dry. In the north, winter feels colder, and snow falls. This variable climate encourages considerable biodiversity in a relatively small geographic area.

After taking all that Crete had to offer, early peoples looked to the north, to Greece, for more land and resources. Fertile valleys became a comfortable home for the early Bronze Age farmers. Crops of grapes, lentils, cabbage, onion, beans, and garlic were plentiful. Fruit and nut trees, like apples, almonds, pears, and figs, were also common. On top of that, savory herbs were also encouraged to grow—sage, mint, and thyme, among others.

Livestock could thrive as well, feasting on the plenteous greenery. Sheep and goats were capable of moving through mountainous terrain, so many ancient Greeks were sheepherders. Other, smaller domestic animals like pigs were common, but cattle were a bit rarer. These livestock provided early Greeks with milk and meat, and one day would become a source of cheese, wool, and leather. Horses, donkeys, and mules were used for transportation.

However, since Greece consisted of large mountain ranges and a widely spread archipelago, it was difficult for its earliest inhabitants to connect their communities into a cohesive whole. Many villages were isolated. Early Greeks who explored for more land and resources in modern-day southern Italy, Turkey, and North Africa were even less connected with the other ancient Greek towns. As a result, each settlement began to form its own culture, laws, and dialects. The birth of the *polis*, the city-state, had begun.

Early Civilization

As far back as the Stone and Bronze Ages, civilization has flourished in Greece and the islands of the Aegean. Over 2.5 million years ago, during the Paleolithic, or Old Stone Age, early humans began to slowly develop tools and early forms of culture. The Neolithic, New Stone Age, generally dated to 7,000–3,000 B.C.E., especially marked a period characterized by simple yet important advancements.

As suggested by the name, tools during this period were made of stone, and agriculture was basic. There are hints that religion and rudimentary culture were present, as well. Thanks to the remaining clay figurines of animals and women at burial sites and sanctuaries, we understand that society was beginning to form at this early stage.

The New Stone Age

Findings on a small island called Melos near Crete show that small boats were in use throughout the Neolithic. These early sailors were scavenging and collecting obsidian for toolmaking, and they were already farming basic grain, domesticating animals, and fishing for tuna. However, thanks to the climate and fertile lands in the area, more technological advancements were made, and humans began to spread throughout the region.

The great advance of the Neolithic was agriculture, and it spread from the Middle East to the Greek islands. Pottery was developed, and the art of firing ceramic vases began to allow for increased development in cooking. At the same time, new tools began to spring up—axes, chisels, and grinding stones. Agricultural crops expanded to oats, lentils, peas, and fruit. Arrowheads dug up in mainland Greece and the Cyclades point to the use of archery. Slings and clubs were used in other areas of the world at the time, including Egypt, so it is believed that these were also probably common.

By this point in time, communities were more settled. At Knossos on Crete as well as at other sites in the Cyclades and in Macedonia, archaeologists discovered ancient sites of Late Neolithic communities. Houses were made of stone, although they were simple rectangles or circular structures. More houses were built next to each other, forming the first acropolis towns; some towns had walls and up to 30 houses. Late Neolithic communities also boasted megarons, which were large central halls, as can be seen at Dhimini, in northern Greece.

With this growth, culture began to once again flourish. Pottery became more complex with patterns of various colors. Social hierarchies began to form, and dominant chiefs led their communities. However, civilization wasn't finished progressing yet.

A new era dawned—the Bronze Age (Townsend Vermeule & Hood, 1999).

The Bronze Age

The Bronze Age is usually dated from roughly 3,000–1,000 B.C.E. As more people traveled westward from the Mesopotamian cradle of civilization, they brought innovations in working with metals. Tools began to transform again as the people of ancient Greece learned how to use copper, bronze, and other metals.

However, since they were more isolated, the Cycladic settlements in the Aegean archipelago developed later. As a result, three cultures arose with many similarities but some distinctive differences— the Cycladic, the Helladic, and a Cretan civilization that would develop into the Minoans of this chapter's introduction.

Cycladic Civilization

The Cycladic culture flourished in the islands of the Aegean to the east of mainland Greece. Although their isolation resulted in some lags in advancement, these people shared many characteristics with other Bronze Age groups. Nevertheless, they were already defining their cultic practices. Family cemeteries began to spring up. White marble sculptures were carved, and stone vases were regularly created. White marble was particularly popular, so these islands had regular exports they could send to the mainland or to Crete.

Toward the middle of the Bronze Age, Cretans began to form definitive colonies on the island of Cythera as well as on Rhodes and in Anatolia, modern Turkey. While the two peoples seemed to coexist fairly peacefully, the original inhabitants of the Cyclades only borrowed pieces of Cretan culture. They maintained their own identity, as can be seen from the artifacts left behind.

During this period, pottery was decorated with flowers and animals, including depictions of bluebirds and dolphins. Frescoes, pictures of animals and fishermen, were discovered on the island of Thera. Paintings show that life, like many cultures around the world, involved a mixture of tranquil civilization and war (Townsend Vermeule & Hood, 1999).

Helladic Civilization

At the same time, the Helladic civilization flourished on the mainland. As in the Cyclades islands, houses became more complex and permanent. Towns began to grow. They began to add balconies to houses, and innovations in roofing led to the first creation of tiles in the region.

With a growth in population, early forms of government began to develop. Religious and cultural rituals became more complex. While burials on the mainland are less well-known, excavations reveal that mainland graves contained several bodies at a time, usually from close-knit families. Many of these tombs were cut into rocks or covered with heaps of stones, called cairns.

At Lerna, a Greek city, archaeological digs reveal that invaders entered the region from the middle of the Bronze Age onwards. After destroying the native settlements, rebuilding wasn't easy, resulting in more primitive housing. These new groups, who might have come from the Balkans or the Black Sea, brought new pottery, rituals, and ornamentation. They were likely the ones who introduced horses to Greece. The pottery was darker, and some of it had linear patterns, suggesting that the invaders shared some affinities with the culture they conquered.

Minoan Civilization

Throughout the Bronze Age, Cretan civilization also developed rapidly. Unlike the more distant communities on Greece's mainland and its islands, Crete had direct connections to Egypt and the Middle East. As a result, it developed alongside its neighbors, creating larger cities, hierarchal social structures, elaborate rituals, and beautiful art. However, the true flower of Cretan civilization would come to a head with the Minoan civilization. The Minoans were about to change the world (Townsend Vermeule & Hood, 1999).

Shrouded in myths, the start of the Minoan civilization begins with a tale of a mighty king. The legendary King Minos appears in myth as the son of Zeus. He is also linked to other deities and supernatural beasts, including the minotaur, a half-man, half-bull figure.

However, ancient historians like Thucydides and recent excavations in Crete suggest that Minos probably did exist, in a sense. The name "Minos" was probably a kind of title, similar to "President" or "King," used for rulers who also fulfilled religious functions.

There were other mysterious religious figures like the Snake Goddess, a gowned woman wearing the Cretan-styled bare-chested top while clutching snakes. Was this a unique goddess, or did this represent a special order of priestesses known to Crete? To this day, no one is certain (German, 2022).

What *is* known is that the legends surrounding bulls and snakes evolved into complex cultural rituals. From the worship of bulls came fascinating sports, including bull-jumping, where athletes would jump through the wide horns of a bull as a show of flexibility and courage.

According to Thucydides, the first King Minos expanded Cretan territory to the Cyclades islands. He expelled the original settlers and began to govern a growing empire of pirates. The Cretan's thalassocracy, a word which translates from the Greek as "sea power," wasn't focused on warfare. His goal was to trade, as evidenced by the number of Cretan artifacts discovered at sites around the Mediterranean.

From the palace in Knossos, the kings of Crete dominated trade in the Aegean Sea. They sent timber, wool, ceramics, and bronze vessels to Egypt, and sent daggers, lamps, and stone and bronze vessels to Cyprus. Italy and the northern lands around the Aegean Sea imported a variety of these Cretan products.

Thanks to the advancements and efficient production of the Minoans, their civilization lasted from around 3,000–1,100 B.C.E. Its art, architecture, tools, and rituals became more complex over time. Larger public buildings in Knossos were painted with gorgeous frescoes depicting religious, mythological, or everyday life scenes. Beyond art, the palace showcased higher advancements in city building and maintenance. The streets were paved, and water was brought to the palace in pipes.

Some archaeologists believe these "palaces" were more like central distribution hubs for the islanders. Most of the people lived in stone, wood, or brick houses, living off the land as farmers, lumberjacks, or artisans. Goldsmithing was one of the highlights of Cretan creativity. Since the Minoans were spread across the island, even larger hubs like Knossos did not raise thick city walls. Their wall was the Mediterranean Sea. Any who approached shore would easily be picked off by experienced Minoan sailors.

Since Crete was isolated but not too distant from larger nations, it was able to maintain independence for a while. Its navy, considered by later historians to be the first of its kind, colonized the Cyclades islands and spread to other corners of the Mediterranean Sea for trade. From this foundational civilization, Greece was given the knowledge of complex city construction, shipbuilding, and other forms of engineering. Studying the Minoans, they clearly impacted the world around them, but there is still so much we don't know (Movellán Luis, 2018).

Early Writing in Greece

The main reason why archaeologists and historians struggle to decipher the details of Minoan culture is because its language remains a mystery.

The first two widespread writing systems to appear in Greece are called Linear A and Linear B. While Linear B has been deciphered, Linear A remains a mystery. What is known is that both languages have been found on thousands of clay tablets and pottery, representing two distinct periods.

In the center and south of Crete, scholars have found many samples of Linear A. Its epicenter was Crete, between 1,900–1,500 B.C.E., though examples have been found on other Aegean islands, mainland Greece, and Anatolia. It was the common writing system used before the arrival of the Mycenaean Greeks.

Another hieroglyphic script was found in the north and eastern areas of Crete. There is debate about whether the two are related or not. To make matters even more confusing, a third script was also discovered by Italian archaeologist Luigi Pernier in 1908 on a famous artifact called the Phaistos Disk.

A few observations have been made about Linear A. Scholars surmise it comprises at least three vowels and around 90 common symbols. Like many Western writing systems, it reads left to right and top to bottom, in rows. The writing symbol is more abstract than Egyptian hieroglyphics and is drawn with lines, giving it the name Linear A (Hirst, 2018).

However, the difficulty in translation is that there is no obvious key. While there are many examples of Linear A, no Rosetta Stone-like translation has been found. Another problem is that Linear A texts are mostly just lists of words, not full sentences, which means that it isn't as easy to crack as many other languages.

Additionally, Linear A is an early representation of language writing systems built on syllables, like modern-day Japanese or Cherokee. When Linear B was deciphered, it helped identify some things, such as which symbol represented which sound. However, it can't tell what the sounds combined mean.

Overall, Linear B has proven less of a puzzle. Studies of the writing system prove it was borrowed from the Minoans around 1,600 B.C.E. and co-opted by the Mycenaeans, who had settled in southern Greece by about 1750 B.C.E. It was deciphered in the 1950s, and is considered to be the Mycenaean civilization's major writing system, representing their archaic dialect of the Greek language (Hirst, 2018).

In 2023, linguist Dr. Ester Salgarella pioneered new translation techniques to definitively prove the link between the two writing systems. Drawing on linguistics, archaeology, and paleography techniques, as well as a digital database, Dr. Salgarella was able to analyze the mysterious Linear A in detail. Salgarella hoped to provide a foundation for future linguists to work from, clarifying the symbols used and ensuring that no misclassification of signs would happen.

At the same time, Salgarella realized that both writing systems are directly linked. After a sharp decline of Minoan civilization shortly after 1500 B.C.E., there was a 50-year gap where no writing seemed to happen. During this period, there was a switch, where the writing more or less remained familiar, but the actual language it represented dramatically changed. The closest comparison today might be the difference between Cantonese and Mandarin Chinese, languages that share similar writing systems but whose pronunciation is different and whose underlying languages are not mutually intelligible (Claus, 2023).

There is a lot of work to be done. With the number of Linear A's symbols, it may never be fully decipherable. However, what linguists are able to guess is that the Minoan civilization thoroughly dedicated to record keeping, a testament to their mercantile tendencies. Their language system would inspire other people's writing and evolve into the Greek alphabet we are familiar with today—the origin of the Latin alphabet that is so influential in the modern world.

The Timeless Impact of Crete

We may never hear the voices of the Minoan civilization; their words are locked behind coded messages. Their myths and rituals may have been lost to time, and their enigmatic figures, like the Snake Goddess, may never be fully understood. One thing is for certain, however—the impact of their advancements on the early settlers of Greece. Not only did they help usher in a new age of metalwork, but they also diversified the world around them through their trade.

Between 1,500 and 1,400 B.C.E., the Minoan culture fell into sharp decline. A century is a long time to experience in person, but, in archaeological terms, it is almost like the Minoans disappeared overnight. Why? No one is certain.

Some posit that a volcano on Santorini disrupted the area, leading to earthquakes and potential tsunamis. Others suggest that signs of fire and desecration at the Knossos ruins point to marauders. Either way, the ancient city of Knossos fell, and Crete lost its grip on the Mediterranean Sea. Yet, in a way, their story was not over.

From the hands of the Minoans came knowledge and tools that empowered the next civilization—the Mycenaeans. Known for fortified palaces and military prowess, this new group dominated the Greek landscape for centuries, playing a central role in one of the most-remembered myths of antiquity— the Trojan War. In the next chapter, we will explore the rise of the Mycenaean civilization and the world of heroes and legends it left behind.

Chapter 2: The Mycenaean Age

"Goddess, sing the wrath of Peleus' son Achilles,
destructive, that brought boundless suffering to the
Achaeans.
For it sent to Hades many stouthearted souls
of heroes, and made their corpses carrion for all manner
of dogs and birds. Thus was the will of Zeus fulfilled."
(Homer, *Iliad*, 1.1-5)

This is a tale of desperate men, besieging one of the largest cities of antiquity—Troy. The famous warriors Achilles, Hector, Paris, and Odysseus clashed blades, leading armies in an epic siege. Pushed to the edge, the Greek army of King Agamemnon was faced with two choices: return home in disgrace, or risk everything to take the city.

Odysseus hatched a plan: Build a large hollow horse and pack it with the surviving heroes of the Greek army. Hopefully, the city would open its gates and bring it in. Despite the warnings of some Trojans, Odysseus's plan succeeded. With the help of one "survivor" who spun a tale, the Trojan people welcomed the gift and dragged the horse into the city. The rest is history. Sort of.

The historicity of the Trojan War remained unquestioned throughout antiquity and the Middle Ages. However, by the end of the Renaissance, the stories of Troy were considered myths. Nevertheless, archaeological data over the decades has filled in the gaps, bringing to light more information about the civilization that rose to dominance after the Minoan's decline.

The Mycenaeans were warriors, architects, and traders who left an indelible mark on Greek history and mythology. They dominated the late Bronze Age in Greece, and they played a central role in one of the most famous (hi)stories ever told—the Trojan War.

Rise of the Mycenaeans

Partially overlapping the Minoan culture, the Mycenaeans flourished in mainland Greece from 1,600–1,100 B.C.E. Although they stuck to the mountains and valleys of the peninsula, the Mycenaeans mingled with visiting Minoans. And even as the Minoan civilization precipitously declined after about 1450 B.C.E., the Mycenaeans persevered. They adapted the Minoan writing system to fit their needs and continued to develop the tools and advancements that the Minoans had introduced.

How closely related were the Mycenaeans to the Minoans? After extracting and analyzing DNA from 19 individuals, researchers discovered that the Minoans and Mycenaeans were, in fact, genetically related. They appear to have both come from Anatolia.

Furthermore, although the Minoan culture disappeared, significant traces of Bronze Age DNA (both Minoan and Mycenaean) have persisted in modern-day Greeks (*Ancient DNA Reveals Origins of the Minoans and Mycenaeans*, n.d.). However, the Mycenaeans didn't just impact the gene pool. They also helped to define Greek culture with their political organization and cultural development.

Although many people place the Mycenaean civilization after the Minoan, the truth is that the Mycenaeans were around for quite some time. For 150 years, between 1,600–1,450 B.C.E., the two civilizations flourished concurrently. It was only in the final 350 to 450 years of the Bronze Age that the Minoans fell into decline, allowing the Mycenaeans to take center stage. Some scholars even suggest it was the Mycenaeans who conquered the Minoans.

Either way, what is certain is that Mycenae began to dominate the Mediterranean Sea in matters of trade. They picked up where the Minoans left off, selling pottery and other articles to Egypt, Sicily, and the Mesopotamian civilizations. Like the Minoans, they also assumed ownership of the Cycladic islands.

At the same time, the Mycenaeans were very observant. Just as they learned from the Minoans, so they also learned from other neighboring civilizations. This allowed them to flourish for almost 500 years (Greek Boston, 2017).

Spreading across the Aegean Sea and the peninsula, the Mycenaeans built cities, including Mycenae, Pylos, Thebes, Argos, Athens, and Sparta. Mycenae, their largest city, was built on a high hill around 900 feet above sea level. On top of this hill, they built a massive citadel complete with walls, tombs, and large, palace-like buildings. Another important city linked to Mycenae is Athens. Some scholars believe that modern-day Greece's capital was originally a Mycenaean fortress.

The Mycenaeans didn't just settle the peninsula and the Cycladic islands. Relying on the naval advancements of the Minoans, they traveled further afield, eventually re-settling Crete and rebuilding Knossos. In this way, the fledgling civilization began to truly make an impact on the cultural landscape of the Aegean Sea (Cartwright, 2019).

Daily Life in Mycenae

What was life like in Mycenae and its far-flung outposts of hilltop citadels? Thanks to archaeological discovery and research, we are able to piece together a picture of Mycenae's vibrant culture. This was a tough, hard-working people who plied their trade around the Mediterranean.

With the flow of goods and wealth, farming and the domestication of animals continued, tools and weapons were developed further, settlements were able to solidify, and faith and political organization were codified. Their daily lives, marked by an increase in wealth and luxury commodities, were comfortable. The Mycenaeans might have been a profoundly warlike civilization, but the late Greek Bronze Age was a time of abundance.

Technological Innovations and Advancements

The greatest advancements heralded by the Mycenaeans were the formalization of monumental architecture like palaces and tholos tombs, the development of ceramics, and the evolution of Linear B script. Of course, the Minoans' influence continued to impact the Mycenaean people's production, but the Mycenaeans were invested in improving what they already knew.

The Mycenaeans improved architecture and defined how later Greek states would envision the building of structures. The Minoans had large cultural centers, to be sure. However, the more war-like Mycenaeans invested time and money to develop new types of walls, palaces, and fortified buildings in major cities like Mycenae, Thebes, and Tiryns. In these ancient ruins, you will find massive stone blocks placed to form thick walls, corbel-arched doorways, and large palace complexes.

Also, Mycenaean dig sites reveal that the civilization improved pottery and ceramic production. For as long as humans have eaten, they have also had to develop ways to store food. In Mycenae, ceramic production increased in innovation and intricacy. Pots like the "Warrior Krater" that have been dug up reveal that some were quite large and richly decorated with pictures of people or scenes of daily life.

Finally, the Mycenaeans appear to have adapted Linear A, the Minoans' writing system, to their dialect of Greek, producing Linear B. They preserved the Minoan tendency to keep meticulous records, but they also put writing on some of their pottery. This became one of the hallmarks of what we recognize today as Classical Greek pottery (Stirn, 2022).

Religion and Politics

Thanks to the development of agriculture and trade, humans had now been settled for quite some time. As populations grouped together to form larger settlements, society became more organized, hierarchical, and stable. Concepts like family lineage and class were now considered the norm.

Upper-class Mycenaeans would take part in military, religious, or political affairs. The lower class was more involved in trade, production, and farming. During this period of time, slavery also existed, and the lower classes, as well as women, were allotted fewer rights and privileges.

The Mycenaeans may not have had computers, the Internet, or cameras, but they were still involved in running governments, creating bureaucratic structures, and keeping records. Excavations of Mycenae have revealed that bureaucracy played a key role in Mycenaean daily life as well as in war.

From tablets and death masks, we now know that the head of each settlement was called the wanax. Ruling from a massive palace, the wanax was considered a priest-king who ruled over the city and its surrounding land. Other classes identified in Mycenaean culture include:

- ***lawagetas***: leaders or administrators

- ***heqetai***: aristocratic warriors

- ***telestas***: landowners

- ***demos***: common classes (artisans and tradesmen)

- ***doeri***: slaves and women

Perpetuating the common social hierarchies of their times, the Mycenaeans preferred to give importance to their wealthy aristocratic warriors and landowners. This social structure would persist for millennia (Roberts, 2023).

Archaeologists have also identified traces of structured religion during this period. In tombs, golden masks highlighted important figures, such as the *wanax*. Jewelry, swords, and crowns also reveal the beautiful craftsmanship of the Mycenaean people. Frescoes depict the Mycenaeans sacrificing animals on alters, enjoying feasts together, offering food, and pouring libations (wine or other liquids) to the gods. Carrying forward many Minoan ideas, the symbol of the bull persisted (Klaeser, 2021).

Life and Culture

During this period, art, fashion, and cultural activities flourished. In frescoes, jewelry, and pottery, we can see how the Mycenaean artisans enjoyed using geometric or decorative patterns like spirals, rosettes, and lines. Homes were decorated with sculptures, paintings, and figurines that hint at common scenes of daily life—boar hunts, bull leaping, and battle scenes.

Fashion and clothing at this time reflected Minoan influence. The women still wore floor-length gowns that were often tiered in multicolored flounces. Sometimes they would cover their plunging necklines with a thin bodice.

Men's fashion changed more drastically. Instead of wearing just a loin cloth and helmet, Mycenaean men began to wear boat-necked tunics that fell to their thighs or knees. This style would set a fashion trend that would last millennia (*What Did They Wear in Ancient Greece? Mycenaean Attire*, n.d.).

Trade

When the massive trading empire of the Minoans fell into ruin, the Mycenaeans stepped in and took over. Not only did they continue to trade with the isolated communities found among the islands of the Aegean Sea and the shores of Turkey, but they continued to ferry their wares to Sicily, Cyprus, and other nations and empires in the Middle East. In the ruins of these ancient civilizations, Mycenaean artifacts have been found—gold, glass, copper, and ivory. Other important exports included wine, olive oil, and perfume.

In order to produce special wares, the Mycenaean people had to import exotic goods. While there aren't a lot of Linear B records to read, archaeologists found other ways to figure out what these new traders ferried around the Mediterranean Sea. A shipwreck off the coast of Turkey tells a fascinating tale. It sank sometime during the 1300s B.C.E. Its hold carried raw materials that would have been turned into specialty items, such as ivory, glass disks, tin ingots, and copper. All of these discoveries point to a time of bustling activity, commercial life, and creative expression (Cartwright, 2019).

Mycenaean Architecture

With social and political organization as well as relative economic and agricultural stability, the Mycenaeans were able to focus on other ways to express themselves creatively, take part in rituals, or highlight their social standing. One of the most fascinating legacies of Mycenae and its sister fortresses was its architectural achievements. The walls, *tholos* tombs, and *megarons* have defined Greek notions of beauty, stateliness, and power for millennia.

As migrants or invaders themselves, Mycenaeans understood the importance of a good wall. Unlike the Minoans who did not employ fortification walls around their civic centers and palaces, the Mycenaean civilization wanted to keep new invaders out. One such type of wall, known as the Cyclopean wall, helped to protect Mycenaean interests.

In Mycenae, Thebes, and Tiryns, remnants of Cyclopean walls can still be seen today. Named after the giant Cyclops of mythology, the unworked blocks that made up these walls were so huge that it was said (by later Greeks) that only a Cyclops could lift them. Reaching to heights of 42 feet and widths of up to 26 feet, these walls were incredibly thick. They marked an increased interest in security and allowed the Mycenaeans to live in relative security during a time when other empires began to expand (Cartwright, 2019).

Besides building walls, Mycenaeans began to evolve their burial rituals. At first, they used shaft graves, dug into the rock, where they placed their dead with important belongings at the bottom of a vertical shaft that would then be filled in with rubble and dirt. Some shaft graves were dug close together in circles, signifying kinships. Later on, however, horizontal tombs cut into rock and family sepulchers were built. These circular vaults, called *tholos* (plural: *tholoi*) tombs, were cut into hills and accessed by an arched door.

The largest of the tholoi are impressive, even today. The tholos at Mycenae called the "Treasury of Atreus" is around 50 feet in diameter and almost as high. The lintel of the doorway is an enormous monolith weighing 120 tons. The central circular room was used to house the tombs and later to conduct rituals. Even after the people connected to the dead were long gone, others would return to tholoi to continue rituals for hero-based worship (Hoffmann, 2000).

Mycenaeans also organized social and political spaces clearly. Their permanent settlements included massive palace structures for the *wanax* and society's elite, which followed common patterns. In the center of the palace, a large rectangular central hall, the *megaron*, would be erected to hold the *wanax*'s court.

Each megaron would have an entrance porch, a foyer or vestibule, and then the hall itself. In the center of the main hall, a round hearth surrounded by columns would be set into the floor, while above it a hole in the ceiling allowed for ventilation. The megaron would also have smaller versions for the queen as well as a host of side rooms for work, storage, and daily life activities.

A symbol of power and authority, the megaron's walls were limestone blocks covered with plaster; its ceilings were vaulted with wood and bronze. Painted with frescoes and other decorative motifs, the palace complexes spoke to a wealthy and artistic civilization.

Later in history, the Archaic and Classical Greeks would look to these forms for inspiration, and the Mycenaean palaces would become templates for Greek halls and temples. The power and art of the Mycenaean civilization would live on (Cartwright, 2019).

The Trojan War

The Mycenaens also left for posterity one other important thing—their stories. Classical and later Greeks didn't question the historicity of the Trojan War, neither did the Romans or Medieval Europeans.

But belief in the veracity of heroic tales about the war waned by the 19th century AD. For a long time, the story seemed implausible. Did it really happen? Or was it just some kind of folk hero tale, epic saga, or myth-inspired text?

Although there were many texts describing the events of the Trojan War, including Homer's famous works, the *Iliad* and the *Odyssey*, as well as Virgil's *Aeneid*, many scholars doubted that the events of these epic tales were real. Homer wrote in the 8th century B.C.E., 400 years after the events of the Trojan War, while Virgil, a Roman poet, lived much later, from 70 to 19 B.C.E., more than 1,000 years after the war. As a result, many scholars doubted the truth of their tales. Then, Heinrich Schliemann, a German archaeologist, revealed a massive discovery in the late 1800s—the fabled city of Troy.

The Story of Troy

The story of Troy, as told by Homer, was fantastical. There were gods, goddesses, handsome warriors, and beautiful queens. There was drama, manipulation, intrigue, and death. Homer and Virgil's writings depicted convoluted plots, highlighted ancient places, and described a war between two peoples. On one side were the Greeks, led by King Agamemnon of Mycenae and his brother King Menelaus of Sparta; on the other, the people of Troy, led by King Priam, and his sons Hector and Paris.

The siege of Troy lasted 10 years and resulted in many deaths on both sides. According to Homer and Virgil, Troy eventually fell due to cunning strategy and deceit. The Greeks, packed into a hollow horse, were dragged into the city. At nightfall, they emerged to lay the great city of Troy to waste.

While the stories of the Trojan War sound exciting, it was a matter of debate over centuries of scholarship. To begin with, the active presence of gods, like Poseidon, Athena, Aphrodite, and Zeus, sets the epic poems directly in the realm of myth. Furthermore, the famous people mentioned, like King Agamemnon and King Priam, hadn't been found in any ancient burial site.

Also, Homer's Iliad only focused on a short period near the end of the 10-year war. The Odyssey, set after the Trojan War, chronicled the return of Odysseus to his family home. Neither appeared to have been written with historicity in mind. As a result, scholars weren't certain whether to treat the stories about Troy as fact. It wouldn't be until the late 1800s that Troy was definitively identified.

Discovering Troy

In 1870, Heinrich Schliemann led a group of archaeologists at a dig site at Hissarlik in western Turkey on the shores of the Aegean Sea. As the team dug deeper, they began to reveal older layers of history. The layers revealed a pattern of settlement, wherein a city was abandoned, then new settlers would arrive at the ruins, fill them in, and then build on top. The process created what is known as a mound, or "tell." There was about 80 feet of debris to sift through in some places, but the team managed to locate Bronze Age ruins far below.

Over 46 buildings were uncovered. Further excavations revealed that a city 10 times larger than the citadel surrounded the central ruins that were uncovered. Was this Troy?

Schliemann's hunch may have been correct. The site's origins were dated as far back as 3,000 B.C.E. Signs suggested that one of the largest layers had been abandoned around 1,100 B.C.E., around the time later Greeks believed the war to have taken place.

If the poets and local lore about the dating of the Trojan War were correct, it would place this site as a reasonable location for Troy. What was clear was that during Homer's time in the 8th century, the city's ruins would have been visible, kindling the imagination of one of history's greatest poetic traditions. Over time, it was covered in debris, waiting for Schliemann to stumble across it (History.com Editors, 2023).

For some people, the site of Troy might not look particularly exciting. The statuary is in bad shape, weathered by wind and destructive human force. Many walls are intact, but beyond a few small areas, no vaulted palaces remain. Paving stones are cracked with grass, and only a few pieces are inscribed with ancient lettering. However, for scholars, the discovery of Troy rocked the world.

The idea that there had been many versions of Troy helped cement the concept of borrowed settlements and mounds, where later inhabitants would move in or build on top of older structures. It also allowed archaeologists and historians to properly study the permutations of Anatolian and Greek civilizations. It was clear that later Greek, Anatolian, Middle Eastern, and Roman populations revered the site as the fabled city. King Xerxes and Alexander the Great personally visited the area. Later on, Romans would go on pilgrimages to visit the place where Aeneas, the ancestor of Romulus and Remus, had started his own epic adventure.

Finally, the site of Troy was able to reveal what challenges the people of that time faced. Scholars were able to make some guesses as to what really brought about the fall of Troy—earthquakes and political conflict (Jarus, 2017).

The Significance of Mycenae

Given how distant the Mycenaean civilization lies in the past, the fact it had a massive long-term impact on Greece might sound extreme. However, by continuing to pursue the Minoans' trading, writing system, and commercial practices, the Mycenaeans were able to nurture the growth of human civilization in the Aegean. Their willingness to communicate with and learn from neighboring cultures allowed them to flourish.

In this way, their stories, later preserved by oral traditions, became the myths that later Greek culture wrote down. Furthermore, by preserving the budding system of coherent small urban centers, the Mycenaeans set the stage for political drama for centuries to come.

On top of that, we can see how the Mycenaeans perpetuated increasingly complex architecture and agricultural techniques. Their walls, agricultural terraces, gates, and bridges signaled the arrival of more established public spaces. Mycenaean architectural innovations would inspire Greek religious, civic, and military structures for millennia.

The Mycenaeans were one of the great Bronze Age civilizations, but even so, they would fall into dark times. When the Mycenaean Age came to an end, Greece entered a period of decline known as the Greek Dark Ages.

It was a time of cultural regression, but it also set the stage for the emergence of the Classical Greek civilization that would follow. In the next chapter, we'll explore the Greek Dark Ages and how they shaped the world of ancient Greece.

Chapter 3: The Bronze Age Collapse and Greek Dark Ages

A weathered shepherd whistles tunelessly as he follows his small flock of sheep along a narrow, dusty path. The sun is sinking behind the now-shadowed mountains. As he moves quickly down the path, making his way home, his gaze rests on ancient ruins rising on the hill.

Long ago, it was said, they had housed kings and warriors. Heroes had fought armies, and the gods themselves came down to meddle in the affairs of men. The shepherd shivers. But that's all they are, he reminds himself. Tales. There are no more heroes, kings, epic battles, or visits from gods. Greece is abandoned. Its darkest days have arrived.

After the fall of the Mycenaean civilization, Greece plunged into centuries of obscurity and silence—an age so dark that it would forever be enshrouded in myths, legends, and unanswered questions. From about 1,150–800 B.C.E., Greece experienced a difficult transition into the Iron Age. Trade contracted, and many of the advancements of the Minoans and Mycenaeans would be forgotten. Some, for a time. Others, forever. Most importantly, writing ceased.

During this period, the Greeks lost their social structures as their political leaders were removed, their population decreased, and their survival threatened. Culture-making was put on hold. But how did this happen? What caused such a drastic shift? The mystery only deepens (Mark, 2015).

The Dorian Invasion

Beginning with the advancements of the Minoan culture and iterating on what they had learned from their many neighbors, the Mycenaeans should have continued their upward trend, conquering new lands, establishing new trade routes, improving their military, and shoring up their defenses. However, for some unknown reason, the civilization collapsed over a period of about 200 years, from 1,200 to 1,000 B.C.E. For many scholars, the reasons for the decline of the Mycenaean culture are still not certain. One strong theory emerged—the Dorian Invasion.

The Causes and Effects of Collapse

What exactly happened to the Mycenaeans? Several theories have been suggested, ranging from climate change to natural disasters to direct human intervention.

Climate change has been a long-term factor in history-making. Difficult living conditions, such as an ice age or increased temperatures, can result in human migration. According to anthropologists and climate scientists, the Mediterranean Sea underwent a rapid cooling phase around 1,100 B.C.E. Consequently, less rain fell. The dry periods wrecked the Mycenaean economy and made it tougher to survive.

There are some hints that natural disasters may have hit the region hard, too. Earthquakes and volcanic eruptions disrupted civilization, causing devastation evidenced in the damaged walls of palace complexes. Broken pottery was also found, shattered in a way that points to earth-based disruption (*Decline of the Mycenaean Civilization (1250-1050 B.C.E.)*, 2022).

Finally, human patterns of migration, or invasion, may have unsettled the previously wealthy, advanced Mycenaeans. With population declines and the shifting of resources to basic survival, the Mycenaeans would have been swamped by incoming "Dorian" migrants, or the more war-like Sea Peoples who appeared during the same time period.

These two groups were less technologically and culturally advanced. Called the Dorian Invasion, this mass migration appears to have impacted the native Mycenaean culture, demolished the palace complex system, and led to a decline in cultural activity.

Theories About the Dorian Invasion

The word invasion brings to mind war. You might be envisioning armies charging down hills, pitched battles on the slopes of Greece's mountains, or perhaps long, punishing sieges. The Dorian Invasion, however, is a bit of a misnomer since there is no evidence of large-scale military involvement. The "invasion" would be more aptly named "migration," since the people who moved in with the Mycenaeans were not further advanced in military matters. The Mycenaeans were not conquered.

Historical accounts of this time by ancient historians are now considered to be unreliable at best. After all, knowledge of this period was passed down orally and may have suffered from errors accrued over time. Imagine a telephone game lasting centuries. Facts are certain to have been lost along the way.

Therefore, when Herodotus recounts "The Return of the Heracleidae," or the "Return of Hercules," many scholars suggest taking his story with a grain of salt. Hercules? Isn't he a myth? Indeed, many of the people involved in the story are considered mythical in nature or only barely representative of real people.

In Herodotus's story, Hercules's descendants decided to take back the Peloponnesian peninsula and reclaim Greece for their own. Their efforts were not initially rewarded with success. Several battles resulted in failure, and lives were lost. However, when they teamed up with the Dorians, the descendants of Hercules were able to take over the entire peninsula, thus plunging the original inhabitants into a dark age.

By all accounts, and from the evidence of ruins and artifacts dated to this period, no such invasion took place. It is clear, though, that the Dorians did come from the north, possibly Macedonia or

Thessaly. This part of the world was a large region. Today, it would cover the eastern edge of Albania, northern Greece, eastern Bulgaria, North Macedonia, and the southern portion of Kosovo. Still, even if a large portion of migrants appeared on the doorstep of Greece, the robust Mycenaeans should have handled it easily enough. Perhaps something even more devastating had happened—revolution.

Evidence of fires in the great palaces points to some kind of social upheaval. Some scholars believe that constant attacks from the Sea People, a piratical group, might have destabilized the region. Others suggest that in-fighting among the Mycenaean leaders may have torn the war-like civilization apart. Another theory still posits that an uprising of a slave class, which could have included Dorians, brought the social system down. Any of these theories explain why the upper class, including the elite warriors, disappeared so quickly, and why the entire peninsula was overrun with northern tribes (*Dorian Invasion*, 2023).

To this day, there has been no single satisfactory answer, leading many to believe that there may have been a confluence of events that triggered Mycenae's collapse. Regardless of how it happened, it is evident that the decline of the Mycenaeans and an increase of Doric culture signaled a rapid shift. Overnight, in archaeological terms, the world of ancient Greece had changed.

Life in the Dark Ages

Silence. Uncertainty. Struggle. Chaos. These are four words that many might attach to the Greek Dark Ages.

After millennia of keeping records and other writing, creative work, and trade, the post-Mycenaean landscape looks eerily silent in comparison. Archaeological digs have revealed the abandonment of city centers, pointing to an era of uncertainty and struggle. But was the Dorian Invasion as chaotic as some historians have made it out to be?

Social Structures Reorganized

With the Dorian Invasion, society was turned upside down. The *wanax* and the *heqetai* disappeared, leaving a power vacuum for any who might wish to seize control. Depending on the region, the migrating Doric culture either integrated with the native Mycenaeans or overruled them.

Corinth, Argos, and Rhodes saw the two merging cultures blend together relatively well. On the other hand, evidence in Crete and Sparta suggests that the incoming northern tribes ruled the native population through a militarized political system (Varsity Tutor, n.d.).

In other places, political organization crumbled even further with a return to tribal factions and large family clans. These kinship groups or households, known as *oikoi*, split up the regions and fragmented the more cohesive units that the Mycenaeans had built. In Nichoria, for example, archaeologists discovered that a previous Mycenaean town had been abandoned and then rebuilt as a smaller village a century later. Some artifacts at Nichoria suggested that the village had been led by a chieftain, but there was no significant gap in wealth between the leader and his village (McLean, n.d.).

Literacy and Arts Transformed

The state of visual and literary art throughout Greece's Dark Age provides a complex picture of loss and recovery. Since the previous rulers and elite were removed, access to the literacy of Mycenaean culture was lost. The spoken and written language of Linear B faded, replaced by Doric Greek.

This new dialect eventually adopted a new writing system. By the 700s B.C.E., the Phoenician alphabet was most widely used. It wasn't based on pictures, like pictograms, or syllables, like logograms, but instead introduced the idea of having a character for specific sounds. This was the Greeks' first alphabetic writing system (McLean, n.d.).

This change did not happen overnight. As a result, for a long period of time, no accounts were written, and literacy languished. Similarly, the arts also struggled at first as the two cultures figured out how to recover the lost advancements of the late Bronze Age.

That said, the Dorians had forms of art and architecture, as well. Dorian styles of poetry would impact forms of Greek tragedy. It was during this period that Homer wrote his famous epics. In 776 B.C.E., the Olympics were also held for the first time (*History of Greece: The Dark Ages*, 2023).

Dorian ideals of art were linked to simplicity, restraint, and large proportions that would later influence Roman architecture. Compared to the *megarons* and *tholoi* of the Mycenaeans, these new buildings might have seemed rudimentary, but the Dorian people's architecture spoke to a rebirth of creative vision.

Economy Redefined

Another common belief about the Dark Ages was that everyone became a bit poorer. This is true for the most part, as the social hierarchies crumbled and the necessary infrastructure to maintain trade also died. In the beginning, the remaining populations as well as the new migrants were more likely to focus on farming and raising livestock as a means to survive (Greek Boston, 2017b).

At first, these newly created communities couldn't trade or conquer other areas around the Aegean Sea. However, over time, the Dorian civilization began to reach across the ocean. They not only settled in the Cycladic Isles but also sailed further to Rhodes and Crete.

By the 700s B.C.E., trade was once again beginning to flourish. Archeological sites dated to the same period have revealed that the Levant, in particular, began to reestablish trade with the ancient Greeks. With the rise in economic stability, other cultural activities like making art, decorating homes, and investing in nicer burial sites also restarted (McLean, n.d.).

Athens Reborn

Compared to the breadth of the Minoan and later the Mycenaean civilization, the Dorian Invasion period was characterized by a lower population density. As noted before, this might have been due to natural disasters, civil war, or difficulties with farming during arid seasons. What is interesting is that major settlements appear to have been abandoned wholesale at first (Greek Boston, 2017b).

Not only were the palaces and military fortifications abandoned, but many of the major settlements fell into disrepair, some into complete abandonment. When archaeologists looked at the various ancient sites across the Peloponnese, they noted that 90% of the sites had been abandoned. This suggests that the population must have declined sharply (McLean, n.d.).

However, as time went on, the area began to fill once again. Some cities, like Athens, remained dominant. Athens, like a few others, managed to keep a certain level of wealth, and life went on as usual. Its rise to power would set the stage for a new world order.

A New World Order on the Horizon

While the Mycenaean civilization might be praised as being entrepreneurial and cultivated, there was an aspect of their society that was immensely rigid. The class system resulted in a serious divide between those who had power, those who had land, and those who had neither. That all changed during the Dorian Invasion.

With the disappearance of the elite leaders and warriors of the Mycenae, a more loose-knit formation emerged within the new communities. Once again divided by geography, these isolated settlements would form what would become known as the *polis*, or Greek city-state.

However, unlike the fortress settlements of Mycenae, the residents were much more independent, and the social stratification of the previous millennium relaxed slightly. Hereditary rule was forgotten, and new forms of government emerged, paving the way for Greece's first form of democracy (*History of Greece: The Dark Ages*, 2023).

The Origins of Homer

Although the people of Greece's Dark Ages were not writing books or making records, like all humans, they loved a good story. The practice of passing stories down by word of mouth was common during this time as the Dorians and Mycenaeans shared their tales of the past. Through the centuries, some of the best stories evolved into long tales of heroic warriors and the gods, perhaps recalling historical events of the earlier Mycenaean and Minoan civilizations.

Homer's Tales

As noted in the previous chapter, the tales of Homer were an attempt at inscribing oral traditions of mythical-historical accounts. Modern-day scholars initially believed it was no more than a myth because of the references to the Greek pantheon. The dates linked to Homer also suggested that the time period between Homer (8th century B.C.E.) and the actual events he recounted was over 400 years. Homer's two famous poems, the *Iliad* and *Odyssey* would inspire the ancient Greeks and form part of the backbone of Western literature. But their origin is problematic.

In the *Iliad*, Homer describes the war between the armies of King Agamemnon of Mycenae and King Priam of Troy. The source of the conflict was Menelaus's beautiful wife, Helen. According to the English playwright Christopher Marlowe, Helen was so beautiful, she had a "face that launched a thousand ships" (Marlowe, 1604).

When she left Menelaus to be with Paris of Troy, the king of Sparta and his brother Agamemnon decided to get her back. They gathered armies, and with a cohort of warriors, such as Achilles and Odysseus, they laid siege to Troy for 10 years. Many died on both sides, but eventually, relying on the cunning of Odysseus, the Greeks were able to deceive the Trojans, enter the city hidden in a wooden horse, and sack Troy.

In Homer's *Iliad*, the poet describes the first part of the war, the death of Paris's brother Hector at the hands of Achilles, and the treaty that brings the siege to a short pause. Virgil's work *Aeneid* describes in detail how the Greeks deceived Troy and the aftermath. Virgil's poem describes more of the connection between the Romans and Greek history, probably as a way to affirm the political and cultural legitimacy of Rome.

The other major poem Homer wrote, the *Odyssey*, focuses on Odysseus' return home. During this saga, Odysseus endures a long, winding journey home to Ithaca. It is filled with adventures and obstacles, which he has to overcome with his wisdom, experience, and cunning.

When he finally reaches home, he discovers that his wife is being courted by other men because she is considered a widow. However, his faithful wife and son, Penelope and Telemachus, are waiting for him. Together, father and son unite to kill the suitors and reestablish Odysseus as King of Ithaca (The Editors of Encyclopedia Britannica, 2019).

Oral Traditions

While we might find the stories of the *Iliad* and *Odyssey* exciting and inspiring, they are, unfortunately, not the complete picture. They are all that remains of a larger body of work that has been lost to time.

Most scholars believe that many stories were spoken and not written down during the earlier centuries of the Dark Ages. Passed down by word of mouth, the poems were probably memorized and shared by professional bards called *rhapsodes* who would stitch together stories from memorized poetic formulae. They may have been used as entertainment during religious festivals. In later periods, at school, they were some of the first stories read by students (Homer's World, 2011).

In many ways, the oral traditions (and then, later, Homer's poems) were similar to what we call historical fiction or historical epics. Like the "historical fiction" films *Braveheart* and *Gladiator*, these orally transmitted stories took the seeds of what might have been historical events and added a load of exciting drama and adventure that says as much about the culture producing the new versions as the original events the stories portray, perhaps more. Initially, this caused confusion among modern scholars, who saw the tales as simply made up.

However, with the discovery of the actual site of Troy, it became clear that oral poetry played an important role in culture-making during and after the Dorian Invasion. The poems highlight the sense of nostalgia that arose during the Dark Ages when Greeks looked back at a golden era for inspiration. These stories more than likely helped to unify the groups who settled in the area and to validate political ambitions as the city-states, the *poleis*, emerged at the end of the Dark Ages. Even more importantly, the passing down of oral tales allowed future Greeks to preserve the stories of the Dark Ages. During the Archaic Period, Homer's transcription of the poetry would play an important role in culture-making once again.

The Emergence of the Polis

In the last century of the Dark Ages, between 850–750 B.C.E., the previously loose-knit communities, isolated by mountains and sea, began to stabilize politically once again. However, instead of returning to the rigid hierarchies of the *wanax*, the *heqetai*, and the other ancient strata, the new communities, now formed of Dorian migrants and

Mycenaean natives, began to organize themselves into new forms of governance.

As before, the villages and cities struggled to form a single nation. The mountains and the Aegean Sea proved to be obstacles yet again for unity, particularly after the breakdown of the Mycenaean social order. The emergence of the *polis*, the city-state, formalized as one of the most important political frameworks in ancient Greece, each with its own unique cultural and political landscape.

While some city-states were ruled by monarchs, others were ruled by groups of select people, forming what is called an oligarchy. Less fortunate cities were seized by tyrants. Tyrannies generally did not end well, but for some of these cities, they were a welcome change from the anarchy and chaos of the previous centuries. Indeed, some poleis installed their tyrants by popular acclamation. The popular tyrants, in turn, often provided housing and jobs.

However, after years of upheaval, a new form of government took the stage—the first form of democracy. The democracy of these new city-states wasn't the same as the voting rights and processes that we enjoy today. However, the small advances leading out of the Greek Dark Ages signaled a step forward into a brand-new form of government that would change history and transform the world.

Darkness Before the Dawn

For a long time, scholars depicted Greece's Dark Age as a time when poverty ruled, literacy disappeared, and culture struggled to survive. While it is true that the Mycenaeans faced a time of economic and cultural struggle, new research and investigations reveal that the Dorian Invasion did not spell an absolute end.

Instead, the Dark Ages repositioned Greece economically, socially, and politically. As the Dark Ages lifted, a new dawn approached for Greece. The forthcoming era, known as the Archaic Period, ushered in unparalleled innovations in art, politics, and society. Join us in the next chapter as we explore the foundations of the classical civilization that would inspire the world.

Part 2: The Rise of the *Polis* and Classical Greece

Chapter 4: The Archaic Period

A wide grey road wound its way through the rolling green hills of Greece's countryside, past rustic farmhouses huddled in villages, and toward the walled fortification of an early city. Then, it arrived at the heart of every Greek *polis*—the *agora*.

The large square was filled with wooden stalls where the citizens of the *polis* gathered every day to do business. Here, they bought the latest catch of fish, bartered for cloth, pottery, and farm produce, and caught up on the latest gossip. Around the agora, other citizens involved in the governance of the city met—in the law courts, where disputes were settled; the stoa, where the citizens of the *polis* gathered to talk; the *bouleuterion*, where the city council met; and the *prytanikon*, where members of the council lived.

This was the heart of the *polis*, but also the heart of Greece. What fueled the emergence and expansion of the Greek city-states? By answering this question, we will understand how the many *poleis* transformed Greece and thus, the world.

The Foundation and General Characteristics of the Poleis

From about 800–480 B.C.E., Greek culture and society emerged from the shadows of the Dark Age into what scholars call the Archaic Period. Human records and cultural activity began to proliferate once again as the populations coalesced back into larger settlements. The mountainous landscape ensured that these new cities would remain isolated, and ambitious aristocrats and kings were less likely to give up authority over their growing city-states.

Of the 1,000 *poleis* that sprang up, Athens, Delphi, Corinth, Thebes, Rhodes, Syracuse, and Sparta were arguably the most famous influential. Athens and Sparta were the most powerful and held the most territory (The Greek Polis, 2017).

The political and cultural landscape of each *polis* varied, but there were some commonalities. Politically, four major political systems evolved as the city-states proliferated across Greece and the Aegean Sea: monarchies, oligarchies, tyrannies, and democracies (Greek City-States, 2022).

In terms of city planning, most poleis shared common features, including:

- **chora** - which are the surrounding farms and villages.

- **fortification walls** – Sparta was the most notable exception.

- **urban centers** - with gymnasiums, temples, amphitheaters, an agora, and (geography permitting) an acropolis.

The agora, in particular, was a square area in the center of the city where trade and governance were carried out. Public and government buildings surrounded it. On the other hand, temples and theaters were often placed further away, such as on the hills. This was because the locations chosen were either sacred or because they simply looked more aesthetically pleasing in a natural setting.

Most *poleis* were also invested in creating singular identities that all of its inhabitants could be proud of and connected to. Their focus on the agora, *polis*-specific festivals, mythical founders, and patron deities helped to form unique societies for each *polis*. This way, citizens (land-owning males) and non-citizens (everyone else) could feel united under a single banner, regardless of their representation or lack thereof (Cartwright, 2013).

Overall, *poleis* represented groups of people who had gathered for mutual economic and political benefits. Their goods, products, coinage, art, and political organization often varied. Of all of the city-states, three make representative case studies: Corinth, Athens, and Sparta.

Corinth

Strictly transliterated as *Korinthos*, Corinth was an ancient city located at the most important intersection of Greece—the Isthmus of Corinth. The large peninsula of Greece is actually comprised of two parts connected by a thin strand of land, also known as an isthmus. The two-sided harbor city, therefore, fronted the two most important seas in the Greek World—the Ionian Sea to the west and the Aegean Sea to the east (Ancient Corinth, 2023).

As noted earlier, Corinth, like most *poleis*, was filled with government buildings, temples, and other public spaces, like the agora. An important location in Corinth was the Fountain of Peirene, which was considered sacred and was therefore developed over time to become more like a temple (Ancient Corinth, 2023). Other temples honored Apollo, Poseidon, and cult heroes like King Sisyphus, Bellerophon, Jason, and Medea.

Its major features, however, were its two harbors: Lechaion, on the Corinthian Gulf to the west, and Kenchreai on the Saronic Gulf to the east. Between the two harbors, a special stone track was created, called the Diolkos. It allowed the Corinthians to drag large wagonloads of produce—or even ships—from one harbor to the other (Cartwright, 2009). This innovative way of portage allowed traders to avoid sailing around the southern peninsula.

Because of this, Corinth flourished as a trade city. It relied on maritime trade to sell the goods it became known for—glass jars, perfumes, pottery, wine bronze, and furs. Corinthians were able to trade with other parts of Greece and Italy, as well as with the Phoenicians. Their perfume pots became particularly famous when they invented a new form of artistic black-figure pottery (Carr, 2017). They dominated the pottery market for a couple of centuries, boosting their wealth and allowing for a more stabilized society.

Corinth had a dynamic political history. Emerging from a strict monarchical system, Corinth shifted into a time of flux, where it was either run by oligarchs or tyrants. The Cypselid tyrants made a name for themselves, particularly the second tyrant, Periander, who came to power in the early 600s B.C.E.

According to Herodotus, Periander was initially more interested in encouraging the arts and ruled his people reasonably. However, after taking advice from Thrasybulus, another tyrant running the city-state Miletus, Periander began to believe that the only way to consolidate power was to weed out the powerful and rich Corinthian citizens. Periander became increasingly blood-thirsty and suspicious. He killed his wife, ostracized his favored son, and terrorized the citizens of Corinth until his death (Lloyd, 2016). Eventually, Corinth would transform into an oligarchic state with limited democratic elements, including a council of 80 elders. This ensured citizens had some input in the governance of their city (Cartwright, 2018a).

Around the same time, Corinth began to expand culturally. Corinth became famous for the Isthmian Games, which were similar to the Olympic Games. In honor of Poseidon, they were held at Isthmia every two years during the spring. Its horse and chariot races were particularly famous (Cartwright, 2009).

Corinth would never gain the power that Athens and Sparta had, but it is a good example of how ancient Greek politics transformed over time from the Dark Ages onward. It exemplifies the struggles for political freedom, economic independence, and innovation, as well as cultural production. Unlike intellectual Athens or war-like Sparta, Corinth struggled to establish a stable government. In the end, it became a major player in the late 5th-century war between Athens and Sparta (see Chapter 5).

Athens

Athens, also known as *Athenai*, is the most famous city-state of Ancient Greece, founded in the region of Attica. It made its mark on history with its art, culture, and politics. For its time, Athens was an impressive sight to behold. It was a beautiful city, set on a plain surrounded by hills and the Aegean.

Athens had everything most city-states had: a hilltop fort on an acropolis, temples, sacred shrines, monuments, and government buildings. Although it was surrounded by hills, the countryside did not yield enough produce for the city; the climate of Attica was drier than the more fertile regions of Sparta.

Athens, therefore, relied heavily on its harbor to increase its economic and political power throughout the Archaic period. It developed silver mines to increase the value of its products, relied on alliances with other *poleis* for trade, and gained dominance over many of the Cycladic Islands (Williams, 2008).

Internally, Athens struggled at first. Its political scene, tending toward an oligarchical structure, led to corruption, oppression, and a widening class gap. Many lower-class citizens ended up impoverished to the point they would sell themselves into debt slavery.

This led to revolt and systemic changes, led by Draco, an Athenian statesman, who first revised Athenian law. His first statutes, created around 620 B.C.E., were too harsh. Many crimes were punishable by death, leading to the creation of the word "draconian," which means "overly severe" (The Greek Polis, 2017).

Soon after, Solon stepped in to revise Draco's laws. He tried to equalize the political structure and allow the common classes to have a voice. Not only did Solon ease Draco's harsh laws but he also canceled debts, abolished debt slavery, and laid the groundwork for democracy in Athens. The common people were allowed to take part in the government and be heard. Solon divided male Athenians into four classes based on wealth and defining their military responsibility:

- *pentakosiomedimnoi* - the "five-hundred-bushel men" (highest)

- *hippeis* – knights, or the cavalry class

- *zeugitai* - the hoplite class

- *thetes* - the rowing class (lowest)

The state was therefore hierarchical, but no longer based on birth alone. Now, it also took into consideration land-owning or military capabilities (Hornblower, 2023).

The restrictive hierarchy Solon had instituted colored its attempts at democracy. The only citizens who could vote were males who owned land. That meant that of its 300,000 citizens, only 20% were actually eligible to vote (Williams, 2008). Women, foreigners, slaves, and anyone who didn't own land couldn't vote. While debt slavery was abolished, Athens relied on its slave class to cultivate food in the surrounding countryside, do construction work, mine, quarry, and carry out domestic duties (The Greek Polis, 2017).

Women, regardless of their station, did not have many freedoms. They were expected to remain home to tend to their family's households. If they wished to go out or travel, they required a male chaperone. Unlike boys, Athenian girls were not sent to school and faced a life of relative security, depending on their class, but also many restrictions (Athens vs. Sparta - Difference and Comparison, 2019).

Athens wasn't paradise, but after the Dorian Invasion and the Dark Ages, it was considered the height of culture for its time. More educated and intellectual, the city focused on learning, strategy, and cerebral or artistic pursuits. Boys studied history, literature, philosophy, math, science, rhetoric, military strategy, and art, among other things.

As its navy grew in power and its territory increased, Athens became more wealthy and secure, allowing its citizens to foster the arts and pursue academics (Noonan, 2023). Although an outlier in its size and influence, Athens' steps toward democracy are representative of a wider trend in many other Greek *poleis*.

Sparta

If any *polis* offers a sharp contrast to Athens, it's Sparta (also known as *Lakedaimon*). Located in Laconia, a fertile area in the southern Peloponnesian peninsula, Sparta was nestled among fertile hills, perfect for growing crops and raising livestock. Up through the 600s B.C.E., the city, its population, and its territory slowly grew to encompass the whole of Laconia (The Greek Polis, 2017).

However, despite its massive size, Sparta did not gain a huge population. This might have been because Sparta was isolated. And, since it was self-sustainable, it did not contact other city-states or encourage immigration.

Sparta was naturally defended. The city did not require the walled fortifications that Athens and other *poleis* had. Instead, the city clustered about the usual buildings—the agora, the acropolis, the temples, and government buildings.

When excavations of the Archaic period layers were dug up, archaeologists discovered that there weren't as many temples, monuments, and statues as in other *poleis*. This was because Sparta was not as focused on art and intellectual pursuits. As a result, Sparta's pottery tended to be minimalist, geometric, and utilitarian, but with its own beauty. Skilled workers in Sparta created vase paintings, bone or ivory carvings, stone sculptures, and metalwork.

Sparta was more interested in athletics and military prowess. Its entire political structure became centered around its citizens' ability to participate in war. The hierarchical structure of Sparta, however, was rather complex, involving a monarchy and a mild blend of oligarchy and representative council. This hierarchy included:

- **two kings** from two powerful families

- **the gerousia**, a council of elders

- **the ephors**, five representatives chosen by lot from the citizen body

- **the hoplites**, the population of full-citizen males

- **the helots**, the unfree laborers working in the farmland outside the city

The hoplites were very important. Taken at the age of seven, these boys were raised in barracks, away from their families, where they were trained for war.

In their early teens, they would take part in the fighting.

While these males had some rights, inevitably, wealthy families would enjoy more privileges than others. Below, the helots were tied to the land and forced to farm for Sparta while secured by Sparta's warriors.

Since physical strength, size, and military prowess were prized above all else, if you were more intellectually inclined or physically weak, you would struggle to maintain any meaningful status within the city. Sparta became known for being harsh, and their ruthless habit of killing weak or small infants has shocked historians throughout the centuries.

However, although Spartan culture was cruel, it was a culture of paradoxes. The kings, with their oligarchies, listened to the ephors. Similarly, while strong males were preferred, women were given more freedom than in other Greek city-states.

Spartan women could not only own property but were also able to control their own finances when widowed. Dowries were given to women, which they often used to buy land. As a result, half of the Spartan land was owned by women.

Furthermore, women were educated, allowed to take part in athletics, drink wine, travel without a male chaperone, and wear what they wanted (The Greek Polis, 2017). With Sparta, we can see yet again how diverse the city-states of ancient Greece were in terms of their ideas of how to order a society.

Colonization and Expansion

During the Archaic Period, city-states with larger populations or less agricultural land, most notably Corinth, began to look for land elsewhere. They would set up trade centers and free markets, called *emporia*, across islands and other abandoned shoreline locations. This was not a concerted effort to create an empire. Rather it originated from a need for more resources and land for their growing populations. As a result, colonization began slowly at the beginning of the 8th century and gained momentum as the mainland Greek poleis became more affluent.

During the colonization period, Greek settlers also began to extend to southern Italy, calling it "*Megale Hellas*," or "Greater Greece" (*Magna Graecia* in Latin). These colonies were often military in nature, sometimes conquering the locals and impressing their own culture on the populace.

The process of Hellenization, "spreading Greek culture," began. Many of these colonies were sent by Chalcis, Achaeans, Phocaea, Athens, and Sparta. Parts of Sicily were also conquered by Rhodes, Crete, and Corinth, among others (Cartwright, 2018c).

Eventually, the Greeks would spread across the rest of the Mediterranean coastline, settling along the shorelines of modern-day France, Spain, Northern Africa, Turkey, and around the Black Sea. All of these colonies, far away from their mother cities (*metropoleis*), carried on their own systems of culture and government. They were not ruled like their parent government necessarily, but many followed the same forms as mentioned before—monarchies, oligarchies, and tyrannies. From these unique city-states, various new forms of artistry emerged, as well as new resources. For example, in the Black Sea region, gold became an important raw commodity (Hemingway, 2019).

Greece was not an empire, but its *poleis*, out of economic necessity, began to populate the known world, trading and competing with the Phoenicians, the Egyptians, and many Middle Eastern peoples. With each trade contact or conquest, their power grew, building the largest city-states into vessels of power that would one day set the stage for a war that would transform Greece.

The Development of Greek Literature

The Dark Ages represented a loss of literacy. But, emerging from that time, a new script was accepted and evolved to fit the scholars and record-keepers of Archaic Greece. No longer connected to the Mycenaean Linear B script, this new alphabet was formed from the Phoenician writing system, which itself originated in the Middle East. It was related to the Semitic writing systems like ancient Hebrew.

According to Herodotus, Phoenicians introduced the alphabet to Ionian Greeks, the Greek colonists located in Western Asia Minor. From there, it quickly spread to the other *poleis* throughout the Greek world.

Unlike the pictograms and logograms of earlier ancient writing systems, the Phoenician alphabet was phonetic and allowed for greater variation in terms of connecting the spoken word to writing. Initially, the Phoenician alphabet was a utilitarian script, consisting of 22 characters with vowel sounds built into the characters. The Greeks added more symbols to represent vowels and evolved the alphabet to fit their language's phonics.

Since the language and the writing system were more flexible, scholarly writing improved and increased. Greeks began to write about everything— science, math, history, literature, and more. They leveraged the versatility of the Phoenician alphabet to collate information on a large scale. This new alphabet later evolved into Classical Greek, and it later impacted the Latin and English alphabets (Mark, 2015b).

After long centuries plunged into silence, the Greek literary world came alive. Its records, plays, poems, and treatises point to a lively culture. Debate was encouraged, and progress was driven by economic, political, and academic interests.

Many of the ideas the Greeks shared had been developed by earlier minds, but their brilliant synthesis was able to push the boundaries of human knowledge. Even so, there still remain many gaps, particularly in the early part of the Archaic period. Many questions remain, such as the mystery of Homer.

The Rise of Homer

Who was Homer? No one really knows. He is a bit of a mysterious figure. No scholar or archaeologist has managed to uncover where he was born, who he was, or when or where he lived. However, ancient Greek and Roman scholars have suggested that he lived in Greece between 900 and 700 B.C.E.

The island of Chios has been linked to Homer as a place where he might have lived, but there are no definitive clues that he resided there. Another characteristic linked to Homer by ancient scholars is that he was blind. Once again, no data has been able to prove this definitively.

Modern historians have floated another popular theory: Homer was not one singular person. It is very possible that the two poems might have been written by more than one person. Bards would often sing together, making up verses as they went. It is, therefore, probable that the epic poems the *Iliad* and the *Odyssey* were the result of a collaborative effort by talented musicians and poets (Homer's World, 2011). Homer could be just a singular name for a group of people who preserved the dying oral traditions of their ancestors.

Preserving the Homeric Tradition

Greece's epic poems had a long history forged from the oral traditions of the Dark Ages. Thankfully, they were eventually written down and formalized by "Homer" during the Archaic period. Utilizing the newly found Greek alphabet, the Greeks were able to preserve and standardize their oral narratives.

However, since they lived during the end of the Dark Ages and the emergence of the Archaic period, this composite "Homer" undoubtedly put his own spin on the tales. It is possible that his version of the poems differs from the original oral traditions that emerged 400 years earlier, after the Dorian Invasion.

Preserving Homer's version of the oral traditions required the work of many individuals throughout history. As with almost all ancient literary works, there is no original manuscript. But thankfully, others copied the original written poems. Eventually, the poems reached their more or less canonical form in the early 2nd century B.C.E., when Aristarchus edited them and placed them in the famous library at Alexandria.

Even then, the texts were in danger of disappearing. Copies were made once again, and the two poems were shared before the tragic fire that destroyed the Library of Alexandria. The modern versions of Homer's poems, therefore, are the result of careful preservation that may have also altered the details of the stories in the intervening years (Nagy, 2017).

Not a lot may be known about Homer, but it is clear to see that Homer's work, although initially oral, marked the beginning of a cultural recovery. This transformation would take place over the next couple of centuries. By using the new Greek alphabet, he was able to preserve poetry and helped to found renewed literary endeavors. Thanks to Homer's work, not only was a veil drawn back on ancient Greek history, which prompted the search for the city of Troy, but his epic poems also inspired literature, music, and art around the world for millennia (Whelan, 2020).

Setting the Stage

What must this new world have felt like? We can sum it up with two words: the Olympics. Starting in 776 B.C.E., the Olympic Games united the city-states for a short period of time every four years. It provided cities with a chance to show off their athleticism, show civic pride, and honor their patron deity. Winners were gifted with laurels, and the audience enjoyed a rare unity with other *poleis* (International Olympic Committee, 2021).

In many ways, the origins of the Olympic Games highlight the vigor of discovery and growth felt during this period. With the increase of resources and territories, the Greek *poleis* flourished, spread their ideas, and left their imprint on the ancient world.

This was a precursor to what would be known as the Hellenic identity.

Another thing that would unite the city-states during this time of prosperity was the threat of war. Set against the Persian Empire, the *poleis* arranged themselves into loosely knit alliances. The epic confrontations between the Greeks and Persians would forever alter history. Join us in Chapter 5 as we explore the tumultuous era of Classical Greece and witness the splendor of Greek civilization at its zenith.

Chapter 5: Classical Greece

Steep mountainsides cascaded down on either side. Ahead of them, a road led north, now filled with rank upon rank of spears and horses. The forces of the Persian King had arrived. All that stood between them and their goal were several thousand men huddled behind the barely repaired ruins of a wall. It was going to be a piece of cake, they must have thought. A single push, and they'd be through. They were wrong.

From 480 to 350 B.C.E., Greece flourished in more ways than one. Not only was it able to prove to the world at large that it was a military force to be reckoned with, but it also witnessed the growth of sophisticated culture hitherto unseen in these regions of the world. Classical Greece was a time of unparalleled glory and bitter conflict, when mighty heroes and city-states shaped the destiny of Western civilization.

However, the golden age was brought to an end by the greed and ambition of two city-states—Athens and Sparta. Who would be the winner? Or would the so-called victor realize that, in winning, they too had lost?

The Greco-Persian Wars

The Greek *poleis* were flourishing. A period of expansion across the Mediterranean Sea had led to wealth for their citizens and a growing sense of pride in themselves. Greece was not alone, though. There were other nations, like the Persian Empire, who also had dreams of expansion and an equal drive for resources. It was only a matter of time until they would clash.

The origins of the Greco-Persian Wars began when the Persian Empire expanded into Asia Minor (modern Turkey) in the mid-6th century B.C.E. Ionian Greeks had settled there in the age of colonization, creating or immigrating to major port cities like Byzantium, Ephesus, and Sinope. Some of these cities, largely non-Greek, accepted Persian rule and became part of its western provinces, also known as satrapies.

Some colonies with strong ties to their *metropoleis* attempted unsuccessfully to revolt between 499 and 493 B.C.E. (Gill, 2019). The Athenians helped rebel forces besiege the provincial capital of Sardis in 498 B.C.E., torching much of the city. They were ultimately unsuccessful. The revolting colonies were brought in line. King Darius I of Persia, however, wasn't going to forget the interfering role of Athens and her allies (Bliss, 2022).

Two Invasions

The Persian Wars are divided into two major invasions followed by counterattacks. Separated by years of fighting, the invasions pitted Persia against many prominent Greek city-states. Persia, however, invaded the mainland of Greece before being pushed back once and for all.

In order to fend off the Persians, the Greeks uneasily allied with each other. Athens led a new league, the Delian League, which it formed in 479 B.C.E. Most of the city-states joined the Delian League, but Sparta remained independent.

Each *polis* had a single vote in the League, but Athens was the leader. While they battled the Persians together, the Delian League *poleis* and Sparta were also trying to outdo one another. But who would win?

The Battles and Warriors of the Persian Wars

While Persian invasions and the resulting counterattacks involved many battles, four stood out to ancient historians for their cultural and historical significance: the battles of Marathon, Thermopylae, Salamis, and Plataea. These battles were significant in deciding who ultimately won the war. They also highlighted the strength of combined Greek military power, setting the stage for later conquests.

The Battle of Marathon

In 490 B.C.E., the Battle of Marathon was held on a plain outside the city of Marathon. Facing King Darius I's forces (anywhere between 25,000 and 90,000 men), the Greeks proved they could withstand the power of the superior forces of the Persians. Led by an Athenian leader, Miltiades, Greek forces numbered only 10,000.

When the Persian fleet landed on the shores of Marathon, they discovered that the Greeks were waiting for them on the narrow plain just beyond. Miltiades thinned the center of his battle line. In this way, as the Persians pushed through, the more densely manned sides of the Greek wings then enveloped the Persian forces. The plain of Marathon was too narrow for the Persian cavalry to counter the maneuver effectively.

Recognizing defeat, the Persians fought their way back to their ships. The battle was brutal. On the shores of Marathon, Miltiades was slain. Most of the Persian fleet escaped; but the Greeks had won (Cartwright, 2013d).

The Battle of Thermopylae

Darius died in 486 B.C.E., and his son Xerxes I prepared a second invasion of Greece. His target was Athens, and the only viable land route was through Thermopylae, a narrow path with a steep mountain on one side and sea cliffs on the other.

In 480 B.C.E., the Greeks sent a mixed group of Spartans, Corinthians, Thebans, Arcadians, and others to create an army of around 7,000 men. They faced off against a Persian force of 80,000 troops. King Xerxes waited four days for the army to flee. They refused to budge. He ordered them to drop their weapons. King Leonidas of Sparta sent back a suitably laconic reply: *Molōn labe*—come and get them.

The Persians did. Leonidas and the Greek forces held out for three days. However, their time was cut short by a traitorous shepherd who gave intel to the Persian army. Using a hidden path, the Persians looped around and attacked from the south, surrounding King Leonidas and his surviving fighters.

With no one to stop them, the Persians sacked Athens and took a strip of territory on the mainland. Nevertheless, the Greeks were already preparing new forces to halt the Persian invasion. In later years, despite the fact that the Greeks had lost, the Battle of Thermopylae became a popular tale of a band of men fighting for freedom against all odds (Cartwright, 2013a).

The Battle of Salamis

Soon after the loss at Thermopylae, in September of 480 B.C.E., the Greeks were forced yet again to face King Xerxes and his army; this time, at sea. The Battle of Salamis, a naval battle between the Greeks and Persians, was Greece's last chance to stop Persia from taking over the mainland. The Greeks, comprising about 300 ships led by Themistocles, an Athenian general with previous victories under his belt, faced a huge Persian navy of almost 1,200 ships, made up of fleets from Egypt, Phoenicia, Persia proper, and even some Ionian Greek cities.

When the navies drew close, the Greeks deployed, probably in two ranks, with their backs to the island of Salamis. The cramped Saronic Gulf meant that the Persians could not bring their entire fleet to bear at once. The Greek navy drew the Persians into the strait and the ships began maneuvering to ram each other. It is difficult to reconstruct the tactical dispositions of the opposing sides, but the Persian sailors were more experienced, and the ancient sources affirm the Greek ships were heavier and slower than the invaders.

Nevertheless, the Greek navy controlled the battlefield of the waves. Their ships likely carried contingents of 20 heavily armed hoplite marines each, while the skilled crews of the Persians were less well armed. Moreover, while the Persians had been rowing practically all night, the Greeks were relatively fresh.

As more Persian ships moved forward, they cut off exits from their allies who floundered among the Greek ships. Some of Persia's navy ran aground, others were sunk, and some were able to extract themselves and return home. This allowed the Greeks to move their hoplite army to the mainland, where they began to attack the remaining Persians. King Xerxes was forced to retreat (Cartwright, 2013b).

The Battle of Plataea

From Salamis onward, King Xerxes remained at home, leaving the invasion in the hands of General Mardonius, a gifted Persian leader and cousin to the king. It wasn't until 479 B.C.E., the year after the naval victory at Salamis, that the Greeks were able to force Persia off the mainland once and for all. The Battle of Plataea would be the birthplace of Greece's freedom.

During this battle, the Persians fielded around 130,000 men. Opposing them, the combined forces of Athens, Sparta, and other city-states gathered in the mightiest Greek army yet, comprising around 70,000. The two armies were very different from one another. The Persians preferred to soften up their targets with long-range attacks from archers, which they would then follow up with a devastating cavalry charge. The Greeks preferred to use a tight-knit formation on foot, called a phalanx, that was heavily armored but slower in movement.

The leadup to the battle lasted 11 days. It was a cat-and-mouse game. Both sides tried to lure the other into their preferred location. The Greeks wanted to fight the Persians in the foothills while the Persians wanted to lure the Greeks out onto the plain.

As days passed, dwindling water and food supplies became a problem. Led by Pausanius, a Spartan leader, a major part of the army began to retreat in search of water. When the Persians pursued, they found themselves inadvertently flanked by stranded Athenians and Plataeans when the war-ready Spartans turned at bay. The Greeks were outnumbered, but heavily armed. When Mardonius was killed by a rock thrown by a Spartan, the Persian troops nearby began a retreat that swiftly devolved into a rout. The Greeks were finally able to stem the tide of Persia and prepare for a counterattack (Gill, 2019a).

The Fallout

Greece successfully defended itself from a Persian invasion. It sustained attacks from the massive empire, and from the fires of war, it emerged stronger than ever.

Not only was Greece able to stop the Persians from penetrating into Europe, but it was able to reclaim many of its Ionian settlements along the edges of the Black and Aegean Seas. Recognizing the Greeks' combined strength, Persia opted to encourage the tensions between Sparta and Athens.

The widening split between the two grew in the following years. Differences in culture, leadership, and governance became apparent. Joining forces with powerful city-states like Corinth, Sparta reformed the Peloponnesian League that had been first created around 550 B.C.E. On the other hand, Athens ran the Delian League, which became less of an alliance and more of an Athenian hegemony as it browbeat weaker *poleis* to remain loyal (*Effects of the Persian Wars*, 2023). The question was: Which league would win?

The Golden Age

The Greco-Persian Wars were a dark time for Greece. Many lives were lost. However, an awareness of power emerged within the city-states, particularly in Sparta and Athens. National pride began to grow. As the *poleis* began to rebuild, many of their leaders dreamed of a glorious future for their people, and Athens was at the center of it all.

Pericles: The First Citizen of Athens

After the intense conflict of Greco-Persian Wars, Pericles (495-429 B.C.E.) came to power in Athens. He was a studious introvert who did not seek political power. When he met Aspasia of Miletus, the beautiful and wise woman encouraged him to use his skills for the good of the people.

Pericles' influence grew, and from 461 to 429 B.C.E. he exerted a great deal of control over Athens. He was a talented statesman, orator, and general who oversaw a flourishing of Athenian and, by extension, Greek culture. This period of time is often called the Age of Pericles because his influence changed Athens and the rest of Greece, even beyond his death.

Pericles further developed Greece's early forms of democracy. Male citizens of Athens could vote and participate in politics. He also ensured that Athens remained a powerful city-state among the other *poleis*.

Ever conscious of the destruction the Persians wrought on Athens, Pericles carefully used the Delian League to his home city's advantage. This led, in time, to the Peloponnesian Wars between Athens and Sparta. However, it also ensured that Athens' cultural and political achievements would last.

Under Pericles, Athens became a cultural center. Alongside his consort, Aspasia, he promoted Greek art, music, literature, architecture, philosophy, and other advancements. The world he helped nurture would indeed stand the test of time. When Pericles succumbed to the plague in 429 B.C.E., his loss was felt. Athens struggled to replace their leader (Mark, 2018).

The Great Works

During the Age of Pericles, Athens witnessed the growth of cultural, philosophical, and scientific expression. Continuing the trend of the Archaic Period, Greek literary output intensified through the Classical Period, producing some of the most famous pieces of literature in the Western tradition.

In addition to famous Athenian playwrights like Aristophanes and Sophocles, other Greek academics wrote down their advancements in science, history, and philosophy; and many Athenian literary and artistic works are preserved to this day. Some of the most famous writers, thinkers, and artists of this era include (Mamakouka, 2014):

- **Sophocles** (496-406 B.C.E.), a tragic playwright who wrote *Antigone* and *Oedipus the King*, among others.

- **Phidias** (490-430 B.C.E.) was a sculptor, painter, and architect who sculpted for the Parthenon.

- **Herodotus** (484-425 B.C.E.) was an historian who wrote *The Histories* and who was known as "the father of history."

- **Euripides** (480-406 B.C.E.), a tragic playwright who wrote plays about Medea and Helen

- **Socrates** (c. 470-399 B.C.E.) was a philosopher known as the "father of philosophy."

- **Democritus** (460-370 B.C.E.) was a philosopher who developed the idea of atoms as the building block of the material universe.

- **Hippocrates** (460-370 B.C.E.), a doctor who created the Hippocratic Oath and wrote treatises on medicine and doctoral ethics; also known as the "father of medicine."

- **Aristophanes** (446-386 B.C.E.), a comic playwright who wrote *The Birds, The Frogs,* and *Lysistrata,* among others.

- **Plato** (424-348 B.C.E.), a philosopher who wrote *The Republic* and *Symposium,* and who produced philosophical "dialogues" between Socrates and other Greek thinkers.

The Peloponnesian Wars: Athens vs. Sparta

The Age of Pericles marked the growth of Athens in many ways. Now home to around 300,000 people, Athens was fast becoming an important political center. It was the heart of the Delian League, and the source of great wealth thanks to its navy and trade connections.

Although it had been sacked by the Persians, Athens rebuilt stronger than ever under Pericles. Its alliances with other city-states, though soured by its ambitions, remained mostly secure. There was one polis, however, that sought to eclipse Athens—Sparta (Woerner, 2022).

Roots of Conflict

After the end of the Greco-Persian Wars, the uneasy truce between the Delian League and Sparta came to an end. Scholars suggest that Sparta feared

Athens's ambitions and didn't think the Greek *poleis* had the resources to conquer the Persian Empire. In some ways, Sparta was right.

Athens' handling of the Delian League betrayed its intentions. Despite increasing revolts within the League, Athens began to clash with Sparta. Other factors for the Peloponnesian War stemmed from the stark differences between the two city-states. Sparta was a *polis* that focused on military might, while Athens valued education, art, and trade.

Recognizing that Athens held greater power, Sparta worried that Athens would turn its eyes to the fertile lands that Sparta held. Therefore, in 460 B.C.E., the First Peloponnesian War broke out, plunging all of Greece into armed conflict as the two leagues clashed. Fighting continued off and on for 25 years, until 445 B.C.E. During this period, Athens and Argos clashed with Sparta and Thebes.

Athens ruled the seas due to their experience in naval warfare. Sparta fought hard to maintain dominance on land. In the Battle of Tanagra, Sparta beat Athens. It was a sign of things to come.

There were several attempts at peace. Initially, a treaty was brokered by the moderate Athenian general Cimon in 446 B.C.E. It was supposed to last 30 years. However, disputes over land, such as the sacred site of Delphi, as well as revolts in Athenian-held Megara, led to further degradation of the relationship between Athens and Sparta.

The ultimate spark, however, was Corinth, which had long opposed Athens and considered itself

Sparta's ally. When Corinth entered conflict with Athens, Sparta came to its aid, starting a 27-year war that threatened to tear Greek culture down from its lofty height (National Geographic Society, 2022b).

Athens vs. Sparta

In 431 B.C.E., Sparta was back at war with Athens. The Second Peloponnesian War, which lasted from 431 to 404 B.C.E., had begun.

Led by the eloquent and charismatic general Brasidas, Spartan forces clashed with Athenian armies. At first, neither side could gain the upper hand. Athens, struggling with plague in 429 B.C.E., lost its brilliant leader Pericles. Still, it pushed its forces into the Corinthian Gulf and attacked Sparta's allies. At the same time, Sparta began a two-year siege of Plataea, which eventually fell.

In the following years, Athens battled for ground, while Cleon and Demosthenes, two brilliant Athenian generals, led the charge against Corinth and Sparta. Cleon was a particularly important voice during these years. After the death of Pericles in 429 B.C.E., he stepped up to lead Athens. An advocate for war, he beat the Spartans in battle twice in 425 B.C.E., both at Pylos and Sphacteria (The Editors of Encyclopaedia Britannica, 2020).

However, despite their best efforts, Athens' victories ground to a halt in 424 B.C.E. General Brasidas, Sparta's best strategist at the time, was able to fend off Athenian forces in Megara and Boeotia. Reluctantly, a year of peace was brokered.

In 422 B.C.E., war resumed. Brasidas led Spartan forces against Cleon, who was heading the Athenian army. At Amphipolis, the Spartans won, but Brasidas was killed alongside Cleon.

With the death of two pro-war leaders, Nicias, an Athenian politician and general, was able to negotiate for peace in 421 B.C.E. Called the Peace of Nicias, it was hoped that the war would be brought to a close, or at least to a temporary halt (Bloxham, 2016). Unfortunately, by 418 B.C.E., hostilities resumed. Sparta, led by Agis II, defeated Argos, an ally of Athens. In retaliation, Athens attacked Melos for supporting Sparta.

Around the same time, the Athenian generals Nicias and Demosthenes reluctantly mounted an expedition to Sicily. Alcibiades, a brilliant, wealthy, and well-connected Athenian, who proposed the idea, hoped Sicily might provide resources and allies. The expedition did not go well, ending in the deaths of Nicias and Demosthenes as well as most of their men. Alcibiades, realizing that he'd be blamed, fled Athens. He dwelt in Sparta for a time, acting as a military advisor against his native city. His political connivance made him enemies there, so he later fled to Persia to advise the satrap Tissaphernes until 410 B.C.E., when his friends secured a safe return to Athens.

Athens needed his expertise. In 412 B.C.E., Rhodes had successfully revolted and joined Sparta, and Athens great rival was now led by a fierce new general, Lysander. Yet, Alcibiades led the Athenians to several victories, starting with the Battle of Cyzicus in 410 B.C.E. After more victories around the Aegean, Alcibiades returned to Athens and accepted the position of *strategos autokrator*, commander of all Athens' forces on land and sea.

However, Sparta was not giving up. It managed to forge an alliance with Persia in 408 B.C.E. Two years later, Lysander beat the Athenian fleet at Notium, near Ephesus. This failure reflected poorly on Alcibiades, and the talented but erratic general was forced again into exile.

When Lysander overwhelmed Athens' forces in 404 B.C.E. at the Battle of Aegospotami, he showed no mercy, executing 3,000 captives. Lysander cut off Athens from its port, Piraeus. He then destroyed its fortifications and laid siege until the starving city was forced to surrender.

With that, Sparta won the war, replacing the Athenian empire with one of its own. However, Sparta's allies, Corinth in particular, had borne the brunt of the war's destruction. Sparta would soon find, as Athens had, that hegemony is difficult to handle.

Effects of the Peloponnesian War

After Sparta's victory and Athens's surrender in 404 B.C.E., the Delian League disbanded. Athens was thrown into disarray. The democratic system briefly collapsed, and "Thirty Tyrants" were appointed by Lysander to keep the city unified. In the chaos, Athenians were killed, pro-democratic citizens were exiled, and private property was confiscated.

While many Athenians still had the right to bear arms, live in the city, and take part in jury trials, the "Thirty Tyrants" became brutal in their punishments. Neutral citizens began to revolt. A revolution transformed the regime, and Athens finally began to rebuild.

Meanwhile, Sparta's power grew. Not only were their naval forces more honed, but they were able to maintain Athens's old hegemony across the Aegean Sea for a time. At one point, they too began to believe they could invade the Persians.

But the relationship between Sparta and its allies deteriorated quickly, and the destroyer of Athenian power entered a war against an alliance of Thebes, Corinth, Athens, and Argos in 395 B.C.E. The "Corinthian War" lasted for 8 years, but the Greek *poleis* were exhausted after more than 40 years of fighting.

In reality, although Sparta came out nominally on top in the conflict, Persia was the real winner. After hostilities ceased in 387 B.C.E., the Persians were free of Greek meddling in Asia Minor. And in 371 B.C.E., at the Battle of Leuctra, the tactical genius of Epaminondas would lead Thebes in the annihilation of Sparta's military supremacy forever (*Effects of the Peloponnesian War*, 2023).

The end of both Sparta and Athens is best illustrated by the fates of their last heroes— Alcibiades and Lysander. Alcibiades, seeking refuge in Persia from Lysander's forces, died around 404 B.C.E., likely murdered by the Persians in Phrygia. Lysander died in 395 B.C.E., in a small skirmish. He led his troops too close to the walls of the *polis* of Haliartus at the start of the Corinthian War. A nearby Theban force moved to assist the city, and Lysander was killed in the melee. Just as their heroes died after falling from glory, neither of the two greatest *poleis* would fully recover after their decades-long quarrel.

The Philosophical Triumvirate: Socrates, Plato, Aristotle

While the Classical Era reached a high point before the Peloponnesian War, some progress was still made after it. This was particularly true in the field of philosophy. Moving beyond spirituality and traditional cult religion, philosophers like Socrates, Plato, and Aristotle began to explore the big questions of life and reality.

While their fields of interest weren't exactly the same, Socrates impacted Plato, who in turn left an impression on Aristotle. These three men formed the all-important foundation for the field of philosophy. It is a foundation that has lasted up to the 21st century.

Socrates: The Only True Wisdom Is Knowing You Know Nothing

The father of philosophy, Socrates, emerged into a world of upheaval and uncertainty. Born in 469 B.C.E. to a moderately wealthy family, Socrates received a good education, studying rhetoric under Aspasia, Pericles's gifted consort. Despite his interest in his studies, Socrates took part in the Peloponnesian War.

When Socrates returned home, he lived humbly. He tended to move about Athens and talk with people. Barefoot, long-haired, and unwashed, Socrates didn't cut a fine figure in a city that prized beauty above everything else. According to historians, he was not handsome. Socrates was simply more focused on the things he thought were important—discovering truth and exploring ideas about ethics and how to conduct your life.

Always questioning the *status quo*, Socrates talked with people everywhere. He spoke with intellectuals, political leaders, young men, and admiring students. Two of his favored students were Plato, a fellow philosopher, and Xenophon, an historian. They wrote down Socrates's dialogues *Memorabilia*, *Apology*, *Symposium*, and *Crito*, among others.

These works describe how Socrates talked to people. While Plato's *Dialogues* are considered to be accurate, Xenophon's version is often more trusted.

This is due to his historically neutral stance on Socrates (Brinkhof, 2022).

Socrates was famous for many reasons. Although Plato and Xenophon never recorded direct speeches from Socrates on what he believed, some inferences can be drawn. From what we can glean, Socrates:

- formulated a new way of learning by using "the Socratic method," asking questions and creating a dialogue between teacher and student (Kruse, 2022).

- focused on logical consistency, definitions, and virtues.

- believed the soul was more important than our physical bodies or the material world.

- encouraged his listeners to care for their souls and consider how to properly develop virtues (Cooper, 1998).

Despite Socrates' interest in the truth, he became embroiled in politics. This drew Meletus' attention to him. Not much is known about Meletus, but in 399 B.C.E., he charged Socrates with showing a lack of piety and corrupting young men.

Although the 70-year-old provided a passionate defense, trying to prove his way of life was actually in service to the gods, the jury found him guilty. Socrates' students tried to turn the punishment into a hefty fine, but Meletus and his supporters managed to swing the vote in favor of execution. In the end, Socrates chose to drink a cup of brewed hemlock (Standjofski, 2022).

According to Plato, the execution was delayed for a month because of a festival. During that time, Socrates' friends encouraged him to run away. Socrates refused.

Instead, when the time arrived, he willingly drank the brewed poison, walked around until he couldn't feel his legs anymore, lay down, and then, over time, died, surrounded by his friends and admirers. Later scholars and scientists have noted that Plato's noble retelling of Socrates' death fails to mention how the hemlock would have slowly paralyzed his lungs and heart, suffocating him to death slowly (History.com Editors, 2009b).

Why did this travesty happen? There are no clear answers as to why Socrates was targeted. Some scholars suggest it was due to conservative religious sentiment. Socrates stated that if people didn't understand what piety and moral virtue truly were, their faith and actions were a sham. That could have upset some people.

Other scholars believe that Socrates had been too critical of the political establishment, particularly Athenian democracy. Socrates was most prolific in the wake of the Peloponnesian War when Athens was in decline and under the rule of the Thirty Tyrants. During this period, Athenians might not have wanted to hear critiques of their ideas or political ideals. Oddly enough, Critias, the leader of the Thirty Tyrants, was a student of Socrates. Despite that, the Thirty Tyrants didn't save Socrates from death.

Regardless, the father of philosophy transformed the world. He caused people to question their values and ideas. He also raised a generation of philosophers, who would propound ideas that echoed through the centuries down to the present.

Plato: Thinking—The Talking of the Soul with Itself

Born around 428 B.C.E. during the Age of Pericles, Plato grew up in a world of transformation and upheaval, much like his mentor and teacher Socrates. He came from a noble family. His father died when he was a child, and his mother remarried a politician. As a result, Plato was afforded the best education, studying philosophy, gymnastics, and poetry under great teachers.

However, the world he grew up in wasn't easy. Plato came of age during the Peloponnesian War, just about when Sparta defeated Athens once and for all. Therefore, as a young man, Plato saw his city torn apart by competing pro-Spartan and pro-Athenian factions. In the midst of it all, Socrates became a voice of wisdom. Plato, drawn to the wise philosopher, became invested in Socrates' ideas.

When Socrates was forced to commit suicide, Plato left Athens and traveled through south Italy, Sicily, and Egypt. Meeting other scholars, scientists, and academics, Plato began to form his own ideas about life, reality, and virtue. He returned to Athens in 387 B.C.E., bought a plot of land outside the city, and started his Academy, a school for philosophical thinking.

In many ways, Plato's Academy is considered to be the world's first university. Plato gave lectures to students who traveled miles to hear him. One student, hailing from northern Greece, was Aristotle, aged 17.

As an academic teacher, Plato was able to formalize his ideas. Throughout his travels and teaching period, Plato came to grips with his own ideas, based on Socrates's concepts. Not only did Plato carry forward and immortalize some of Socrates' words, but he also began to explore his own ideas and push back against the wisdom of his great teacher (History.com Editors, 2009b).

Plato was prolific. In his writings, he:

- provided a defense for Socrates' ideas, pushing back against contemporary criticism and lampooning.

- discussed general topics like the nature of love or the forgotten wisdom of the soul (*Symposium* and *Meno*).

- theorized about the parts of the soul (reason, spirit, and appetite) and linked them to three main groups of a city-state (*The Republic*).

- proposed that the best city-state would be led by a philosopher-king (*The Republic)* (Meinwald, 2018).

- suggested that virtues, such as goodness or beauty, were based in another plane of reality (known as the Theory of Forms, articulated in *Phaedo* and *Parmenides*) (Turner, 1903).

- encouraged readers to dwell on the true forms in order to bring virtue and lost knowledge from our previous lives.

- encouraged readers to create their own path to self-improvement.

- wrote topical discussions on geometry, politics, and general knowledge (Kraut, 2004).

In 347 B.C.E., Plato died of old age and was buried near the Academy. However, his ideas continued to change the world. Not only did he open the world of philosophy to Aristotle, but his Academy would survive in various forms until the 6th century CE.

Although his Academy would shift focus a few times, from dogmatic, speculative, moral-focused thought to skepticism and then Middle Platonism and Neoplatonism, the Academy provided the world with an ongoing font of philosophic thought (The Editors of Encyclopaedia Britannica, 2017b). The Byzantine Empire and Islamic thinkers particularly enjoyed Plato's work, while the West focused on the writings of his most famous student, Aristotle.

Aristotle: Knowing Yourself Is the Beginning of All Wisdom

Aristotle entered a different world from Socrates and Plato. In 384 B.C.E., Aristotle was born in Stagira, located in the north of Greece. At the age of 17, Aristotle was sent south to Athens to study at Plato's Academy, where he learned from Plato himself. After remaining there as both a student and teacher for 20 years, he left the Academy when Plato died. This may have been due either to rising anti-

Macedonian sentiment in Athens or Academy politics.

For the next five years, Aristotle traveled along the coast of Asia Minor, staying at Assos and Lesbos where former students housed him. He married, had a daughter, and continued his studies. He also tutored King Philip II of Macedon's son, Alexander, starting in 343 B.C.E.

Returning to Athens by 335 B.C.E., Aristotle started his own school, called The Lyceum. Students from all around the Greek world attended to hear his lectures, take his courses, and use his massive research library. Thanks to Aristotle's wide interests, students at The Lyceum studied a wide array of subjects including various fields of science, rhetoric, literature, theology, and the arts (Shields, 2008).

It was during this period that Aristotle did most of his writing. He supposedly wrote around 200 works, but due to poor storage after his death, only 31 survived. What remained of Aristotle's writings was poorly organized, not chronologically ordered, and very dense. However, many scholars break Aristotle's writings into four basic categories: analytical, theoretical, practical, and rhetorical or literary-focused (History.com Editors, 2019).

Like Plato, Aristotle went through phases. He first defended his teacher's ideas, then analyzed and critiqued them, and finally (after 335 B.C.E.) began to formulate his own philosophy. Aristotle moved from examining the natural world, as seen in his biology, marine biology, and botany treatises, and began to think about more existential and philosophical topics (Haskett et al., 2016). Some ideas that Aristotle considered include:

- ways to carry out scientific or philosophical investigations (*On Interpretation, Prior Analytics*).

- empiricism and how to determine truth with the five senses.

- definitions of logic, logical fallacies, as well as the aims and role of logic.

- writings on cosmology, physics, metaphysics, and animals.

- treatises on ethics and politics (*Nicomachean Ethics, Politics*).

- a defense of the role, aim, and therapeutic benefits of literature (*Poetics*).

- explanations on how to create logical syllogism (arguments) with two premises and a conclusion sentence (*Dialectics*).

- exploration of the definitions and techniques of persuasion (*Rhetoric*).

- a proposal that "a good life" is discovered by understanding and fulfilling your individual, unique function, pursuing virtuous living, embracing reason, and achieving some comfort and pleasures in life.

- the definition of different political states, in which he reluctantly supports polity (majority of people ruling in the interest of all) as having the most long-term success.

- the importance of proper environments for individual personal growth.

- defense of humanity's natural tendency to hierarchies.

- a study on nature, being, function, and substance, with a focus on the importance of classification as a way to define and understand the world around us.

- a definition of *telos* (your purpose in life) and the role it plays in helping you understand your function and your path to "the good life."

It is important to note that by focusing on function, on different types of life, and the naturalization of hierarchies, Aristotle became a springboard for justifying unhealthy cultural practices, such as slavery and the unequal treatment of women. Although Aristotle did believe that nonliving machines would one day replace slaves, ideas about "natural" slaves would come into play as justification for slavery centuries later, particularly among the conquistadors (Messerly, 2014).

As he aged, Aristotle faced the usual challenges of life. His wife passed away, and Aristotle found love again with a woman called Herpyllis, who some say was a servant in his home. Herpyllis and Aristotle had a son, Nicomachus, after whom he named his famous treatise, the Nicomachean Ethics. However, after tensions rose between the Greeks and Macedonians, Aristotle fled Athens. A year later, in 322 B.C.E., he died of natural causes.

Following his death, Aristotle's Lyceum, failing to compete adequately against Plato's Academy, collapsed. Aristotle's writings, poorly stored away, were forgotten. Andronicus of Rhodes rescued them in 30 B.C.E. After grouping and editing what he could collect, copies were maintained. Aristotle's works would become popular in Byzantium, the Islamic World, and, centuries later, in medieval Europe (History.com Editors, 2019).

Like his teachers, the importance of Aristotle cannot be underestimated. Not only did he become one of the world's first documented scientists, but he also formalized the identity of scientific disciplines like botany and marine biology. Among the Greeks, Aristotle was the first professor to organize lectures into a course and create a syllabus for his students. His research library was renowned for its accumulated knowledge, which helped preserve the advancements of the era. In this way, the lineage of critical thinking and questioning would be preserved from well beyond the age of the three greatest Greek philosophers.

When the Dust Settles

Despite the great achievements of Athens and the might of Sparta, the city-states could not weather the storm of clashing ambition. Greece had managed to fend off the Persians, proving to the known world that they were a military power to be reckoned with. However, the fall of Athens and Sparta signaled a time of radical transformation.

As the smoke of the Peloponnesian Wars cleared, a new power emerged in the north, ready to change the course of Greek history forever. Chapter 6 will explore the rise of Macedon and the remarkable figure who would go on to conquer the known world.

Part 3: The Rise of Macedon and the Hellenistic Period

Chapter 6: The Rise of Macedon

> I swear this oath by Zeus, Gaia, Helios,
> Poseidon, Athena, Ares, and all the gods and
> goddesses. I shall abide in peace and not break
> these covenants. Neither shall I bear arms
> against any who likewise swear, either on land
> or sea... nor shall I seek to end the dominion of
> Philip and his progeny. (IG II² 236)

These are the words of the oath given to the League of Corinth, formed by an unusual man—Philip II of Macedon. The mercurial rise of this Macedonian king is a thrilling story of a man driven by ambition, bolstered by success, and destroyed by his own appetites. In his 23-year reign, Philip did what none had managed before him—unify Macedonia and Greece.

How did a kingdom in the northern fringes of Greece rise to dominate the entire Hellenic world in such a short span of time? To most Greeks, the Macedonians were no better than other barbarians, even though they spoke a rough dialect of Greek. The answer lies in the figure of Philip himself. His ambitions drove him to extend his territory on the battlefield and at the negotiating table.

Despite his detractors, Philip cultivated diplomatic relations with the Greek *poleis*, provided refuge at his capital city of Pela for great thinkers, and charmed those who met him. He drank hard, fought hard, and lived hard. In many ways, Philip was the rock'n'roll star of his era (Griffith, 2019).

Philip II

Born in Aegae in 382 B.C.E., the youngest of three sons, Philip II was ushered into a world of upheaval and uncertainty. His father, King Amyntas III of Macedonia, ruled a struggling realm. Macedonia would one day grow to include the modern-day Republic of North Macedonia, northern Greece, and parts of Bulgaria, Albania, Serbia, and Kosovo. However, during Phillip's youth, his country was not unified.

Early Career

When the Greeks of Thebes invaded Macedon, they captured the teenage Philip and took him hostage. Living there for three years, he studied under the Greeks. Epaminondas, the great Theban general who had crushed the Spartans at Leuctra in 371 B.C.E., taught Philip about military strategy. The Macedonian was a quick study.

After he returned home, Philip initially helped his second oldest brother, Perdiccas III, rule (his oldest brother had died). When Perdiccas died in battle fighting Illyrians in modern-day Albania, Philip deposed his nephew and took the Macedonian throne at the age of 23.

The first thing Philip focused on was stabilizing Macedonia. It wasn't easy. Relying on a cunning combination of threats and warfare, Philip managed to secure the loyalty of both the core Macedonian nobility and many of the barons of outlying hill regions.

Macedonia, compared to Greece, was not as advanced technologically or culturally. However, Philip saw his people's hidden potential. He believed his family's lineage traced back to Heracles, son of Zeus, so he was determined to prove the royal family's worth.

The new king invested in bringing culture to Macedon's capital city, Pella. Philip invited philosophers and writers to stay. Aristotle was hired to teach Philip's son Alexander for a couple of years.

Philip cultivated Pella as a center of culture and diplomacy.

Philip's Military Innovations

One of the keys to Philip's success was his military prowess. By listening to his tutors, such as the experienced general Epaminondas, Philip was not only able to transform the Macedonian army, but he was also able to pioneer strategies that surprised his Greek opponents.

The first step Philip tackled was the transformation of the Macedonian army. Under Philip, Macedon's army increased from 10,000 to 24,000 men. The cavalry was boosted from a royal guard of 600 to a battalion of 3,500. Philip introduced many other reforms to help increase his military power, including (*The Military Revolution: What Were Philip II's Reforms of the Macedonian Military and How Revolutionary Were They?*, n.d.):

- an oath of allegiance.

- well-made gear and uniforms.

- strict training exercises for improved fitness, including forced marches.

- regular drills to increase tactical flexibility and unity cohesion.

- a fair punishment and reward system.

- allowances for restricted looting.

- good, regular pay.

- education and training in Greek military techniques and strategy.

- a new weapon—the *sarissa* (a 13 to 23-foot-long pike).

- practice in multiple forms of weaponry, including the sarissa, swords, and bows.

- new siege weaponry including towers, catapults, and battering rams.

Philip took care to account for several different types of warfare as he reformed his military apparatus. The Persians had relied on long-range weapons like bows and slings to soften their enemies before charging with heavy lancers and other cavalry. For them, most infantry was poorly armored, but mobile. On the other hand, the Greeks had shown the effectiveness of a heavily armored hoplite phalanx in holding position or attacking straight ahead, especially if its flanks were protected. Philip doubled down on the offensive power of the phalanx, replacing the shorter hoplite spear with the sarissa and reducing his phalangites' armor (Wasson, 2014).

Philip's heavy infantry soldiers were not perfect, however. The phalanx, despite its immense mass and forward impetus, could sometimes struggle on uneven terrain. Moreover, these formations could be easily flanked since larger phalanxes couldn't turn quickly. And while the sarissa was able to fend off oncoming attacks, if the formation lost cohesion and the enemy closed in, the phalangites' sarissa was less wieldy than short swords or smaller spears (Roman Legionary, Macedonian Phalanx, or Spartan Hoplite: Which Was the Better Ancient Warrior?, 2023). Philip's answer was a combined arms approach.

He outfitted an elite corps of infantry called the *pezhetairoi* or "foot-companions." They were highly-trained professionals chosen for their size, strength, and facility with multiple weapons. Scholars debate whether they carried the sarissa or a shorter one-handed spear, but the prominent placement of the *pezhetairoi* at crucial places on the battle line is testimony to the importance Philip placed upon them.

In addition, Philip maintained both light and heavy cavalry squadrons and recruited poorer citizens as javelineers and other light infantry. With these additions, the heavy phalanx formed the iron core of a flexible force capable of operating on any terrain against nearly any opponent. It would lay the foundation for Macedonian power in the age of Philip and beyond.

Eventually, with his new army, Philip subdued the Illyrians, completely defeating them in 359 B.C.E.

Then, Philip turned his eye toward his next concern—Athens. Athens controlled nearby silver and gold mines, and the major city-state was also interfering in Macedonian politics. Philip captured Amphipolis in 357 B.C.E., took its gold and silver mines from Athens, and then moved to capture other *poleis*.

The Unification of Greece

Philip II was invested in stabilizing Macedon and its diplomatic relationships in order to enlarge its territory. But after he captured Amphipolis, Crenides (which he renamed to Philippi), and other city-states, the fragmented Greek *poleis* united against him. However, Philip proved himself adept at leveraging the ongoing divisions among the Greeks.

In 354 or 353 B.C.E., the Thessalian League, a loose confederation of northern Greek *poleis*, asked Philip for help fighting Phocis and its allies, including Athens and Sparta, in the Third Sacred War over the holy sanctuary of Delphi. Philip agreed.

The Greek city-states were cautious about entering open battle. Nevertheless, Philip defeated Phocis and its allies several times, most notably in the Battle of Crocus Field in 353 or 352 B.C.E. Philip's victory saw him named *archon* of Thessalian League, giving him full authority over the considerable army and revenue of Thessaly. Neither side claimed a complete victory, but Philip came out of the Third Sacred War more powerful than he went in. The Athenians took over the pass of Thermopylae barring

Philip from pressing into central and southern Greece.

Philip opted to negotiate over the next six years. As the newly installed *archon* of the Thessalian League, he was able to negotiate a long-term alliance with the Greeks. Despite his capture of more cities and having proven his military might, Philip preferred to find a peaceful resolution between himself and Athens.

Demosthenes, a famous Athenian orator, hated Philip. He constantly warned his fellow Athenians about the danger that the Macedonian king represented. His eloquent venom was such that, to this day, an exceptionally bitter verbal denunciation is called a philippic. Yet, during the lengthy diplomatic maneuvering, Philip continued to expand wherever possible. He annexed Thrace to the east, tightened his hold on Thessaly, and completely took over Illyria.

The Greeks, at length, realizing Demosthenes was right, reopened the war against Philip in 339 B.C.E. They swayed the once-friendly Thebes to their side. Nevertheless, the Battle of Chaeronea in August of 338 B.C.E. settled the matter of Greece's independence for the foreseeable future.

Philip and his 18-year-old son Alexander III crushed a large army of 35,000 formed by Athens, Thebes, Corinth, and several other powerful *poleis*. With a resounding victory, Philip showed his overwhelming supremacy on the battlefield. He then forced a peace treaty that ensured support from the Greeks going forward.

The victory at Chaeronea put Philip in a position to expand the borders of his territory, unite the city-states of Greece into a new political body, and begin planning an expedition to capture the riches of the east. Securing his position in Greece with garrisons in Thebes and Corinth, Philip still needed to tackle the more sensitive issue of how to handle Athens. Without Athens, he couldn't hope to take on Persia.

As a result, in 337 B.C.E., Philip created the League of Corinth, also called the Hellenic League. This organization was formed to help preserve peace between the city-states within the League as well as with Macedon. Most of the Greek island colonies and almost all the city-states on the mainland supported the alliance. Sparta was the most notable exception.

The League's guiding principle was war with Persia in revenge for its invasions of the previous century. For the first time in history, the city-states of Greece (*sans* Sparta) were united under a single political organization. With Philip in power, the city-states would not only behave, but they could rely on Philip's forces combined with Athens's navy to provide proper protection for everyone.

Every city-state had a representative at the *synedrion*, or congress. The only exception was Macedon, since Philip was the head, or *hegemon*, of the League and looked after his homeland's interests. This council decided on matters that best worked to the city-states' advantage. As part of the League, each *polis* was required to provide ships or troops. The amount required depended on their power.

Thanks to Philip's diplomacy and military prowess, Macedon was positioned at the head of large collection of powerful city-states. It had the combined strength, resources, and wisdom of the Greek *poleis*. Unwillingly, Greece had been united, but it was this important step that would lead to the creation of the first, true Hellenic Empire (Griffith, 2019).

Preparing for Empire

If Philip wanted to achieve his dream of taking on the might of Persia, he would need as many allies as possible. The Greeks had formidable armies, a long history of military victories, and academic resources that would provide Philip with the foundation he needed for empire-building. Recognizing that he couldn't do it all on his own, Philip set about to form alliances. Through the League of Corinth, as well as his own marriages, Philip was able to build a robust network of shared interests.

The League of Corinth

The League of Corinth, as noted above, was established later in Philip's life. Formed after years of warfare and treaties, the League represented the first tangible progress toward unifying Greece and consolidating Philip's power. Initially proposed by

Isocrates of Athens in 346 B.C.E., it took years to form. However, it was the first politically unifying institution in Greek history and paved the way for future expansion.

There were three parts to the League of Corinth. In addition to Philip the *hegemon* and the *synedrion* council were the *dikastai*, important judges who aided in decision-making. When decrees were made, they were posted to cities such as Athens, Corinth, Olympia, and Delphi (Chrysopoulos, 2023a).

As part of joining the League, each *polis* swore an oath, stating they would keep the peace, bear arms for their allies, and uphold Philip's position. They also promised punishment for any signatory who violated the oath, stating, "But should any oathbreaker violate these covenants, I shall assist those in need however they demand, and I shall wage war upon the transgressor however the council and *hegemon* (i.e. Philip) should command me" (IG II³,1 318).

Therefore, this council of Greeks decided on major military and political moves and represented the military and naval power of each *polis* proportionately. City-states with less military power were represented less, but they still had a voice at the table. When the first meeting was held, Philip was able to successfully negotiate support from the League in pursuit of war with Persia. Philip was, of course, elected as the chief commander of the armed forces, the *strategos autokrator* (The Editors of Encyclopædia Britannica, 2020).

The Marriages of Philip II

Diplomacy, peace treaties, and the formation of the League weren't the only ways Philip gathered support; Philip was also open to marriages, many of them. Although the chronology of his unions is not certain, how they supported his ambitions for power and territory can be surmised. Each of these women hailed from different regions or cities, and their marriages to Philip more than likely coincided with the acquisition of new territory (Tronson, 1984):

- Audata: from Illyria, bore Cynane (daughter).

- Phila: from Elimeia, no children.

- Philinna: from Larissa, bore Arrhidaeus (son).

- Olympias: from Epirus, bore Alexander (son) and Cleopatra (daughter).

- Meda: from Thrace, no children.

- Nicesipolis: from Thessaly, bore Thessalonika (daughter).

- Cleopatra: from Macedonia, bore Europa (daughter) and Caranus (son).

The two most famous wives of Philip were undoubtedly Olympias and Cleopatra. Olympias was the mother of Alexander III. She was a wise and powerful woman, manipulative and capable. Long after Philip's death, through their son, Alexander, her cunning helped shape the fate of nations.

Cleopatra, on the other hand, was young when she married Philip. She was chosen to bear Philip a true heir with "pure" Macedonian blood. The young woman bore Philip a son, directly threatening Alexander's inheritance. This circumstance enraged Olympias and set things in motion that would unleash the greatest conqueror the world had ever seen (Mann, 2013).

Philip's Final Years

When Philip formed the League of Corinth in 337 B.C.E., Persia was calling. But before he could achieve that dream, personal issues erupted in the warrior-king's personal life. Alexander's intelligence and ambition matched Philip's, sometimes raising tension between the two high-spirited men. Furthermore, Alexander's birth was not considered "pure" enough for the Macedonian throne.

To solve this issue, Philip took the advice of his close friend and commander, Attalus. Therefore, also in 337 B.C.E., Philip married his seventh wife, Cleopatra, the niece of Attalus. She was much younger than Philip, and the marriage made Alexander angry. When Alexander spoke out about it, he and his mother were separated and temporarily exiled. Alexander was sent to Illyria, his mother back to Epirus.

Hoping to properly secure his throne and lineage, personal issues continued to threaten his legacy. Philip's former friend, bodyguard, and (some say) lover, Pausanius of Orestis stabbed him to death during the wedding ceremony of his daughter, Princess Cleopatra. Thus, Philip II died in 336 B.C.E., never fulfilling his dream of conquering Persia and leaving his throne empty for an ambitious son with a destiny that would overshadow his own (Wasson, 2014).

Imperial Premonitions

The year was 344 B.C.E. The evening sun cast long shadows over the grand court of Pella. Philip II of Macedon took his ease and watched his 12-year-old son, Alexander, practicing combat moves with sheer determination. The boy's relentless spirit was evident even at this age. It wasn't just training for battle, but a dance of aspiration. That is what Philip saw: a dream. Every stroke of the sword promised an empire larger than any the world had seen.

With that ambition, Philip unified Greece. But it was this young prince, with fire in his eyes and ambition in his heart, who redefined the very notion of empire, pushing the boundaries of the known world. He faced the might of Persia and ventured into the mysterious lands of India.

Everywhere he went, he spread the telltale marks of Greek culture, intertwining them with local customs. But more than his conquests, his true legacy was a merging of civilizations—an era of Hellenization. In the next chapter, we journey alongside Alexander, not just as a conqueror, but as a catalyst for the fusion of East and West.

Chapter 7: Alexander the Great and the Hellenization of the East

Many men had tried to ride Bucephalus. None succeeded. Alexander, however, fell in love with the magnificent horse, admiring his ferocity and beauty. Despite his youth, he knew he could tame the noble Thessalian beast before him.

Approaching Bucephalus, the sharp-eyed 12-year-old boy noticed that the horse was afraid of his own shadow. He spoke soothingly, coaxing the black charger toward the sun. Alexander tamed the now calm Bucephalus and would keep him as his prized steed for the next 18 years. His determination, cleverness, and keen eyes had won the day. It was a sign of things to come.

Bucephalus and Alexander fought many battles together. It wasn't until 326 B.C.E. that they parted, when Bucephalus succumbed to wounds taken in the heroic crossing of the Hydaspes river in India. Grieving the loss of his dear friend, Alexander founded a city called Bucephala in honor of the horse who had borne him over 3,500 miles from home.

The story of Alexander and Bucephalus has become famous over the centuries. It isn't just about a boy who loved his horse. It also reveals the core of a man who created an empire (*Bucephalus: The True Story of Alexander the Great's Legendary Horse*, 2023).

Capable of greatness, generosity, love, ruthlessness, and cruelty, Alexander III of Macedon put his mark on history. Following in his father's footsteps, Alexander achieved the imperial dreams that Philip had harbored. He created an empire stretching from Greece to Egypt, to the Middle East, and beyond to northern India. In the process, he laid the foundation of Hellenistic culture and laid the groundwork for future empires.

Education and Relationships

Alexander, son of King Philip II and his fourth wife, Olympias, was born in 356 B.C.E. into a world where opportunity—and challenge—waited. As the legitimate son of the king of Macedon, Alexander had a warrior for a father and role model. This was reflected by his upbringing, which was characterized by a blend of military, academic, and artistic education. Alexander's curriculum was designed to form a well-rounded man.

Under Leonidas of Epirus, one of his mother's relatives, Alexander learned how to ride a horse, fight, and march long distances. His early training under Leonidas transformed Alexander into a powerful warrior with stamina and resilience.

Lysimachus of Acarnania taught Alexander how to read, write, and play the lyre. Thanks to Lysimachus, Alexander gained a lifelong appreciation of the arts, and spent much of his spare time reading – even when at war. When Alexander was around 13 years old, Philip hired Aristotle to tutor him.

During Alexander's youth, he made important friends who impacted his life in positive and negative ways. Some of his childhood friends were Cassander, Callisthenes, and Hephaestion. This last was particularly close to Alexander, becoming his second-in-command and most trusted confidant. Many historians have debated the relationship between Alexander and his boyhood friend, but what is known is that Hephaestion remained at Alexander's side until the end of his life (Mark, 2013).

Eventually, Alexander grew up. Like his father before him, Alexander brokered marriages for political and personal reasons. Alexander's polygamy was not as extensive as his father's; he married three times, once for love (Roxana, a Sogdian princess in 327 B.C.E.) and twice for politics (the Persian princesses Stateira and Parysatis in 324 B.C.E.). Roxana and Stateira were particularly powerful consorts who vied for influence after the death of Alexander (Edwards, 2022).

Outside his marriages, Alexander had several possible lovers, including the Thessalian woman Campaspe and the Greco-Persian noblewoman Barsine. The latter was a daughter of the Persian satrap of Phrygia and wife of the famous Greek mercenary Memnon of Rhodes, one of Alexander's greatest adversaries.

Alexander may also have had intimate relationships with the men of his inner circle. He was particularly distraught at the death of Hephaestion, but there are no clear references to a sexual relationship in the ancient sources. Likewise, the Persian eunuch Bagoas, who had been a favorite of the emperor Darius III, was a member of Alexander's Persian court. The ancient sources describe an episode where Alexander was drunk at a festival and kissed Bagoas at the urging of the other Macedonians.

Unfortunately, modern inferences about the sexuality of ancient figures are largely doomed to failure. Primarily, these exercises illustrate the preoccupations of modern scholars more than those of the ancients. Furthermore, even if we could determine with any certainty the social constructs within which ancient sexuality operated (a dubious claim), the sources at our disposal rarely offer enough material to analyze against them. The best we can do is reaffirm what the sources state explicitly: Alexander married three times, had a few love affairs with prominent women, and may have enjoyed similar relationships with a select group of men.

Alexander's Conquests

Alexander began his career on the battlefield at an early age. At 18, he helped Philip win the Battle of Chaeronea by commanding the left wing of the Macedonian battle line. Upon Philip's assassination, the 20-year-old Alexander took the throne and began to work on his own plans for building an empire.

Starting in Thessaly and Thrace, Alexander revisited old territory, ensuring his power was secure in the north. For the rest of Greece, he used Thebes as a warning, razing the once might *polis* to the ground while keeping its temples intact. Athens and other city-states got the message, allowing Alexander to conquer much of Greece and form a strong foundation for his future conquests.

The Battle of the Granicus

In 334 B.C.E., Alexander crossed into Persia. At first, it wasn't easy to maintain a foothold. The Battle of the Granicus was the first great test of Alexander's mettle, and that of the allied Macedonian and Greek army.

His 40,000 men met an equally large force commanded by Arsites, the satrap of Phrygia, on opposite sides of the Granicus River. The armies were fairly well-balanced. So, victory was determined by how well the men were led, whether the army was able to act as a unit, and how disciplined the soldiers were.

Alexander knew he would make for easy bait. Deliberately choosing clothing that stood out, Alexander drew most of the attacks toward his own unit. This involved him in heavy fighting.

According to Arrian, our most reliable source for the battle, Alexander spotted Mithridates, one of Emperor Darius' sons-in-law, and killed him with a spear thrust to the face. However, Rhosaces, one of Darius' satraps, struck Alexander on the helmet with his sword. The young Macedonian king was unbowed and ran the Persian through the chest with his spear.

Another satrap, Spithridates, maneuvered to strike Alexander from behind, but his companion, Cleitus the Black, hewed off the satrap's arm, rescuing his king. The death of so many Persian commanders, Alexander's survival, and the steady pressure of the Macedonian phalangites eventually caused the Persians to rout (Bileta, 2023). Alexander had defeated the only imperial army then in Asia Minor.

For the next year, Alexander fought to pacify the cities of Asia Minor. The Persian fleet was still operating in the Aegean, and he needed to deny them safe ports. Some cities surrendered without a fight, others he needed to take by assault. Nevertheless, his boundless energy enabled Alexander to exert control over most of the region within a year.

The Battle of Issus

In 333 B.C.E., Alexander faced off against King Darius in person. Darius tried to approach the battle with Alexander more strategically than his satraps had the year before. By careful maneuvering, he split Alexander's army, forcing the Macedonian and his men to march over 60 miles in two days to rejoin with one another. Arriving at Issus, Alexander knew his force of 40,000 men was outnumbered by King Darius' army nearly two to one.

The warlords faced each other across the Pinarus River where it met the coast. Alexander deployed his Greek Thessalian cavalry on the left wing, near to the seashore and under command of Parmenion, one of his father's most trusted generals. They stood opposite the more numerous Persian heavy lancers. The phalanx held the middle, opposite a large body of heavily armed Greek mercenaries on Darius' payroll. Alexander himself led his heavy companion cavalry and light infantry on the right wing. They faced off against Persian heavy and light infantry that greatly overextended the Macedonian line. Darius and his bodyguard commanded the Persians from the middle.

The Persian heavy cavalry crossed the river to attack the Thessalians *en masse*, but the Greeks stood firm, buying time under the stalwart Parmenion. The right half of Alexander's phalanx crossed to the Persian side but suffered heavy losses against the hardened Greek mercenaries and had to retreat. Meanwhile, Alexander dismounted and led a force of hypaspists ("shield bearers") to drive a wedge into the Persian line and relieve pressure from his exhausted phalangites. The maneuver successfully opened a gap in the Persian line.

The king re-mounted Bucephalus and led a charge into the gap while his javelineers held off the Persian enveloping force on his right. He completely pierced the formation of the enemy and forced Darius's army into retreat. King Darius himself panicked and fled the scene, leaving his army to flounder. Alexander not only beat the king's army, but he also captured King Darius's wife, mother, and two of his daughters (Bileta, 2023).

The Siege of Tyre

Before going eastward, Alexander consolidated his territory in Syria and Phoenicia, still seeking to neutralize the Persian navy by denying it safe harbors in Asia Minor and the Levant. To that end, in 332 B.C.E., Alexander laid siege to Tyre, a large Phoenician port. This city was important because it was the major base for King Darius's navy.

However, it was not easy to take. All of the women and children had been sent away to Carthage, an ancient colony of Tyre, leaving only strong defenders behind its massive 150-foot walls. Around 40,000 men defended the city, and they settled in for a long siege.

Alexander decided that he needed to build a huge causeway to reach the city walls across the channel that protected it. It wasn't easy, but eventually, Alexander's engineers managed to build siege towers that could withstand Tyre's missiles and a massive land bridge that brought Alexander's armies to the wall. However, without control of the sea, he could not fully blockade the city.

Fortunately, his diligent capture of ports from Asia Minor to Syria gave him control of their navies. More and more squadrons arrived during the course of the siege. In addition, the king of Cyprus sent a fleet to assist him. Within seven months, Tyre fell. It is estimated that 8,000 men were killed and around 30,000 men were sold into slavery. The surrender and occupation of Tyre were considered a massive victory and an indicator of Alexander's power (Bileta, 2023).

The Liberation of Egypt

The next year, Alexander took control of Egypt, which the Persians had conquered in 525 B.C.E. The Macedonian king sought legitimacy; therefore, he restored many of the Egyptian temples that the Persians had let fall into disrepair. He visited the famous oracle of Amun-Ra at Siwa, where he was proclaimed the son of Amun. He commissioned new temples and reduced the tax burden. On the coast, he founded the city of Alexandria, perhaps his greatest cultural achievement. Finally, he was crowned pharaoh with the traditional Egyptian double crown. Now, with control of the eastern Mediterranean and the entire coast, Alexander was ready to take on the rest of the Persian Empire. But Darius was busy raising new armies in the east to check his advance.

The Battle of Gaugamela

The Battle of Gaugamela (sometimes called Arbela) in 331 B.C.E. was Darius' last chance to keep his empire. He chose the time and place carefully—the flat terrain of the Nineveh Plains of northern Iraq. He ordered the entire battlefield to be cleared of debris to give his huge cavalry and scythed chariot contingents freedom of movement. He then formed up his lines to urge a night battle. However, Alexander waited until morning, allowing his men to rest while the Persians waited up all night in fear of attack.

It's impossible to determine the Persian numbers. The only thing modern scholars agree on is that the ancient sources are wholly unreliable on this point. Unfortunately, modern estimates are hardly more useful, since they vary from 50,000 to 250,000. We can observe the same phenomenon in most reconstructions of ancient battles. In any case, every source, ancient and modern, affirms that the Persians hugely outnumbered Alexander, who had about 30,000 heavy infantry, 9,000 light infantry, and 7,000 mixed cavalry.

The width of the Persian line exceeded Alexander's by nearly a mile, making envelopment almost a certainty. Nevertheless, the Macedonian chose to attack a numerically superior force head-on across open terrain while at a disadvantage in cavalry. A full examination of the battle reveals the nature of Alexander's generalship.

He drew up a double battle line. His Macedonian phalanx formed the center, while his lighter infantry, skirmishers, and cavalry took the wings. The second line was a phalanx of mixed Greek allies and native auxiliaries. As the battle unfolded, Alexander would command the entire right half of the line, while Parmenion oversaw the left.

Alexander ordered his Macedonian phalanx forward to engage the Persian center, keeping his light infantry and cavalry forces echeloned back. Darius knew that his infantry was no match for the phalangites head-to-head. Therefore, he committed his center to a holding action and sent an overwhelming cavalry force and his heaviest infantry to outflank and annihilate Parmenion. He hoped a crushing blow would allow his forces to roll up the Macedonian line from the left, neutralizing the moral effect of Alexander.

But the young king wasted no time and led the Companions sharply to the right, extending the Macedonian line in an apparent move to flank the much larger Persian army. As he neared the edge of the territory Darius had cleared for the battle, the Persian king ordered cavalry opposite Alexander to engage, preventing the Macedonian from reaching terrain where the Persian mobility advantage would dissipate.

What followed was an intense cavalry skirmish in which Alexander proved himself one of the great battlefield captains in history. With judicious use of his tactical reserves, incredible discipline, and a willingness to expose himself to physical danger, his mix of cavalry and light foot skirmishers forced the Persian horse to withdraw.

In response, Darius ordered his 200 scythed chariots to engage Alexander directly. However, Alexander moved up the Agrianians, elite javelineers from the Balkans, to screen the Companions. The skirmishers effectively disrupted the chariots who ineffectively drove through lanes in the Macedonian formation. As they emerged in the Macedonian rear, the Companions' horse grooms and a formation of hypaspists annihilated them.

As the Persians committed more and more men to outflank Alexander, he steadily fed new battalions from his second line into the fray. Eventually, a gap opened between the Persian center, still fighting to hold off the Macedonian phalanx, and the forces trying to outflank Alexander's right. The Macedonian king had lured the Persians.

Alexander formed up the Companions into a wedge, putting every man he could spare behind them. Then, he urged Bucephalus forward into the breach in the Persian line, straight at Darius himself. The Persian royal guard and Greek mercenaries guarding the Great King could not withstand the charge, and the front of the Persian center could not help, it was fully engaged with the Macedonian phalanx. Darius panicked and fled, and most of the Persian reserve lines fled with him.

Alexander wanted to pursue and capture Darius, but he received word that Parmenion was finally being overwhelmed by the main Persian offensive after a stalwart delaying action. Choosing to preserve his army, Alexander attacked the troops surrounding Parmenion from behind in a brutal cavalry strike. 60 Companions were killed, and Hephaestion was seriously wounded. But the Persians were eventually beaten back and routed from the field.

Alexander wasn't able to kill the king, but his army smashed Darius's forces and credibility. The Macedonian king's masterclass in battlefield tactics, discipline in command, trust in his subordinates, physical bravery, and unyielding energy all approached the superhuman at Gaugamela, allowing him to defeat a much larger force in open battle with every disadvantage (Bileta, 2023). If Alexander had fought no other battle in his career, we would still consider Gaugamela one of the greatest displays of combat leadership in history. Yes, King Darius escaped again, but his own men were fed up with their monarch. Darius was murdered by one of his generals, leaving Alexander in control of Persia.

To the East

By 327 B.C.E., Alexander spent 4 years eliminating remaining Persian resistance, pacifying peoples that threatened to leave the empire in the chaos of Darius' demise, and even expanding beyond the reach of any Great King before him. As he conquered more territory, he founded many cities, usually naming them after himself.

He married Roxana, a Sogdian princess reputed to be the most beautiful woman in Asia. He also began to embrace the Persian way of life. Not only did he adopt the Persian style of governance, but he also began to wear Persian clothing and enforce Persian court customs. The custom of *proskynesis*, lying fully prostrate before the king, particularly upset the Macedonians. They felt such a display was suitably only for the gods.

By this time, not everyone was happy with Alexander. Even as he planned to take India, the young conqueror had to deal with mutinous troops.

He also began to fear conspiracies against his life. Some threats were real, but some were imagined, making him an unreliable and ruthless ruler.

Eventually, in 326 B.C.E., Alexander reached India. In a hard-fought battle at the Hydaspes River, Alexander outwitted the warrior-king Porus to force a crossing during a stormy night, smashed through a numerically superior advance force, and finally defeated Porus' main force. In the battle, Bucephalus was mortally wounded. Showing clemency, Alexander appointed Porus as satrap, letting him rule the territory over which he had been king, and even enlarging his domain.

At the Hyphasis, his tired army revolted. Forced back, Alexander tried to consolidate his territory, fuse the Persian and Greek cultures, and manage his empire. In many ways, the relatively young man had reached the zenith of his powers, but his happiness did not last long.

In 324 B.C.E., Alexander's best friend, Hephaestion, died. Alexander was overcome with grief. Stories tell of him clinging on to the corpse of his friend until his advisers and other companions dragged him away. After giving his fallen friend a funeral fit for a king, Alexander returned to Babylon.

A year later, on June 13, 323 B.C.E., Alexander fell ill. His life of soldiering, drinking, and feasting finally caught up with him, perhaps. He may also have fallen prey to malaria. Poison is also not out of the question. There is no certainty about what actually happened to Alexander. It is only known that after a night of feasting and drinking, he became sick and died. He was only 32 years old (The Editors of Encyclopædia Britannica, 2021).

Controversies

Although many ancient Greek writers paint Alexander the Great as an incredible warrior and leader, there are accounts—Greek, Roman, and Persian—that hint at a more complex picture. There was a dark side to Alexander. Paranoid, prone to bursts of temper, fanatical, and megalomaniacal, Alexander had a firm belief in his right to rule and wasn't afraid to enforce it. In the earliest days of his kingship, Alexander and his mother likely killed Philip's new wife and her baby daughter. After that, Alexander held to a path that made him a charismatic leader who was equally ruthless and generous. (Gabriel, 2017)

Many stories have been told about Alexander's ruthless, insensitive, harsh, and cruel behavior. Among other things, Alexander was said to have:

- had the eunuch Betis dragged to death behind a chariot after Alexander conquered the city of Gaza.

- burned down the city of Persepolis during a drunken victory celebration after the Battle of Gaugamela.

- killed his friend Cleitus the Black in a drunken rage over an argument.

- imprisoned his childhood friend Callisthenes, who died in prison.

- slaughtered an entire town as a sacrifice for Hephaestion's funeral.

In some cases, Alexander regretted his drunken behavior. His grief after killing Cleitus appeared genuine. However, some of the reasons behind the revolt against Alexander as he headed further into India are interesting. Notably, his army no longer supported him due to his behavior.

With the loss of Hephaestion, Alexander became a loose cannon. While he had always drunk and taken drug-like substances, his abuse became worse after the death of Hephaestion. Instead of holding to a more reliable and wiser lifestyle, Alexander became reckless, stubborn, and impulsive (Jarus & Gordon, 2017).

How did Alexander end up this way? Theories abound. Alexander may have believed the prophesies and rumors about his divinity. He may also have been psychologically troubled or chronically overstressed. Perhaps he missed the support of his mother who had not joined him on his campaigns. The death of Hephaestion clearly caused further distress, as well.

However, some suggest that Alexander never felt confident, despite his charisma and charm. His own lineage had been brought into question by his father. His early education under Aristotle was also more Athenian and, therefore, more cerebral than a normal Macedonian boys' education.

Furthermore, Alexander was depicted as being average (or shorter than average) in height and having other less robust physical characteristics. Other descriptions, coinage portraits, and sculptured busts depict him as being fair-skinned and beardless, pointing to more feminine features.

Even more interestingly, although Alexander enjoyed the company of women, married, and had children, he was very controlled about his sexual encounters. His own mother allegedly pushed him into his first intimate relationship with the Thessalian courtesan, Callixeina. This points to a deeply sensitive or reserved nature, which might not have been initially suited for sustained imperial warfare.

Therefore, Alexander may have been plagued by deep-seated doubts. He needed the support of his mother and close friends. As paranoia caused him to lash out, he undercut the foundations that he relied upon. After the death of his closest and dearest friend, Hephaestion, it was only a matter of time before Alexander, too, would collapse (Gabriel, 2017).

The Legacy of Alexander

Alexander wasn't a perfect person. Even in the eyes of his own people, the young conqueror was a walking contradiction. He pursued war and fulfilled his father's ambitions, but he also loved music and books. He was paranoid and trusted few, but the ones he loved and lost, he grieved deeply. Similarly, while his cruelty is easily tallied, so are the legacies he left behind.

The first major impact of Alexander was the final destruction of the Persian Empire. While Persian culture itself did not disappear, the nation no longer posed a threat to the West. Alexander was able to exact the revenge that was the founding mission of the League of Corinth.

Alexandria was another of Alexander's major contributions to the world. Founded in 332 B.C.E., Alexandria not only became a massive naval base but also became a center for learning. The Alexandrian Library was the ultimate ancient library. Famous academics like Euclid, Archimedes, and Eratosthenes studied philosophy, mysticism, science, and geography there (Reimer & Mackie, 2019).

Thirdly, in many ways, Alexander's expeditions paved the way for the Roman Empire. The knowledge of Middle and Far Eastern geography and cultures gave the Romans a better understanding of a world they eventually conquered (The Editors of Encyclopædia Britannica, 2020a).

Finally, and most importantly, Alexander and his conquests were responsible for the spread of Greek culture. Alexander the Great came from Macedonia, but he was raised largely by Athenian tutors and scholars. When he conquered new territory, he didn't replace the political structures or customs of the region, but he encouraged the spread of Greek culture. Toward the end of his life, Alexander pursued a more Persian lifestyle to appease the foreigners he ruled, but the impact of his ideas continued to spread beyond his death (*Alexander's Empire*, 2023).

Alexander's reign sowed the seeds of the Hellenistic Age. Greek culture influenced all of the people Alexander encountered, from the matrilineal

Meroitic kingdom in Nubia to the Egyptian and Indian peoples. The Greek language and coins became a necessity for trade from Greece to Persia and to India beyond. Alexander might be gone, but Hellenism was now fully underway (*Alexander the Great*, 2019).

The Dawn of the Hellenistic Era

With the passing of Alexander, a new era dawned on the Greek world. The world of trade, politics, and culture would be transformed, paving a path through upheaval to a new world order underneath the Romans. However, power still remained in the Middle East and beyond. India and China now made contact more regularly with the Greeks, Persians, and Egyptians. A common language, the Greek language, would shape economic and political policies for centuries to come.

Before he died, someone asked Alexander, "Who is your empire going to go to?"

Alexander replied, "To the strongest man."

The question then became: Who was the strongest man?

In the next chapter, we'll examine the Diadochi, or "successors," of Alexander the Great: Cassander, Ptolemy, Antigonus, and Seleucus. Beyond the Succession Wars lay the Hellenistic period, where the cultural and political legacies of Alexander took on new forms and spread even further.

Chapter 8: The Hellenistic Period

The sun dawns in the east, glinting on the dark waters of the Mediterranean Sea. Sandy beaches run up to the great walls of the port city of Alexandria, the jewel of the Hellenistic world. Close by, the Lighthouse of Alexandria rises on the nearby isle of Pharos as a monument to the city's grandeur, as well as a practical beacon for the ships coming into port.

Behind Alexandria's walls, streets follow the straight lines of a grid system in an organized layout. This is uncommon in other ancient Egyptian cities. Gorgeous edifices of theaters, public buildings, and temples line the bustling streets.

From the shadows of a great conqueror emerged an age of culture. The Hellenistic period lasted from 323 B.C.E. to 31 B.C.E. It set the stage for future advancements and political change.

The Successor Kingdoms

Alexander's death came as a shock. It was too sudden and too soon. People back in Greece refused to believe the news at first.

Alexander and Roxana's son was still just a baby. Alexander hadn't left a regent clearly in control. Whatever Alexander's choice, any decision, either in favor of his infant son or his friend, Perdiccas, was ignored.

Chaos plunged his fledgling empire into a struggle for power. Friends battled friends, and wives battled wives, allying themselves with different factions. Among the leaders of Alexander's empire, known as the Daidochi, or "successors," four major names vied for power: Cassander, Ptolemy, Antigonus, and Seleucus.

In the following years, Cassander hunted down and killed Olympias, Roxana, and Alexander's son, Alexander IV, who was around 12 years old at the time. Cassander was swiftly routed by Antigonus. This left three major figures to claim and fight for territory.

Over a period of 40 years, Seleucus, Ptolemy, and Antigonus stabilized their chosen regions. This ushered in a new era of cultural and economic advancement. While none of these men matched Alexander's charisma, intelligence, or military genius, their dynasties were secured until the arrival of the Romans (Mark, 2013).

The Seleucids

The Seleucid Empire (312–63 B.C.E.) was the largest territory left after Alexander's death. Claimed by Seleucus, it included a large portion of Mesopotamia, Anatolia, and northwestern India. After a two-year war and negotiations with King Chandragupta Maurya in the east, Seleucus looked back to the other successor kingdoms.

Seleucus contested territory with Antigonus, beating his old friend in 310 B.C.E. By 301 B.C.E., Seleucus controlled the largest portion of Alexander's old empire. He founded a new capital city, Antioch, on the Orontes River. His son helped him rule from the other capital city, Seleucia, in the east.

In 281 B.C.E., circumstances gave Seleucus the chance to take Anatolia from Lysimachus, another, less successful Daidochos. After defeating and killing Lysimachus, Seleucus was the last of the surviving Diadochi and the new ruler of Anatolia. Later that year, Seleucus was busy with preparations to invade Greece. He never achieved that dream, assassinated by Ptolemy Ceraunos, the oldest son of his friend Ptolemy, in a bid for control over Anatolia.

Out of the four men, Seleucus was able to not only hold the largest portion of land but also achieve what Alexander had dreamed of—a multicultural empire, where Western and Eastern culture fused. Underneath the Seleucid Dynasty, Seleucus and his heirs successfully encouraged cultural fusion, religious tolerance, organized governance, and lucrative trade (Mark, 2019).

The Ptolemies

The Ptolemaic Dynasty (305–30 B.C.E.) wasn't as big as the Seleucid Empire. Ptolemy, known for being "enterprising," claimed Egypt. A close friend and bodyguard of Alexander, Ptolemy realized that

Alexander's son would never rule. He instantly went to Egypt.

Ptolemy believed Egypt was perfect since it was ideally positioned and rich in resources. The Egyptians didn't seem to mind. After all, Alexander had freed them from an oppressive Persian rule, had worshipped at their temples, had built a new temple to honor Isis, and had given them the freedom to worship their preferred faith and preserve their cultural traditions.

Like Alexander, Ptolemy continued to reign in a tolerant way. He focused on stabilizing the country. Although he found himself caught up in the Successor Wars, Ptolemy worked to revive Egypt, create a haven for Greek and Macedonian culture in Alexandria, and bring prosperity to his people.

When he died in 282 B.C.E., his successor Ptolemy II came to power. The start of Ptolemy II's reign was rough. He got caught up in a war with Lysimachus and Antiochus I, among other conflicts.

However, at home, Ptolemy II continued his father's program. He created trading posts along the coast of the Red Sea, finished the lighthouse, Pharos, made the Alexandrian Library even larger, and improved the famous museum located there. Both Ptolemy I and his son, although Macedonian by blood, were considered the last two great Pharaohs of Egypt (Wasson, 2016).

The Antigonids

The Antigonid Dynasty (306–168 B.C.E.) did not last as long as the others. The homeland of Macedonia was a hotly contested territory. Back in 333 B.C.E., Alexander had put Antigonus I in charge of Phrygia as a satrap. He received the governorship of other areas upon Alexander's death. However, with allies at his back, Antigonus was able to take control of Macedonia.

Antigonus' ambitions to rebuild Alexander's empire did not go unnoticed. His old allies, such as Ptolemy, switched sides in an effort to stop Antigonus from taking over. The war didn't last long. By 312 B.C.E., Antigonus recognized that peace was necessary. Excepting Seleucus, Antigonus created treaties with the rest of his opponents.

However, this peace ended as ambitions between the Diadochi came to the surface yet again. Antigonus and his son Demetrius went to war, once again pursuing old enemies. In 301 B.C.E., the armies of Lysimachus and Seleucus attacked Antigonus at the Battle of Ipsus. The 80-year-old king was killed, leaving Demetrius in charge (Volkmann, 2019a).

Despite the death of Antigonus I, he left behind a strong legacy for his descendants. Not only had he expanded his territory, but he had also created new cities from united smaller communities, such as Teos and Lebedus. However, like the other successor kingdoms, the Antigonid Dynasty experienced its ups and downs under strong and weak rulers.

One of its strongest rulers, the grandson of Antigonus I, Antigonus II Gonatas, worked hard to stabilize the territory he claimed. A student of Zeno, the father of Stoicism, Antigonus II's views on governance and rulership were rather different from the other dynasties and empires. Antigonus II believed that rulers ought to serve the people and the law. Besides inviting Zeno to his court, Antigonus II also encouraged the arts and other academic pursuits (Volkmann, 2019b).

Greco-Bactrians and Indo-Greeks

While Alexander's reign as a king and emperor was cut short, the warrior-king was able to realize many of his imperial dreams. Thanks to his conquests, Alexander ensured that Greek culture would flourish and evolve in places far outside the Aegean. While he didn't forcefully impose much of his culture on his newly acquired territories, cross-pollination of ideas and cultural activity was bound to happen.

The Greco-Bactrian Kingdom, also known as "the land of a thousand cities," is a prime example of Alexander's effect on history. Despite its distance from Greece, Greeks had settled in the area before Alexander's conquests. Since then, the Greek colonies there had been subjugated by the Persians, as far back as the Greco-Persian Wars in the mid-400s B.C.E.

This kingdom gathered more power as the post-Alexandrian dynasties faltered. The Bactrian Kingdom gained independence around the 3rd century B.C.E. Its first king, Diodotus I Soter was a Bactrian-born Greek. Over time, the kingdom grew to include modern-day eastern Iran, Turkmenistan, Uzbekistan, Tajikistan, Afghanistan, and Pakistan.

Many of the cities in the Greco-Baktrian Kingdom, such as Ai-Khanoum, looked like other *poleis* in the Greek homeland. They had large urban centers complete with theaters, gymnasiums, gateways, mausoleums, and main streets. Surviving Greek-styled art, mosaics, and sculpture reveal aesthetics similar to what was produced in Greece. Scholars from Greece traveled to the largest urban centers of the Greco-Bactrian Kingdom, bringing with them philosophical writing, maxims, and even plays (Fernandes, 2022).

Around 190 B.C.E., another Greco-Bactrian king, Demetrius I, extended his borders southward into modern-day northwestern India. The Indo-Greek Kingdom that arose there became its own nation, spreading across parts of modern-day Pakistan and northern India. However, by 130 B.C.E., the Greco-Bactrian Kingdom was fragmented under invasions from the rising Parthians (Stamatios, 2023).

In the Indo-Greek Kingdom, the Greeks and Indians mixed freely. Over time, the Greeks, also known as Yonas, took on more Indian characteristics.

The kingdom survived civil wars and invasions, outlasting the Greco-Bactrian Kingdom from which it derived by more than a century. It was eventually vanquished around 10 B.C.E. by Indo-Sakan invaders. By then, the Indo-Greek culture was far from its origins in Greece. But while their culture eventually faded, artifacts remain, pointing to a diverse and vibrant culture (Simonin, 2011).

Hellenistic Culture: Art, Science, and Philosophy

What does "Hellenistic" mean? Hellenism, or Hellenization, refers to the spread of Greek culture, particularly its language and people. Thanks to Alexander's conquests, Greeks were now living in Asia Minor, the Middle East, North Africa, and the Far East. While many fused with the native cultures, intermarrying and sharing traditions, the Greeks and their new neighbors began to rely on Greek ways of doing commerce, among other traditions.

Evolving Art and Culture

During the Hellenistic Period, the Greeks didn't just spread their ideas to other nations and peoples. Their art, architecture, and literature also began to shift and expand. New forms of art, music, and writing emerged in the two centuries after Alexander's death.

For example, architecture became more dramatic. The Corinthian aesthetic became incredibly popular. The Corinthian order was characterized by slender, fluted columns sitting on a base. The column's capital (the broad section at the top of columns or pillars) was shaped into stylized acanthus leaves or tendrils. It was very delicate and natural looking.

Another popular architectural element that emerged was the stoa, a covered walkway, usually with one side lined with columns. These walkways, or, porticos circled an open space or agora.

Hellenistic sculpture advanced even further. One fine example is the Gigantomachy, which shows the Titans and the Olympian gods fighting each other. Other sculptures, like the Dying Gaul, show how sculpture changed dramatically during this period. In one rendition of the Dying Gaul type, a Gallic chief holds his wife, whom he just killed to avoid slavery. He has taken his knife to himself, committing suicide right after.

Nike of Samothrace. Venus de Milo. The Barberini Faun. All of these are a testament to the lasting power of Greek art. Instead of having human bodies standing stiffly (in stark contrast to Minoan, Mycenaean, Archaic, and even Classical statuary) the figures from the Hellenistic period are emotive and natural-looking. The clothing details, poses, and even textured skin created a powerful sense of dynamism. Since these sculptures were so dramatic, the art during this period became the primary inspiration for European art for centuries to come (Buis, 2023).

The Role of Alexandria

Alexander founded quite a few cities (most named Alexandria), but the greatest city he created was undoubtedly Alexandria in Egypt. For more than 2,000 years, Alexandria remained the largest and most important city in Egypt. On the shores of the Mediterranean Sea, this city was an important port, where navies and traders alike could gather.

Scholars from all walks of life gathered there, from Greek philosophers to Eastern mystics and Jewish leaders. The Alexandrian Library was its main draw. It was said to have around 500,000 books, an astronomical number in days before the printing press. As a result, philosophers, scientists, writers, mathematicians, and religious men visited Alexandria to study and write. In Alexandria, famous thinkers like Archimedes and Euclid formulated philosophical and mathematical theories.

When Alexander died, his body was eventually laid to rest in Alexandria. Ptolemy, taking control of Egypt, nurtured the city. He continued work on its infrastructure, organizing it into a grid system, ensuring that the port was designed for maximum efficiency, and building beautiful public spaces for its citizens. Its public buildings, theaters, and temples fused Greek and Egyptian aesthetics in glorious harmony. In many ways, Alexandria represented the fruition of the Hellenistic endeavor (Mason, 2023).

Emergence of Schools of Thought

During Philip's exploits, Alexander the Great's conquests, and the Successor Wars, the Greek field of philosophy continued to develop. Plato's Academy and Aristotle's Lyceum continued the work of developing concepts around general philosophy as well as virtues, ethics, and other ways to "live a good life." During the Hellenistic period, however, other schools of thought began to emerge: Epicureanism, Cynicism, and Stoicism.

Epicurus (341–271 B.C.E.) pursued an extreme materialist philosophy. He believed everything, including the soul, was made of atoms. He also believed that these atoms were not designed to follow predetermined paths, nor that they were passive. Therefore, he posited, there was an element of chance in the universe.

His scientific beliefs about physics and chance led him to believe that humans had free will and the right to pursue a good life. Good living, he said, could be achieved by pursuing pleasure (*hedone*). However, it was limited by an equal respect for reason, tranquility, and delayed gratification.

According to Epicurus, pain, if the end result would bring more pleasure, shouldn't be avoided. Unfortunately, many people came to believe that Epicureans were allowed to just do whatever they wanted. As a result, "Epicurean" became the byword for hedonism (a word that derives from *hedone*), although Epicurus's initial hedonism was, in fact, nuanced and limited (Graham, 2023).

Antisthenes (c. 445–366 B.C.E.) and, more famously, Diogenes of Sinope (c. 404–323 B.C.E.) espoused the philosophy of Cynicism. This school of thought was never formalized. This was because Cynics didn't believe that formalities, social conventions, or cultural expectations were healthy.

Pushing some of Socrates' ideas to the extreme, Diogenes believed that you didn't need a lot to be happy. Diogenes, among other cynics, pursued a minimalist life that was close to nature and natural self-expression. Diogenes didn't wear great clothing or eat a lot. He spent much of his time mocking the everyday life and choices of his fellow Greeks.

This got Cynics into trouble. Diogenes' pursuit of contentment in all circumstances was embraced by other Cynics. However, the Cynics would never become a fully formed school because of its inherently individualistic and fragmented nature (Graham, 2023).

Zeno of Citium (c. 334–242 B.C.E.) founded the first Stoic school. Focusing on science, logic, and ethics as a way to make sense of the world, the Stoics followed the same path as the Cynics in some ways. Like the Cynics, they recommended a life that is simpler and closer to nature. Furthermore, while they were materialists; they did not see matter as active, and they believed that God (*logos*) energizes matter as an organizing principle (Graham, 2023).

Since the universe was deterministic with limited free will, the Stoics believed that the path to a good life involved contemplation and acceptance. They encouraged their disciples to recognize when to exercise free will and when to accept things they couldn't change. The four basic tenets of Stoicism include courage (the ability to act in the face of fear), temperance (self-control), justice (how to relate well to people), and wisdom (the use of philosophy to know how to act in good or bad situations) (Lake, 2022).

Like Epicureanism, Stoicism became misunderstood over time. Many people today link it to emotional neglect or repression. This is far from what Zeno and other Stoics originally intended-a way to therapeutically gain perspective and spark self-empowerment.

Hypatia and the Hellenistic Tradition

One of the best examples of the lasting influence of the Hellenistic flowering of Greek culture is the life and work of Hypatia. Born in Alexandria around the year 355 C.E., about 300 years after the end of the Hellenistic period, Hypatia was the daughter of a well-known astronomer and mathematician. After spending years in his tutelage, Hypatia continued his work after he died, also tackling projects that interested her.

Hypatia became known for her work in the fields of mathematics, philosophy, and astronomy. The young woman preserved Greek knowledge during a period when the political landscape was in the midst of upheaval. She wrote commentaries on geometry, numbers, and astronomical tables, and synthesized information from numerous sources to preserve knowledge that might otherwise have been lost. At the same time, Hypatia lectured on philosophy to a loyal audience.

While not many of her philosophical works have remained, it appears that Hypatia was a Neoplatonist: one of a series of thinkers who borrowed heavily from Plato and later Hellenistic philosophers. Many great religious figures were influenced by Neoplatonic thought, including St. Augustine, Avicenna, and Maimonides. Due to Hypatia's philosophy and desire to pursue the One, the underlying reality Plato had spoken of, Hypatia embraced a life of celibacy.

Unfortunately, when the moderate governance of Alexandria collapsed in 414-415 C.E., the Roman prefect and ally of Hypatia, Orestes, struggled to keep control. In support of the newly appointed Cyril, patriarch of Alexandria, Christian cultists, most likely fanatical Nitrian monks or followers of a populist preacher named Peter, took to the streets to cleanse the city.

Hypatia was brutally murdered by one such gang. There is no consensus among scholars whether she died because of her paganism, her scholarship, or her political connection to Orestes. Nevertheless, Hypatia later became an example of early feminist scholarship as well as martyred academics in general. Whatever the case, Hypatia was an influential scholar in the Hellenistic tradition dedicated to learning and knowledge (Deakin, 2019).

New Powers Rising: Rome and Parthia

Inevitably, the power of the Ptolemaic Dynasty, the Antigonid Dynasty, and the Seleucid Empire all dwindled. Faced with new threats from the Parthians and the Romans, these kingdoms had to make a decision. Would they ally themselves with the new world powers, or would they fight?

Of the three, the Antigonid Dynasty ended first, in 168 B.C.E. Macedonia was Rome's first target in the east. After conflict and uneasy truces, Perseus, the last king of the Antigonid Dynasty, was defeated by the Romans at the Battle of Pydna in 168 B.C.E. (The Editors of the Encyclopaedia Britannica, 2021).

The Seleucid Empire proved too difficult to unite for many of Seleucus' descendants. Headed by kings more concerned with enjoying life and looking good, the Empire proved lethargic while invaders annexed territory satraps rebelled. Like many Seleucid kings after the brief resurgence under Antiochus III (241-187 B.C.E.), the last king, Philip II, lost his territory to the Parthians. The vision of a Greek empire in the east was gone after 56 B.C.E.

The Ptolemaic Dynasty didn't fare much better. Increasingly, the Ptolemaic monarchs struggled with civil war, family feuding, and the threat of Rome. When Rome began to extend eastwards, the Ptolemaic Dynasty became uneasy puppets of the new imperial power from the west. The last Ptolemaic pharaoh of Egypt was the infamous and tragic Cleopatra VII (Wasson, 2016). She died in 30 B.C.E., caught up on the losing side of Rome's civil war.

Parthians: The Eastern Buffer

One of the two powers that confronted the Seleucid, Ptolemaic, and Antigonid dynasties was the Parthian Empire (247 B.C.E.–224 C.E.), which lasted around 500 years. The Empire stretched from the Mediterranean Sea, including the old territory of Persia, all the way to India in the east. Initially, Parthia was part of the Seleucid Empire as one of the satrapies. The nomadic Parni tribe, however, managed to control the area, and by 247 B.C.E., had gained quite a bit of territory by the Caspian Sea. After defeating Antiochus VII of the Seleucid Dynasty at the Battle of Ecbatana in 129 B.C.E., they were able to expand even more.

Rome, however, had different plans. The two clashed over Armenia. The Parthians won, enlarging their territory. For a while, it seemed like the Parthians would be able to hold their own. This was due to their very unique fighting strategies. They used incredibly mobile fighting units that could pretend to retreat and then turn quickly or do hit-and-run strikes on the enemy. Using horse archers, the Parthians learned how to twist in the saddle and shoot from the back of a horse. This way, they could retreat and attack at the same time. This style of warfare frustrated many other opponents; and, to this day, a verbal zinger sent to an opponent to get the last word in is called a "Parthian Shot."

At the Battle of Carrhae in 53 B.C.E., the Parthians soundly defeated the Romans, taking the Roman standards captive. This was a severe blow to Roman morale. Crassus, who led the Roman army, was an ambitious politician and general who wanted the resources and wealth of the East for himself.

After facing Surena and his army on a tributary of the Euphrates River near the city of Carrhae, Crassus overestimated his power. Surena had successfully hidden the true size of his army behind hides, cloaks, and a wide frontline. Upon the death of his son during an unsuccessful counterattack, Crassus collapsed. His army of 43,000 was decimated in a day. Their retreat to Carrhae ended in refusals to accept a ceasefire. Crassus ended up dead, and Rome reeled from the loss of a powerful political leader and a large army (Hudson, 2019).

In the meantime, Parthia continued to enjoy the fruits of their territorial consolidation. By taking care of the roads and governmental infrastructure that they took from the Seleucid Empire, the Parthians were able to pick up old alliances and encourage the continuation of trade. They were also able to establish control over the Silk Road, allowing them to capitalize on the lucrative trade between China and the Mediterranean (Smith, 2019). The Parthians wouldn't survive forever, but for now, they managed to hold their own. It was only a matter of time before Rome returned.

Rome: Republic to Empire

Ultimately it was the second power, the Romans, that ended the three dynasties. The early days of the Roman Republic were rocky. As Greece reached the height of the Classical Period in the mid-5th century B.C.E., Rome was struggling with its Latin, Etruscan, and other Italic neighbors for control of central Italy. However, it slowly became dominant, absorbing many of the surrounding peoples and dealing with the consequent social and economic fallout through the 4th and early 3rd centuries B.C.E. Finally, after its first two major wars with Carthage (264-201 B.C.E.), Rome became a true imperial power.

Administering provinces outside Italy strained the political apparatus of a city-state, and the Roman Republic struggled to accommodate the growing influence of its generals and magistrates, leading to an increase in political violence after 133 B.C.E. A century of intermittent civil war followed.

However, Roman civil strife did not derail its expansion, and the internally dysfunctional Republic was an externally unstoppable military power that encroached on the Successor Kingdoms more and more.

The Fall of Macedon and the Seleucid Empire

A series of 4 Macedonian Wars (214-148 B.C.E.) thoroughly dismantled the Antigonid kingdom of Macedon, culminating in the complete sack of Corinth in 146 B.C.E., the same year Rome razed Carthage. Rome had conquered mainland Greece. Many Greek cities in western Anatolia followed when the Hellenistic King Attalus III of Pergamum left his kingdom to the Roman Republic in his will in 133 B.C.E. The territory became the Roman province of Asia.

The Greek independent spirit flared up again in 88 B.C.E., when another Hellenistic king, Mithridates VI of Pontus, declared war on Rome and invaded Asia. To expel Rome's influence from the East permanently, Mithridates massacred 100,000 Roman citizens in Anatolia, an episode now called the "Asiatic Vespers." He sent forces into Greece, and many *poleis* revolted against Roman control. Rome declared war.

The Mithridatic Wars raged until 63 B.C.E. Mithridates proved to be one of the Roman Republic's great antagonists, holding his own both politically and on the battlefield. Nevertheless, the Hellenistic phalanx could not stand toe-to-toe with the Roman legion. The Roman politician and general Gnaeus Pompeius Magnus (Pompey the Great) formally incorporated Anatolia and the last remaining dreg of the Seleucid Empire into the Roman provinces of Asia, Bithynia and Pontus,

Cilicia, and Syria. Rome ruled the Near East, and 2 of the great Hellenistic powers were no more.

The End of the Republic and the Fall of Ptolemaic Egypt

In 60 B.C.E., Pompey formed a political alliance with Gaius Julius Caesar and Marcus Licinius Crassus (who would later die at Carrhae fighting the Parthians). Despite Rome's republican structure, the three men forced through the measures they preferred over the next decade. After Crassus was killed at the Battle of Carrhae, Pompey and Caesar remained in power, gaining influence—which eventually drew them into direct conflict with each other (Appleton, 2022).

Crossing from Gaul (modern France) into Italy over the Rubicon River in 49 B.C.E., Caesar returned to Rome at the head of his army. It was an act of war, but Pompey fled. Caesar pursued him, beat him at the Battle of Pharsalus in 48 B.C.E., and forced him to again flee to Ptolemaic Egypt. Pompey, however, was killed by the Egyptians, who believed the gods favored Caesar. Julius Caesar was furious at the murder of his one-time friend.

At this point, Caesar was approached by the infamous Cleopatra VII. After deposing (and effectively killing) the teenage Ptolemy XIII, Caesar aligned himself with her. Cleopatra, born of the Ptolemaic line, understood Egypt. She was the only Ptolemaic ruler to learn how to read and write Egyptian. She was also more in touch with Egyptian culture even though she descended from a long line of Macedonian Greeks.

Recognizing that she needed Caesar's support to keep her throne, Cleopatra practiced careful diplomacy, showing herself to be one of the most formidable politicians of her era. Caesar accepted Cleopatra's support, giving her the regency of Egypt, which she was to co-rule with her younger brother, Ptolemy XIV. Caesar and Cleopatra maintained a passionate love affair until his assassination, producing a son, whom she named Caesarion.

Caesar returned victoriously to Rome in 46 B.C.E. Two years later, he was assassinated on the Ides of March (March 15th). Now Rome was beset by another power struggle between the most influential men left in Caesar's wake: Brutus, Cassius, Antony, and Octavian. Brutus and Cassius were forced to face Octavian and Antony, who temporarily teamed up to beat them at the Battle of Philippi in 42 B.C.E.

Mark Antony then joined Cleopatra in Egypt. At first, Antony harbored ambitious plans, hoping to invade Parthia. His expeditions only granted him temporary ownership of Armenia. Antony's triumphant return to Alexandria coincided with the announcement that Cleopatra's son, Caesarion, was in fact Julius Caesar's son, and therefore heir to Roman rule. Ptolemy XIV, with whom she shared rulership over Egypt, died, likely assassinated by Antony and Cleopatra.

Octavian, the nephew and adopted son of Julius Caesar, recognized the two as a threat. In a bid to consolidate his position, he challenged Antony and Cleopatra's forces at the Battle of Actium in 31 B.C.E. Octavian won, forcing the two to retreat to

Alexandria and fight a rearguard defense (Tyldesley, 2019).

Ultimately, the love of Antony and Cleopatra was their one weakness. Hearing fake news of Cleopatra's death, Antony fell on his sword. He was taken to Cleopatra, where he died in her arms. Although Antony begged her to make peace with Octavian, Cleopatra committed suicide right after, allowing herself to be bitten by a poisonous snake. After killing Cleopatra's 17-year-old son, Caesarion, Octavian was now in control. The Roman Republic was dead, and the Hellenistic Period was over (Mark, 2011).

The Decline of the Hellenistic Period

The dissolution of Hellenistic political power was largely due to the fact that, as Rome conquered new territory, its language, culture, and political organization dominated the regions. Of course, Alexandria and the other Hellenistic cities were not entirely destroyed. Many retained their Greek influences and language. Rome, for example, encouraged hybrid cultures, as long as the people were loyal to the Roman emperor.

In fact, Romans admired Greek culture. They tried to connect themselves to some of the most famous Greek stories. The Aeneid is an example of this tendency, placing a Roman ancestor at the Battle of Troy as a way to culturally validate their authority.

Greece and most of its colonies and kingdoms were now vassal states of Rome. But Greek culture persisted (and persists), impacting nearly every aspect of Roman life. It raised the Roman citizens to new heights of artistic, musical, and philosophical appreciation (Hoekstra, 2021).

Far to the east, the Sassanid Persians (224-651 C.E.) also kept remnants of the Hellenistic influence with their own art, writings, and academic pursuits. The Sassanid rulers were tolerant, allowing multiple faiths to flourish, although they mainly supported Zoroastrianism. Khosrow I (531-579 C.E.) was particularly famous for supporting the Academy of Gundeshapur, where Iranian literature and religious texts, Greek philosophical texts, and Indian writings were gathered. Here, they translated many of these texts into several languages, which were shared with Europeans centuries later (Cervantes, 2013).

Foundation Not Forgotten

As the sun set on the Hellenistic period and the dawn of Roman dominance began, the indelible imprints of Greek thought, art, and governance continued to resonate throughout history. Although the reins of power now lay in different hands, their stories, art, advancements, and philosophy continued to shape the minds of Roman youths and future politicians. The tales of bravery, the questions of existence, the beauty of sculptures, and the rhythm of Greek dramas were not just tales of an era gone by;

they were the foundations for many civilizations to come.

Conclusion

King Minos. Achilles. Homer. Solon. Leonidas. Pericles. Lysander. Socrates. Plato. Aristotle. Alexander. Cleopatra. Hypatia. The list could continue, did continue, for ages. These are just a few of the great men and women who directed the dramatic and epic history of ancient Greece. Their tales are filled with dangerous, heartbreaking, and shocking events. Their dreams and desires cost lives, expanded territory, and transformed the world.

Yet, there was another world in ancient Greece— the scholars, the creatives, and the humble workers. They tirelessly toiled to produce and consolidate the knowledge they had gathered, perpetuating it for future generations. The artists, musicians, and writers inspired each other, other countries, and many peoples throughout the centuries. Even more importantly, it was on the backs of the diligent laborers, artisans, and farmers of Greece that the enduring edifice of the Western tradition arose.

The Legacy of Greece

From their combined power, Greeks entrusted to the future a glorious heritage. Their legacy will always be remembered. For, thanks to Greece, art, architecture, academia, and politics will never be the same.

As we discovered, Greek art affected the entire ancient world. Their exported pottery, sculptures, jewelry, paintings, mosaics, clothes, and musical instruments influenced their neighbors. Furthermore, the art and music of Greece were perpetuated by their Roman successors. Through that Latin lineage, the cities of Venice, Florence, Paris, and even London were beautified with art and sculpture reminiscent of Greek aesthetics.

Greek architecture can also be seen across Europe and around the world. The Greek styles of Corinthian, Ionian, and Doric columns and capitals spread throughout the ancient world and are still used in modern times. Their monuments and public building designs were shared, inspiring future architects to attempt their own forms of beauty.

Academia was heavily impacted by Greek scholars. Math, science, medicine, philosophy, and history all exist on a Greek foundation. Thanks to Socrates, Aristotle, Plato, and many other Greek thinkers, ideas on how to learn, how to use logic, and how to define and classify the basis of the modern scientific method.

The philosophies they shared impacted secular and religious thought through the medieval era and even beyond, to modern thinkers. Furthermore, facts that we take for granted today—the heliocentric solar system, planetary movement, the Golden Ratio, and Pythagoras' theorem—were all formalized by the Greeks. The Hippocratic Oath was the first time medicine and ethics combined to make a vow "to do no harm."

Besides all that, Greek people and scholars also impacted the literature and linguistics of many cultures beyond their own. Thanks to the Greeks, the earliest Phoenician script evolved into what we know as Classical Greek today. Coopted and further evolved by the Romans, the more phonetic alphabet ended up becoming an important piece of the English and other European languages.

In the literary world, Greece inspired future writers with their own epic tales of Troy and Odysseus. Ancient Greek playwrights formalized play structures, genres, and literary concepts, like irony; any word ending in "onomy" or "ology" is rooted in the Greek language. Other words like stadium, gymnasium, drama, and democracy originate from their culture, as well.

History as Their Story

We owe a lot to the Greeks. When we read their histories, it is important to remember that these people once lived as we did, with their own dreams, ambitions, strengths, and flaws. Seen in this light, it might become easier for you to recognize the inherent drama of Greek history. Their stories, adventures, and tragedies are ready and waiting for us to explore.

As the echoes of Ancient Greece resonate within these pages, remember that the past holds treasures that illuminate the paths of the future. If the tales, art, and philosophy within this volume stirred your spirit, share your insights and reviews. Recommend this book to friends, family, and anyone with a thirst for knowledge. The legacy of Greece is not just in its past, but in how its tales inspire the present.

Every era might have an end, but its stories, lessons, and inspirations endure. Dive deeper, discuss more, and let the spirit of inquiry guide your journey through history and life.

References

Achievements. (n.d.). Foundation of the Hellenic World. http://www.fhw.gr/chronos/02/mainland/en/mg/a chievements/index.html#:~:text=The%20Mycenaea ns%20adopted%20the%20numeration

Alexander the Great. (2017). Khan Academy. https://www.khanacademy.org/humanities/world-history/ancient-medieval/alexander-the-great/a/alexander-the-great

Alexander the Great. (2019). Ushistory. https://www.ushistory.org/civ/5g.asp

Alexander's empire. (2023). Lumen Learning. https://courses.lumenlearning.com/atd-herkimer-westerncivilization/chapter/alexanders-empire/

Alphabet (Early Greek). (2007, December 13). Joukowsky Institute for Archaeology. https://www.brown.edu/Departments/Joukowsky_I nstitute/courses/greekpast/4739.html#:~:text=The %20early%20Greek%20alphabet%20was

Ambury, J. M. (2022). *Socrates.* Internet Encyclopedia of Philosophy. https://iep.utm.edu/socrates/

Ancient Corinth. (2023). CyArk. https://www.cyark.org/projects/ancient-corinth/in-depth#:~:text=The%20Greek%20city%20of%20Cori nth

Ancient DNA reveals origins of the Minoans and Mycenaeans. (n.d.). Max-Planck-Gesellschaft. Retrieved August 31, 2023, from https://www.mpg.de/11419864/origins-of-minoans-and-mycenaeans#:~:text=The%20Mycenaean%20civiliza tion%20

Ancient Greece. (n.d.). *Discovery Techbook.* https://www.lee.k12.nc.us/cms/lib03/NC01001912/ Centricity/Domain/1464/Ancient%20Greece%20geo graphy%20mod.pdf

Ancient Greece geography: Landscape & map. (2023). Study.com. https://study.com/learn/lesson/anicent-greece-geography-landscape.html#:~:text=Many%20of%20the%20Greek%20city

Ancient Greece: Impact of geography. (n.d.). East Ramapo Central School District. https://www.ercsd.org/site/handlers/filedownload.ashx?moduleinstanceid=195&dataid=2330&FileName=03-022---Ancient-Greece--Impact-of-Geography-handout.pdf

Ancient Greek farming lesson for kids. (2022). Study.com. https://study.com/academy/lesson/ancient-greek-farming-lesson-for-kids.html#:~:text=Wheat%2C%20barley%2C%20olives%2C%20and

Ancient wisdom: 21 famous Aristotle quotes. (2023). DSF Antique Jewelry. https://dsfantiquejewelry.com/blogs/interesting-facts/ancient-wisdom-21-famous-aristotle-quotes

Ansari, A. (2012, July 14). Alexander the not so great: History through Persian eyes. *BBC News.* https://www.bbc.com/news/magazine-18803290

Appleton, S. (2022, September 28). *Rome's transition from republic to empire.* National Geographic Society. https://education.nationalgeographic.org/resource/romes-transition-republic-empire/

Archaeological site of Troy. (1998, December 2). UNESCO World Heritage Centre. https://whc.unesco.org/en/list/849/

Archaic Greece. (n.d.). Lumen Learning. https://courses.lumenlearning.com/atd-herkimer-westerncivilization/chapter/archaic-greece/

Armstead, K. (2023). *Peloponnesian War: Causes & results.* Study.com. https://study.com/learn/lesson/peloponnesian-war-causes-results.html#:~:text=What%20were%20the%20three%20main

Athens vs Sparta - difference and comparison. (2019).
Diffen.
https://www.diffen.com/difference/Athens_vs_Sparta

Bencze, A. (2014). *Art and craft in Archaic Sparta*. The
Met's Heilbrunn Timeline of Art History.
https://www.metmuseum.org/toah/hd/spar/hd_spar.htm#:~:text=In%20fact%2C%20in%20the%20seventh

Bennett, A. (2020, December 5). *10 reasons the ancient
city of Alexandria was an intellectual powerhouse*.
TheCollector.
https://www.thecollector.com/ancient-city-alexandria-intellectual-powerhouse/

Betancourt, P. P. (1969). *The age of Homer: An exhibition
of geometric and orientalizing Greek art*. Expedition
Magazine.
https://www.penn.museum/sites/expedition/the-age-of-homer/#:~:text=Herodotus%20suggested%20that%20he%20lived

Bileta, V. (2023, February 28). *4 battles from Alexander
the Great's legendary Persian campaign*.
TheCollector.
https://www.thecollector.com/alexander-greatest-battles/

Blakeley, S. (2022a). *Plato's Theory of Forms*. Study.com.
https://study.com/learn/lesson/plato-theory-forms-realm-physical.html#:~:text=Plato

Blakeley, S. (2022b). *The Iliad & The Odyssey by Homer*.
Study.com. https://study.com/learn/lesson/iliad-odyssey-homer-summary-characters.html

Bliss, R. (2022). *The Greco-Persian Wars: Causes &
results*. Study.com.
https://study.com/learn/lesson/greco-persian-wars-results-significance.html

Bloks, M. (2015, July 22). *The seven wives of Philip II of
Macedon*. History of Royal Women.
https://www.historyofroyalwomen.com/the-royal-women/the-seven-wives-of-philip-ii-of-macedon/

Bloxham, J. (2016, April 12). *Nicias*. World History Encyclopedia. https://www.worldhistory.org/Nicias/

Boeree, C. G. (2000). *Epicureans and Stoics*. Shippensburg University. https://webspace.ship.edu/cgboer/latergreeks.html

Brinkhof, T. (2022, March 1). *Socratic problem: How Plato and other Greek writers invented Socrates*. Big Think. https://bigthink.com/the-past/socratic-problem-plato-socrates/

Brown, T. (2022, September 21). *The lasting legacy of ancient Greek leaders and philosophers*. National Geographic Society. https://education.nationalgeographic.org/resource/lasting-legacy-ancient-greek-leaders-and-philosophers/

Bucephalus: the true story of Alexander the Great's legendary horse. (2023). History Skills. https://www.historyskills.com/classroom/ancient-history/bucephalus/#:~:text=Bucephalus%20accompanied%20Alexander%20on%20many

Buis, A. (n.d.). *Mycenaean art*. British Columbia/Yukon Open Authoring Platform. https://pressbooks.bccampus.ca/cavestocathedrals/chapter/738/

Buis, A. (2023). Hellenistic Period. *PressBooks*. https://pressbooks.bccampus.ca/cavestocathedrals/chapter/hellenistic/

Carr, K. (2017a, July 7). *Ancient Corinth - Mycenaean and Archaic*. Quatr.us Study Guides. https://quatr.us/greeks/ancient-corinth-mycenaean-archaic.htm#:~:text=In%20the%20early%20Archaic%20period

Carr, K. (2017b, July 7). *Corinth, Greece in the Classical period*. Quatr.us Study Guides. https://quatr.us/greeks/corinth-classical-period.htm

Cartwright, M. (2009, September 2). *Corinth*. World History Encyclopedia. https://www.worldhistory.org/corinth/

Cartwright, M. (2013a, February 8). *Alcibiades*. World History Encyclopedia. https://www.worldhistory.org/Alcibiades/

Cartwright, M. (2013b, April 16). *Battle of Thermopylae*. World History Encyclopedia. https://www.worldhistory.org/thermopylae/

Cartwright, M. (2013c, May 5). *Battle of Salamis*. World History Encyclopedia. https://www.worldhistory.org/Battle_of_Salamis/

Cartwright, M. (2013d, May 11). *Battle of Plataea*. World History Encyclopedia. https://www.worldhistory.org/Plataea/

Cartwright, M. (2013e, May 19). *Battle of Marathon*. World History Encyclopedia. https://www.worldhistory.org/marathon/

Cartwright, M. (2013f, June 6). *Polis*. World History Encyclopedia. https://www.worldhistory.org/Polis/#:~:text=The%20polis%20emerged%20from%20the

Cartwright, M. (2016a, March 18). *Lysander*. World History Encyclopedia. https://www.worldhistory.org/Lysander/

Cartwright, M. (2016b, July 25). *Food & agriculture in Ancient Greece*. World History Encyclopedia. https://www.worldhistory.org/article/113/food--agriculture-in-ancient-greece/

Cartwright, M. (2018a, March 20). *Ancient Greek government*. World History Encyclopedia. https://www.worldhistory.org/Greek_Government/

Cartwright, M. (2018b, March 29). *Minoan Civilization*. World History Encyclopedia. https://www.worldhistory.org/Minoan_Civilization/

Cartwright, M. (2018c, May 7). *Greek colonization*. World History Encyclopedia. https://www.worldhistory.org/Greek_Colonization/

Cartwright, M. (2019, October 2). *Mycenaean civilization*. World History Encyclopedia. https://www.worldhistory.org/Mycenaean_Civilization/

Cartwright, M. (2020, April 27). *The legacy of the Ancient Greeks*. World History Encyclopedia.

https://www.worldhistory.org/collection/75/the-legacy-of-the-ancient-greeks/

Cason, T. S. (n.d.). *Cycladic, Minoan, and Mycenaean civilization*. Florida State College. https://fscj.pressbooks.pub/earlyhumanities/chapter/cycladic-and-minoan-civilization/#:~:text=The%20Minoan%20Civilization%20

Cervantes, A. C. (2013, May 17). *Sasanian Empire*. World History Encyclopedia. https://www.worldhistory.org/Sasanian_Empire/#:~:text=Although%20certainly%20still%20Hellenized%2C%20the

Chaliakopoulos, A. (2021, March 26). *Who were the Diadochi of Alexander The Great?* TheCollector. https://www.thecollector.com/who-were-the-diadochi-of-alexander-the-great/

Chrysopoulos, P. (2023a, January 2). *The first time all Greek people united together*. Greek Reporter. https://greekreporter.com/2023/04/02/league-corinth-greek-people-united/

Chrysopoulos, P. (2023b, January 28). *Decoding Linear A, the writing system of the ancient Minoans*. Greek Reporter. https://greekreporter.com/2023/01/28/decoding-linear-a-the-writing-system-of-the-ancient-minoans/

Classical Greek culture. (2018). Khan Academy. https://www.khanacademy.org/humanities/world-history/ancient-medieval/classical-greece/a/greek-culture

Claus, P. (2023, August 20). *Minoan language Linear A linked to Linear B in groundbreaking research*. Greek Reporter. https://greekreporter.com/2023/08/20/minoan-language-linear-a-linear-b/

Cleopatra, Julius Caesar and Mark Antony: how the last pharaoh's love affairs shaped Ancient Egypt's fate. (2020, August 21). HistoryExtra. https://www.historyextra.com/period/ancient-

egypt/cleopatra-love-affairs-julius-caesar-mark-
antony/

*Cleopatra's relationships with Julius Caesar and Mark
Antony.* (2013, September 16). Scholaradvisor.com.
https://www.scholaradvisor.com/essay-
examples/cleopatra-relationships/

Cooper, J. M. (1998). *Socrates (469–399 BC).* Routledge
Encyclopedia of Philosophy.
https://www.rep.routledge.com/articles/biographica
l/socrates-469-399-bc/v-1

Coumoundouros, A. (n.d.). *Plato: The Republic.* Internet
Encyclopedia of Philosophy.
https://iep.utm.edu/republic/

Cox, T. (2017). *Ptolemy XIII Theos Philopator.* World
History Encyclopedia.
https://www.worldhistory.org/Ptolemy_XIII_Theos
_Philopator/

Daniel, J. F., Broneer, O., & Grey, H. T. W. (1948). The
Dorian Invasion: The setting. *American Journal of
Archaeology, 52*(1), 107–110.
https://doi.org/10.2307/500556

Davis, Dr. J. L. (2023, March 13). *Agriculture and
settlement: Farm and field at Ancient Mycenaean
Pylos.* Brewminate: A Bold Blend of News and Ideas.
https://brewminate.com/agriculture-and-
settlement-farm-and-field-at-ancient-mycenaean-
pylos/

Deakin, M. (2019). Hypatia. *Encyclopædia Britannica.*
https://www.britannica.com/biography/Hypatia

Decline of the Mycenaean Civilization (1250-1050 BCE).
(2022, July 13). Climate in Arts and History.
https://www.science.smith.edu/climatelit/decline-
of-the-mycenaean-civilization-1250-1050-bce/

Dmitriev, S. (2011). The Macedonian peace of Philip II
and Alexander the Great. *Oxford University Press
EBooks,* 67–111.
https://doi.org/10.1093/acprof:oso/9780195375183.
003.0002

Dorian Invasion. (2023). Academic Accelrator.
https://academic-
accelerator.com/encyclopedia/dorian-invasion

Duignan, B. (2019a). Democritus. *Encyclopædia Britannica.*
https://www.britannica.com/biography/Democritus

Duignan, B. (2019b). Plato and Aristotle: How do they differ? *Encyclopædia Britannica.*
https://www.britannica.com/story/plato-and-aristotle-how-do-they-differ

Edwards, A. S. (2022, October 19). *Alexander's relationships: Facts and myths.* British Library.
https://www.bl.uk/alexander-the-great/articles/alexanders-relationships-facts-and-myths

Effects of the Peloponnesian War. (2023). Lumen Learning. https://courses.lumenlearning.com/atd-herkimer-westerncivilization/chapter/effects-of-the-peloponnesian-war/

Effects of the Persian Wars. (2023). Lumen Learning. https://courses.lumenlearning.com/atd-herkimer-westerncivilization/chapter/effects-of-the-persian-wars/

Everything you ever wanted to know about the Rosetta Stone. (2017, July 14). The British Museum.
https://www.britishmuseum.org/blog/everything-you-ever-wanted-know-about-rosetta-stone#:~:text=The%20importance%20of%20this%20to

Example questions. (n.d.). Varsity Tutors. Retrieved September 1, 2023, from
https://www.varsitytutors.com/ancient_history_greece-help/fall-of-mycenaean-civilization-and-the-greek-dark-ages

Feen, R. H. (1996). Keeping the balance: Ancient Greek philosophical concerns with population and environment. *Population and Environment, 17*(6), 447–458. https://www.jstor.org/stable/27503492

Fernandes, F. (2022, March 16). *The Bactrian Kingdom: Greeks at the extremities of the known world.* TheCollector. https://www.thecollector.com/bactria-greek-hellenistic-kingdom/

Gabriel, R. (2017, July 14). *Alexander the Great: Monster of Macedonia.* Historynet.

https://www.historynet.com/alexander-the-monster/

Garrett, E. (2019). *The Socratic Method*. University of Chicago Law School. https://www.law.uchicago.edu/socratic-method

Geography of Ancient Greece. (n.d.). Students of History. https://www.studentsofhistory.com/geography-of-ancient-greece#:~:text=The%20Geography%20of%20Ancient%20Greece&text=The%20mountains%20of%20Ancient%20Greece

German, S. (2022). *Snake Goddess*. Khan Academy. https://www.khanacademy.org/humanities/ancient-art-civilizations/aegean-art1/minoan/a/snake-goddess

Gill, N. S. (2019a). *A timeline of the Peloponnesian War's major battles*. ThoughtCo. https://www.thoughtco.com/timeline-battles-treaties-peloponnesian-war-112444

Gill, N. S. (2019b). *Introduction to the Persian Wars*. ThoughtCo. https://www.thoughtco.com/introduction-to-the-greco-persian-wars-120245

Golden, J. (2012). *Chapter 16: Battle of Carrhae Romans versus the Parthians*. O'Reilly. https://www.oreilly.com/library/view/winning-the-battle/9780071791991/ch16.html#:~:text=The%20Battle%20of%20Carrhae%2C%20fought

Graham, J. N. (2023). *Ancient Greek philosophy*. Internet Encyclopedia of Philosophy. https://iep.utm.edu/ancient-greek-philosophy/#H5

Greek Boston. (2017a, March 22). *Rise of the Mycenaean Civilization in Ancient Greece*. Greek Boston. https://www.greekboston.com/culture/ancient-history/rise-mycenaean-civilization/

Greek Boston. (2017b, May 26). *About the Dorian Invasion of Ancient Greece*. Greek Boston. https://www.greekboston.com/culture/ancient-history/dorian-invasion/

Greek city-states. (2022, May 20). National Geographic Society.

https://education.nationalgeographic.org/resource/greek-city-states/

Greek Ministry of Culture. (1999). *The archaeological sites of Mycenae and Tiryns.* https://whc.unesco.org/uploads/nominations/941.pdf

Griffith, G. T. (2019). Philip II . *Encyclopædia Britannica.* https://www.britannica.com/biography/Philip-II-king-of-Macedonia

Groarke, L. F. (n.d.). *Aristotle: Logic.* Internet Encyclopedia of Philosophy. https://iep.utm.edu/aristotle-logic/

Gulati, A. (n.d.). *Delian League.* Brown University. https://www.brown.edu/Departments/Joukowsky_Institute/courses/greekpast/4773.html

Hall, E. (2021, May 27). *Cynics, Stoics, Epicureans.* Gresham College. https://www.gresham.ac.uk/watch-now/cynics-stoics-epicureans

Hanselman, S. (2020, October 6). *Stoicism vs. Epicureanism.* Daily Stoic. https://dailystoic.com/stoicism-vs-epicureanism/

Haskett, D. R., Racine, V., & Yang, J. (2016, July 7). *Aristotle (384-322 BCE).* The Embryo Project Encyclopedia. https://embryo.asu.edu/pages/aristotle-384-322-bce#:~:text=During%20Aristotle

Hatch, P. (n.d.). *Tholos tomb.* Brown University. https://www.brown.edu/Departments/Joukowsky_Institute/courses/greekpast/4904.html

Hays, J. (2018). *Seleucids and the division of Alexander's empire after his death.* Facts and Details. https://factsanddetails.com/world/cat56/sub366/entry-6412.html

Hellenistic Art: Hellenism in Classical Antiquity. (n.d.). Encyclopedia of Art and Classical Antiquities. http://www.visual-arts-cork.com/antiquity/hellenistic-art.htm

Hemingway, C. (2019a). *Ancient Greek colonization and trade and their influence on Greek art.* Metmuseum.org.

https://www.metmuseum.org/toah/hd/angk/hd_an
gk.htm

Hemingway, C. (2019b). *Art of the Hellenistic Age and
the Hellenistic Tradition*. The Metropolitan Museum
of Art.
https://www.metmuseum.org/toah/hd/haht/hd_ha
ht.htm

Hemingway, S., & Hemingway, C. (2004). *The rise of
Macedon and the conquests of Alexander the Great*.
The Met's Heilbrunn Timeline of Art History.
https://www.metmuseum.org/toah/hd/alex/hd_ale
x.htm#:~:text=Phillip%20II%20instituted%20far%2
0reaching

Hirst, K. K. (2018). *Linear A: Early Cretan writing
system*. ThoughtCo.
https://www.thoughtco.com/linear-writing-system-
of-the-minoans-171553

Historical context for Homer. (2019). Columbia College.
https://www.college.columbia.edu/core/node/1744

History of Corinth. (2023). American School of Classical
Studies at Athens.
https://www.ascsa.edu.gr/excavations/ancient-
corinth/about-the-excavations-1/history-timeline

History of Greece during Stone and Bronze Age. (n.d.).
Greeka. Retrieved August 30, 2023, from
https://www.greeka.com/greece-history/stone-
bronze-age/#:~:text=The%20Stone%20Age

History of Greece: The Dark Ages. (2023). Ancient
Greece. https://www.ancient-
greece.org/history/dark-ages.html

History.com Editors. (2009a, November 9). *Cleopatra*.
History. https://www.history.com/topics/ancient-
egypt/cleopatra

History.com Editors. (2009b, November 9). *Pericles*.
History. https://www.history.com/topics/ancient-
greece/pericles

History.com Editors. (2009c, November 9). *Plato*.
History. https://www.history.com/topics/ancient-
greece/plato

History.com Editors. (2009d, November 9). *Socrates*. History. https://www.history.com/topics/ancient-greece/socrates

History.com Editors. (2018, August 21). *Stone Age*. History. https://www.history.com/topics/pre-history/stone-age

History.com Editors. (2019, August 22). *Aristotle*. History. https://www.history.com/topics/ancient-greece/aristotle

History.com Editors. (2023a, May 31). *Trojan War*. History. https://www.history.com/topics/ancient-greece/trojan-war#section_3

History.com Editors. (2023b, August 23). *Alexander the Great: Empire & death*. History. https://www.history.com/topics/ancient-greece/alexander-the-great#section_2

Hoekstra, K. (2021, November 5). *What brought about the end of the Hellenistic Period?* History Hit. https://www.historyhit.com/what-brought-about-the-end-of-the-hellenistic-period/

Hoffmann, H. (2000, January 12). *Western architecture - Mycenaean Greece*. Encyclopedia Britannica. https://www.britannica.com/art/Western-architecture/Mycenaean-Greece

Homer's World. (2011). Camel Unified School District. https://moodle.carmelunified.org/moodle/pluginfile.php/81883/mod_resource/content/1/Odyssey%20Textbook%20Homers%20World%202015-16.pdf

Hornblower, S. (2023, September 4). *Ancient Greek civilization*. Encyclopedia Britannica. https://www.britannica.com/place/ancient-Greece/Solon

Hudson, M. (2019, September 10). *Battle of Carrhae*. Encyclopedia Britannica. https://www.britannica.com/event/Battle-of-Carrhae

Hutton, S. (2023). *6.4 The spread of Hellenistic culture*. Teaching California. https://www.teachingcalifornia.org/inquiry-sets/6-4-the-spread-of-hellenistic-culture/#:~:text=First%20the%20Greeks%20

Hypatia. (2018). Famous Scientists.
https://www.famousscientists.org/hypatia/

International Olympic Committee. (2021, April 27). *Welcome to the Ancient Olympic Games.* International Olympic Committee. https://olympics.com/ioc/ancient-olympic-games

Jarus, O. (2017, August 26). *Ancient Troy: The city and the legend.* Live Science. https://www.livescience.com/38191-ancient-troy.html

Jarus, O., & Gordon, J. (2017, August 31). *Alexander the Great: Facts, Biography & accomplishments.* Live Science. https://www.livescience.com/39997-alexander-the-great.html

Jones, E. J. (2018). Long Distance Trade and the Parthian Empire: Reclaiming Parthian Agency from an Orientalist Historiography. *Western Washington University.* https://cedar.wwu.edu/cgi/viewcontent.cgi?article=1717&context=wwuet

Juma, N. (2019, July 22). *Socrates quotes on life, wisdom & philosophy to inspire you.* Everyday Power. https://everydaypower.com/socrates-quotes/

Kampouris, N. (n.d.). *Odyssey: Homer's epic poem is the world's most influential story.* Greek Reporter. https://greekreporter.com/2022/04/01/odyssey-homer-epic-poem-is-officially-the-worlds-most-influential-story/

Kirk, G. S. (2023, July 7). *Homer.* Encyclopædia Britannica. https://www.britannica.com/biography/Homer-Greek-poet#ref524682

Kivilo, M. (2010). *Early Greek poets' lives: The shaping of the tradition.* Brill. https://library.oapen.org/bitstream/handle/20.500.12657/29586/1000346.pdf

Klaeser, M. (2021, July 7). *Mycenaean society.* World History Encyclopedia. https://www.worldhistory.org/Mycenaean_Society/#:~:text=Mycenaean%20society

Kordas, A., Lynch, R. J., Nelson, B., & Tatlock, J. (2023, April 19). *3.1 Early Civilizations*. Openstax. https://openstax.org/books/world-history-volume-1/pages/3-1-early-civilizations#:~:text=The%20development%20of%20early%20civilizations

Koutoupis, P. (2018, January 6). *In search of the mythical King Minos, did the legendary ruler really exist?* Ancient Origins: Reconstructing the Story of Humanity's Past. https://www.ancient-origins.net/myths-legends-europe/search-mythical-king-minos-did-legendary-ruler-really-exist-009394

Koy, M. (2021, June 21). *The Greco-Bactrian Kingdom.* The History Inquiry. https://medium.com/the-history-inquiry/the-greco-bactrian-kingdom-c4c37c87fc7

Kraut, R. (2004, March 20). *Plato*. Stanford Encyclopedia of Philosophy. https://plato.stanford.edu/entries/plato/

Kraut, R. (2019). Socrates - Background of the trial. *Encyclopædia Britannica.* https://www.britannica.com/biography/Socrates/Background-of-the-trial

Kraut, R. (2022, July 2). *Aristotle's ethics*. Stanford Encyclopedia of Philosophy. https://plato.stanford.edu/entries/aristotle-ethics/

Kruse, S. (2022, April 13). *The Socratic Method: Fostering critical thinking*. The Institute for Learning and Teaching. https://tilt.colostate.edu/the-socratic-method/

Kuznetsov, I. (n.d.). *Greek ranges*. PeakVisor. Retrieved August 30, 2023, from https://peakvisor.com/range/greek-ranges.html

Lake, T. (2021, October 26). *Socrates' philosophy: The ancient Greek philosopher and his legacy*. TheCollector. https://www.thecollector.com/socrates-philosophy-ancient-greek-philosopher-legacy/

Lake, T. (2022, December 20). *An in-depth understanding on the four virtues of Stoicism.*

TheCollector. https://www.thecollector.com/four-cardinal-virtues-stoicism/

Largo, M. (2014, August 21). *Big, bad botany: Hemlock (Conium maculatum), the philosopher's choice.* Slate. https://slate.com/technology/2014/08/poisonous-plants-socrates-drank-hemlock-tea-as-his-preferred-mode-of-execution.html#:~:text=When%20his%20blood%20touched%20the

Leeming, D. A. (2023). *Who were the Cycladic and Minoan peoples and what was their history?* Papertrell. https://www.papertrell.com/apps/preview/The-Handy-Mythology-Answer-Book/Handy%20Answer%20book/Who-were-the-Cycladic-and-Minoan-peoples-and-what-was-their-/001137032/content/SC/52caff2e82fad14abfa5c2e0_default.html#:~:text=the%20Cycladic%20civilizati on%20had%20developed

Legacies of Ancient Greece. (2023). Study.com. https://study.com/learn/lesson/legacies-ancient-greece-contributions-influences-examples.html#:~:text=Euclid%20built%20off%20t he%20number

Legacy of Ancient Greece. (2023). History for Kids. https://www.historyforkids.net/legacy-of-ancient-greece.html

Legacy of Ancient Greece: Art, government, science & sports. (2020). Study.com. https://study.com/academy/lesson/legacy-of-ancient-greece-art-government-science-sports.html

Leonard, B., & Zimbler, S. (2016, April 13). *Homer: inspiration and controversy [Infographic].* OUPblog. https://blog.oup.com/2016/04/homer-inspiration-and-controversy/#:~:text=Since%20then%2C%20scholar s%20have%20used

Lewis, D. M. (2019). Pericles. In *Encyclopædia Britannica.*

https://www.britannica.com/biography/Pericles-Athenian-statesman

Linder, D. O. (2019). *The trial of Socrates*. Famous Trials. https://www.famous-trials.com/socrates/833-home

Lloyd, J. (2016, December 22). *Periander*. World History Encyclopedia. https://www.worldhistory.org/Periander/

Logo-. (2017, April 19). Online Etymology Dictionary. https://www.etymonline.com/word/logo-?ref=etymonline_crossreference

Lomas, K. (2014). Greek Colonialism, Archaeology of. In: Smith, C. (eds) Encyclopedia of Global Archaeology. Springer, New York, NY. https://doi.org/10.1007/978-1-4419-0465-2_1435

Lonsdale, D. M. (2011). The campaigns of Alexander the Great. *Oxford University Press EBooks*, 14–34. https://doi.org/10.1093/acprof:oso/9780199608638.003.0002

Mamakouka, I.-A. (2014, March 25). *10 of the most significant writers of Ancient Greece*. Greek Reporter . https://greekreporter.com/2014/03/25/10-of-the-most-significant-writers-of-ancient-greece/

Mann, M. J. (2013, October 30). *The bullet point Alexander: Philip II's wives*. The Second Achilles. https://thesecondachilles.com/2013/10/30/the-bullet-point-alexander-philip-iis-wives/

Mark, J. (2011, April 28). *Julius Caesar*. World History Encyclopedia. https://www.worldhistory.org/Julius_Caesar/

Mark, J. (2018, March 28). *Pericles*. World History Encyclopedia. https://www.worldhistory.org/pericles/

Mark, J. J. (2013, November 14). *Alexander the Great*. World History Encyclopedia. https://www.worldhistory.org/Alexander_the_Great/

Mark, J. J. (2015a, January 30). *Greek Dark Age*. World History Encyclopedia. https://www.worldhistory.org/Greek_Dark_Age/

Mark, J. J. (2015b, February 5). *Greek alphabet*. World
    History Encyclopedia.
    https://www.worldhistory.org/Greek_Alphabet/
Mark, J. J. (2019, October 22). *Seleucid Empire*. World
    History Encyclopedia.
    https://www.worldhistory.org/Seleucid_Empire/
Marlowe, C. (1604). *From Doctor Faustus ("Was this the
    face that launched a thousand ships?")*.
    Representative Poetry Online.
    https://rpo.library.utoronto.ca/content/doctor-
    faustus-was-face-launched-thousand-ships
Mason, M. K. (2023). *Alexandria and the Hellenistic
    World*. Www.moyak.com.
    https://www.moyak.com/papers/ancient-
    alexandria.html
McLean, J. (n.d.). *Greek Dark Ages*. Lumen Learning.
    https://courses.lumenlearning.com/atd-herkimer-
    westerncivilization/chapter/greek-dark-ages/
Meinwald, C. C. (2018). Plato. *Encyclopædia Britannica*.
    https://www.britannica.com/biography/Plato
Messerly, J. (2014, October 17). *Summary of Aristotle's
    theory of human nature*. Reason and Meaning.
    https://reasonandmeaning.com/2014/10/17/theorie
    s-of-human-nature-chapter-9-aristotle-part-1/
Metaphysics summary. (n.d.). SuperSummary. Retrieved
    September 9, 2023, from
    https://www.supersummary.com/metaphysics/sum
    mary/
Meyer, I. (2022a, April 13). *Hellenistic Art – Ancient
    Greek multiculturalism*. Art in Context.
    https://artincontext.org/hellenistic-art/
Meyer, I. (2022b, May 6). *Archaic Greek art - an
    overview of the Greek Archaic period*. Art in
    Context. https://artincontext.org/archaic-greek-art/
Movellán Luis, M. (2018, January 31). *Rise and fall of the
    mighty Minoans*. History.
    https://www.nationalgeographic.com/history/histor
    y-magazine/article/Minoan_Crete
Muscato, C. (2019). *Pericles of Athens: Facts,
    achievements & death*. Study.com.

https://study.com/academy/lesson/pericles-of-athens-facts-achievements-death.html

Mycenae architecture: Info & photos. (n.d.). Greeka. https://www.greeka.com/peloponnese/mycenae/architecture/#:~:text=One%20of%20the%20distinctive%20features

Mycenaean architecture: History, characteristics & influences. (2021, December 5). Study.com. https://study.com/academy/lesson/mycenaean-architecture-history-characteristics-influences.html

Mycenaean civilization. (2023). Study.com. https://study.com/learn/lesson/mycenaean-civilization-social-structure.html#:~:text=The%20Mycenaeans%20flourished%20c.

Mycenaean warrior vase, 12th century BCE. (n.d.). Brock University. https://brocku.ca/blogs/brock-odyssey-2017/2017/06/17/mycenaean-warrior-vase-12th-century-bce/#:~:text=Mycenaean%20Clay%20is%20well%20oknown

Myers, C., Caldwell, E. C., Taylor, A. J., Phelps, M., & Soccio, L. (2021, July 7). *8.3: Mycenaean*. Humanities LibreTexts. https://human.libretexts.org/Bookshelves/Art/Introduction_to_Art_History_I_(Myers)/08%3A_The_Ancient_Aegean/8.03%3A_Mycenaean

Nagy, G. (2017). *Homer, Odyssey*. Columbia. https://edblogs.columbia.edu/worldepics/project/homer-odyssey/

Nails, D. (2018). *Socrates*. Stanford Encyclopedia of Philosophy. https://plato.stanford.edu/entries/socrates/

Nair, S. S. (2017, March 2). *Philosopher Plato quotes on knowledge and learning*. YourStory. https://yourstory.com/2017/03/29-quotes-by-plato#:~:text=%E2%80%9CTruth%20is%20the%20beginning%20of

National Geographic Society. (2022a, May 20). *Greek city-states*. National Geographic Society.

https://education.nationalgeographic.org/resource/greek-city-states/

National Geographic Society. (2022b, May 20). *Philip II of Macedon*. National Geographic Society. https://education.nationalgeographic.org/resource/philip-ii-macedon/

National Geographic Society. (2022c, May 20). *The Peloponnesian War*. National Geographic Society. https://education.nationalgeographic.org/resource/peloponnesian-war/

National Geographic Society. (2022d, September 28). *Key components of civilization*. National Geographic. https://education.nationalgeographic.org/resource/key-components-civilization/

Noonan, M. (2023). *Athens vs. Sparta in Ancient Greece*. Study.com. https://study.com/learn/lesson/athens-sparta-differences-life.html#:~:text=Athens%20was%20a%20democratic%20state

O'Connor, J. J., & Robertson, E. F. (2020). *Hypatia of Alexandria*. Maths History. https://mathshistory.st-andrews.ac.uk/Biographies/Hypatia/

orwell1627. (2013, June 30). *Aristotle's purpose of life*. The Great Conversation. https://orwell1627.wordpress.com/2013/06/30/aristotles-purpose-of-life/

Peloponnesian War timeline. (n.d.). World History. https://www.worldhistory.org/timeline/Peloponnesian_War/

Piper, G. (2020, June 9). *After Alexander: The wars of Succession*. Exploring History. https://medium.com/exploring-history/after-alexander-the-wars-of-succession-ecf843c949ca

Rappe, K. (n.d.). *The Greco-Bactrian Mirage: Reconstructing a history Hellenistic Bactria*. Retrieved September 13, 2023, from https://uwarchive.files.wordpress.com/2010/12/kirk-rappe.pdf

Reimer, M. J., & Mackie, J. A. (2019). Alexandria.*Encyclopædia Britannica*.

https://www.britannica.com/place/Alexandria-Egypt

Roberts, C. (2023). *Mycenaean civilization*. Study.com. https://study.com/learn/lesson/mycenaean-civilization-social-structure.html#:~:text=The%20Mycenaeans%20flourished%20c.

Roman legionary, Macedonian phalanx, or Spartan hoplite: Which was the better ancient warrior? (2023). History Skills. https://www.historyskills.com/classroom/ancient-history/legion-vs-phalanx-vs-hoplite/

Roos, D. (2019, September 9). *How Alexander the Great conquered the Persian Empire*. HISTORY. https://www.history.com/news/alexander-the-great-defeat-persian-empire

Ryder, M., & Salim, M. (2012). A Middle Eastern vision of progress. *World Pumps*, *2012*(5), 28–31. https://doi.org/10.1016/s0262-1762(12)70128-1

Schools of philosophy in antiquity: Cynics, Epicureans & Stoics. (2023). Study.com. https://study.com/academy/lesson/schools-of-philosophy-in-antiquity-cynics-epicureans-stoics.html

Schroeder, S. (2017). *The Roman Republic*. Khan Academy. https://www.khanacademy.org/humanities/world-history/ancient-medieval/roman-empire/a/roman-republic

Shewey, D. A. (2004, June 2). *Athenian ambitions & the Delian League*. Western Oregon University. https://wou.edu/history/files/2015/08/David-Shewey.pdf

Shields, C. (2008, September 25). *Aristotle*. Stanford Encyclopedia of Philosophy. https://plato.stanford.edu/entries/aristotle/

Simonin, A. (2011, April 28). *Indo-Greek*. World History Encyclopedia. https://www.worldhistory.org/Indo-Greek/

Smith, P. S. (2019, September 30). *Parthia: Rome's ablest competitor*. World History Encyclopedia.

https://www.worldhistory.org/article/1445/parthia-romes-ablest-competitor/

Smith, R. (2017). *Aristotle's logic*. Stanford Encyclopedia of Philosophy. https://plato.stanford.edu/entries/aristotle-logic/

Stamatios, D. (2023, February 5). *Greco-Bactrian Kingdom*. Trenfo. https://www.trenfo.com/en/history/civilizations/greco-bactrian-kingdom

Standjofski, A. (2022, October 20). *What happened during the trial of Socrates?* TheCollector. https://www.thecollector.com/the-famous-trial-of-socrates/

Stirn, M. (2022, October 3). Unearthing everyday life at an ancient site in Greece. *The New York Times*. https://www.nytimes.com/2022/10/03/travel/iklaina-archaeology-greece.html

Struck, P. (2000). *The Trojan War*. University of Pennsylvania. https://www2.classics.upenn.edu/myth/php/homer/index.php?page=trojan

Tai Engen, D. (2019). *The economy of Ancient Greece*. Eh.net. https://eh.net/encyclopedia/the-economy-of-ancient-greece/

Tang, W. (2019, September 19). *The comprehensive Greek islands travel guide*. Going Awesome Places. https://goingawesomeplaces.com/the-comprehensive-greek-islands-travel-guide/

The dark side of Alexander the Great. (2022, September 24). Hellenistic History. https://www.hellenistichistory.com/2022/09/06/the-dark-side-of-alexander-the-great/

The development of Archaic, Classical, and Hellenistic sculpture compared to Medieval, Renaissance, and Baroque. (n.d.). Google Arts & Culture. https://artsandculture.google.com/usergallery/the-development-of-archaic-classical-and-hellenistic-sculpture-compared-to-medieval-renaissance-and-baroque/swIyh2aIVVDXJg

The Editors of Encyclopaedia Britannica. (2017a, December 11). *polis*. Encyclopaedia Britannica. https://www.britannica.com/topic/polis

The Editors of Encyclopaedia Britannica. (2017b, December 15). *Academy*. Encyclopedia Britannica. https://www.britannica.com/topic/Academy-ancient-academy-Athens-Greece

The Editors of Encyclopaedia Britannica. (2018). Minos. *Encyclopædia Britannica.* https://www.britannica.com/topic/Minos

The Editors of Encyclopaedia Britannica. (2019a). Brasidas. *Encyclopædia Britannica.* https://www.britannica.com/biography/Brasidas

The Editors of Encyclopaedia Britannica. (2019b). Linear A and Linear B. *Encyclopædia Britannica.* https://www.britannica.com/topic/Linear-A

The Editors of Encyclopaedia Britannica. (2019c). Trojan War. *Encyclopædia Britannica.* https://www.britannica.com/event/Trojan-War

The Editors of Encyclopaedia Britannica. (2020, April 3). *Cleon*. Encyclopedia Britannica. https://www.britannica.com/biography/Cleon-Athenian-politician

The Editors of Encyclopaedia Britannica. (2021, April 29). *Achievements and decline of the Hellenistic Age.* Encyclopaedia Britannica. https://www.britannica.com/summary/Hellenistic-Age

The Editors of Encyclopædia Britannica. (2009, April 1). *Minoan*. Encyclopedia Britannica. https://www.britannica.com/topic/Minoan

The Editors of Encyclopædia Britannica. (2015). Delian League. *Encyclopædia Britannica.* https://www.britannica.com/topic/Delian-League

The Editors of Encyclopædia Britannica. (2018a). Greco-Persian Wars. *Encyclopædia Britannica.* https://www.britannica.com/event/Greco-Persian-Wars

The Editors of Encyclopædia Britannica. (2018b). Peloponnesian War. *Encyclopædia Britannica.*

https://www.britannica.com/event/Peloponnesian-War

The Editors of Encyclopædia Britannica. (2019). Aristotle - Political theory. *Encyclopædia Britannica.* https://www.britannica.com/biography/Aristotle/Political-theory

The Editors of Encyclopædia Britannica. (2020a, August 28). *Alexander the Great's achievements.* Encyclopedia Britannica. https://www.britannica.com/summary/Alexander-the-Greats-Achievements

The Editors of Encyclopædia Britannica. (2020b). League of Corinth | Facts, History, & Definition | Britannica. *Encyclopædia Britannica.* https://www.britannica.com/topic/League-of-Corinth

The Editors of Encyclopædia Britannica. (2021a, April 21). *Parthia.* Encyclopedia Britannica. https://www.britannica.com/place/Parthia

The Editors of Encyclopædia Britannica. (2021b, April 29). *Explore the military campaigns of Alexander the Great.* Encyclopedia Britannica. https://www.britannica.com/summary/Alexander-the-Great

The Editors of Encyclopædia Britannica. (2023, February 27). *Spear.* Encyclopedia Britannica. https://www.britannica.com/technology/spear-weapon#ref186595

The Editors of Encyclopedia Britannica. (2018). Phidias. *Encyclopædia Britannica.* https://www.britannica.com/biography/Phidias

The Editors of the Encyclopaedia Britannica. (1998, July 20). *Archilochus.* Encyclopedia Britannica. https://www.britannica.com/biography/Archilochus-Greek-author

The Editors of the Encyclopaedia Britannica. (2021, August 30). *Antigonid dynasty.* Encyclopaedia Britannica. https://www.britannica.com/topic/Antigonid-dynasty

The great debate: Who would win if the Roman legions fought Macedonian phalanxes? (2023). History Skills. https://www.historyskills.com/classroom/ancient-history/legion-vs-phalanx/

The Greek polis. (2017). Khan Academy. https://www.khanacademy.org/humanities/world-history/ancient-medieval/classical-greece/a/the-greek-polis#:~:text=The%20rise%20of%20the%20polis

The military revolution: What were Philip II's reforms of the Macedonian military and how revolutionary were they? (n.d.). https://www.ed.ac.uk/files/atoms/files/the_military_revolution_-_what_were_philip_iis_reforms_of_the_macedonian_military_and_how_revolutionary_were_they.pdf

The Phaistos Disc. (2022, April 19). Heraklion Archaeological Museum. https://www.heraklionmuseum.gr/en/exhibit/the-phaistos-disc/#:~:text=The%20Phaistos%20Disc%20is%20one

Theory of Forms. (n.d.). Saylor Academy. https://learn.saylor.org/mod/book/tool/print/index.php?id=30538

Tomb of Leonidas. (2016, January 9). Dodeka. http://grecorama.com/en/tomb-of-leonidas/

Townsend Vermeule, E. D., & Hood, M. S. F. (1999, July 6). *Aegean civilizations.* Encyclopedia Britannica. https://www.britannica.com/topic/Aegean-civilization

Trelawny-Cassity, L. (n.d.). *Plato: The Academy.* Internet Encyclopedia of Philosophy. https://iep.utm.edu/plato-academy/

Tronson, A. (1984). Satyrus the Peripatetic and the Marriages of Philip II. *The Journal of Hellenic Studies, 104,* 116–126. https://doi.org/10.2307/630283

Tsagalis, Christos C. (2020). The Homeric question: a historical sketch. *Yearbook of Ancient Greek Epic Online, 4*(1), 122–162. https://doi.org/10.1163/24688487-00401006

Turner, W. (1903). *Chapter IX: Plato.* History of Philosophy. https://maritain.nd.edu/jmc/etext/hop09.htm

Tyldesley, J. (2019). Cleopatra. *Encyclopædia Britannica.* https://www.britannica.com/biography/Cleopatra-queen-of-Egypt

Vanderpool, E., & Ehrlich, B. (2018). Athens. *Encyclopædia Britannica.* https://www.britannica.com/place/Athens

Virgil. (2019). *Virgil: The Aeneid, Book II.* Poetry in Translation. https://www.poetryintranslation.com/PITBR/Latin/VirgilAeneidII.php

Volkmann, H. (2019a, November 12). *Antigonus.* Encyclopedia Britannica. https://www.britannica.com/biography/Antigonus-I-Monophthalmus

Volkmann, H. (2019b, November 12). *Antigonus II Gonatas.* Encyclopedia Britannica. https://www.britannica.com/biography/Antigonus-II-Gonatas

Walbank, F. W. (1951). The problem of Greek nationality. *Phoenix, 5*(2), 41. https://doi.org/10.2307/1086119

Walbank, F. W. (2018). Alexander the Great. *Encyclopædia Britannica.* https://www.britannica.com/biography/Alexander-the-Great

Wasson, D. (2016, September 29). *Ptolemaic Dynasty.* World History Encyclopedia. https://www.worldhistory.org/Ptolemaic_Dynasty/

Wasson, D. L. (2014, July 31). *Philip II of Macedon.* World History Encyclopedia. https://www.worldhistory.org/Philip_II_of_Macedon/

What did they wear in Ancient Greece? Mycenaean attire. (n.d.). National Clothing. https://nationalclothing.org/europe/42-greece/579-

what-did-they-wear-in-ancient-greece-mycenaean-attire.html

Whelan, E. (2020, September 8). *The Age of Homer, or the Dark Ages (12th-9th century)*. Classical Wisdom Weekly. https://classicalwisdom.com/culture/history/the-age-of-homer-or-the-dark-ages-12th-9th-century/

Wilburn, H. (2020). *An introduction to Aristotle's metaphysics*. Philosophical Thought. https://open.library.okstate.edu/introphilosophy/chapter/__unknown__/

Williams, J. K. (2008, February 12). *Athens - birthplace of democracy*. New York Post. https://nypost.com/2008/02/12/athens-birthplace-of-democracy/

Williams, R. (2019, August 6). *Macedonian combined arms warfare*. Medium. https://medium.com/@robert.f.williams/the-macedonian-army-exhibited-a-tactical-brilliance-that-set-a-precedent-in-the-employment-of-9f8548657045

Woerner, J. (2022). *What was the Delian League?* Study.com. https://study.com/learn/lesson/the-delian-league.html#:~:text=The%20Delian%20League%20was%20created

Woodard, T. M., & Taplin, O. (2018). Sophocles. *Encyclopædia Britannica*. https://www.britannica.com/biography/Sophocles

Image References

Atlantios. (2018). Spartan, private, statuette image. In *Photograph*. [Image.] https://pixabay.com/photos/spartan-private-statuette-3082537/

bigfoot. (2013). Fresco, bull, Palace of knossos image. In
    Photograph. [Image.]
    https://pixabay.com/photos/fresco-bull-palace-of-
    knossos-111056/
brianneises. (2015). Trojan horse, Troy, Trojan image. In
    Photograph. [Image.]
    https://pixabay.com/photos/trojan-horse-troy-trojan-
    horse-607574/
DiscoverMacedonia. (2018). Water, nature, river image. In
    Photograph. [Image.]
    https://pixabay.com/photos/water-nature-river-travel-
    mountain-3133678/
ExplorerBob. (2017). Statue, Philip of Macedon, Skopje image.
    In *Photograph*. [Image.]
    https://pixabay.com/photos/statue-philip-of-macedon-
    skopje-2540966/
fietzfotos. (2019). Crete, Greece, amphitheater image. In
    Photograph. [Image.] https://pixabay.com/photos/crete-
    greece-amphitheater-ancient-4217004/
flutie8211. (2023). Ai generated Alexander the great king
    royalty-free stock illustration. In *Photograph*. [Image.]
    https://pixabay.com/illustrations/ai-generated-
    alexander-the-great-8222225/
GDJ. (2021). The Death Of Socrates Socrates painting royalty-
    free vector graphic. In *Photograph*. [Image.]
    https://pixabay.com/vectors/the-death-of-socrates-
    socrates-6471743/
Gina_Janosch. (2016). Mycenae, Lions tomb, wall image. In
    Photograph. [Image.]
    https://pixabay.com/photos/mycenae-lions-tomb-wall-
    1350376/
Hans. (2016). Italy Alps Alpine region royalty-free stock
    illustration. In *Photograph*. [Image.]
    https://pixabay.com/illustrations/italy-alps-alpine-
    region-map-1804893/
HeikoAL. (2017). Crete, museum, historical image. In
    Photograph. [Image.] https://pixabay.com/photos/crete-
    museum-historical-old-minoan-2391755/
rickytolt186. (2022). Bucephalus, the war of the heavenly
    horses, Ferghana horse image. In *Photograph*. [Image.]
    https://pixabay.com/photos/bucephalus-6952339/

Louis le Grand. (2007) Marble bust of Cleopatra VII of Egypt from ca. 40-30 BC. marked as public domain, details on Wikimedia Commons: https://commons.wikimedia.org/wiki/Template:PD-old [Image.] https://commons.wikimedia.org/wiki/File:Kleopatra-VII.-Altes-Museum-Berlin1.jpg

Rita E. (2017). Sea, Aegean sea, outlook image. In *Photograph*. [Image.] https://pixabay.com/photos/sea-aegean-sea-outlook-nei-pori-2729955/

stux. (2013). Ancient, temple, nature image. In *Photograph*. [Image.] https://pixabay.com/photos/ancient-temple-ruin-corinthian-170183/

symvol. (2014). London, British museum, Ancient Greece image. In *Photograph*. [Image.] https://pixabay.com/photos/london-british-museum-ancient-greece-244263/

user32212. (2017). Acropolis, Parthenon, ancient image. In *Photograph*. [Image.] https://pixabay.com/photos/acropolis-parthenon-ancient-columns-2047093/

VIVIANE6276. (2019). Homer, Odyssey, Ancient Greece image. In *Photograph*. [Image.] https://pixabay.com/photos/homer-odyssey-ancient-greece-a%C3%A8de-4570409/

Vlachos, N. (2022). A statue of a man riding a horse. In *Photograph*. [Image.] https://unsplash.com/photos/nfSsyAkYgcs

wpaczocha. (2017). Terrace cultivation, terrace, Greece image. In *Photograph*. [Image.] https://pixabay.com/photos/terrace-cultivation-terrace-greece-2745920/

The Wolves of Mars

---

*An Introductory History of Rome
from the Rise of the Monarchy to
the Fall of the Western Empire*

Aeon History

Introduction

If Twitter (or X, as it's called these days) had existed during the fall of the Roman Empire, #RomeIsFalling would probably have trended. But behind this mighty collapse was a centuries-old saga of ambition, intrigue, and innovation that laid the foundation for every empire that followed. Unlike the trending topics of modern social media, the destiny of the Roman Empire didn't vanish within a few hours. As it is said, "Rome wasn't built in a day," and it certainly didn't disappear in a flash. Dive deep into the chronicles of Rome, and you might just see reflections of our world today.

The Roman Empire wasn't the first in human history, and it wasn't even the largest. However, it had certain features that made it unique, and its legacy is enduring and influential in the contemporary world, far beyond its old boundaries. While empires like the Mongols or the British had larger territories, the Roman Empire's longevity was unmatched. For over two millennia, its institutions and laws have directly influenced a large portion of the modern world, including foundational aspects of legal systems in places ranging from the UK to parts of Africa (Kinder & Hilgemann, 1996).

Rome in Modern Culture

Rome has captivated people's attention for ages. The stories of the Romans reflect their virtues and glory but also highlight their vices and weaknesses. Films, media, and pop culture have taken popular figures from ancient Rome to depict controversial (therefore attractive) aspects of the Romans' lives. Yet, most of these modern interpretations are guided by marketing rules rather than historical rigor. The attempt to move the audience seems to be more important than a reliable academic background. This type of content plays a valuable role in introducing people to historical knowledge, but it is usually fraught with errors that lead to misconceptions.

For history enthusiasts, it is a great challenge to find resources that can balance reliable and relevant information with an engaging storyline. History is a colossal collection of facts, battles, important figures, and processes that are hard to digest for those who aren't used to academic works. But those who don't belong to the academic world shouldn't need to suffer through those heavy-reading books of many volumes to unravel the most interesting secrets of our history. They need to find some better-researched sources to learn about our past than a series from a streaming service. That should be left as a means of entertainment and perhaps a way to foster our curiosity to learn the truth behind the artificial modern plots.

The past is always a source of endless intrigue. What is true and what is not about the good (or bad) old days? Have we left savage practices behind, or do we still resemble our ancestors from over 2500 years ago? Is humankind really moving forward to a promising future? These are the types of questions that move us to learn history. We want to understand the past to explain our present. But over 2500 years of history encompass too many topics to delve into. Almost 2,000 years of Roman history seem unfathomable. How can we discriminate between the "need to know" and the "nice to know"?

The Purpose of This Book

This book aims to zoom in on the prominent figures, milestones, and fundamental processes that marked the evolution of the history of Rome and elucidate how our Western civilization developed out of its rich legacy. However, this doesn't mean that the understanding of Roman history and its long-lasting heritage is restricted by a Eurocentric scope. On the contrary, it aims to broaden the scope and provide insightful explanations of how different cultures were blended throughout history, making today's world what it is. The Romans interacted in many different ways with neighboring cultures and learned from other civilizations, and their influence persists in present-day cultures all over the world.

By reading this book, you will not only gain knowledge but also a newfound appreciation for the monumental influence of the Roman Empire on the modern world (*Traces of Ancient Rome in the Modern World*, n.d.). New perspectives on the distant past that lies beneath the ground of our modern culture are at the core of this book. It's a comprehensive guide to a fascinating past that shaped our mindset and values. The framework for understanding the empire laid the foundation of a timeless ideal: one nation, one power. Somehow, it still summarizes the current objectives of order, peace, stability, and progress.

To facilitate comprehension of the long and complex evolution of Roman civilization, the book is organized into three parts that condense major periods: The Monarchy (753–509 B.C.E.), The Republic (509–27 B.C.E.), and The Roman Empire (27 B.C.E.– 476 C.E.). The first part covers prehistoric Italy, including the primitive peoples who lived on the peninsula, the mythical beginnings of ancient Rome, and the first political organization: the Roman Monarchy.

The second part covers the Roman Republic. The political and social organization of this period not only laid the foundation for the greatest empire of antiquity but also formed the basis of Western political and legal structures down to the present.

The third and last part is dedicated to exploring and explaining the details of the Roman Empire, beginning with the progressive concentration of power in the figure of Augustus until its final collapse (at least in the West).

It is impossible to understand Rome without considering the interplay between politics, culture, military conquests, and social dynamics. Each part is divided into chapters that explain the evolution of social, economic, and political changes in a chronological format to simplify the complex progression of Rome for a non-specialist reader. Instead of slogging through multiple academic texts, this book provides an integrated insight, alternating relevant details with a depiction of the big picture.

The approach to analyzing this evolution is not a mere collection of facts. Instead, *The Wolves of Mars* aims to give a human face to historical events. This version of Rome's history is based on the Romans' stories of ordinary people being part of the legions and attending the amphitheaters, as well as extraordinary leaders like Romulus (if he existed),

Scipio, Caesar, Augustus, Marcus Aurelius, and Constantine.

The Enduring Legacy of Rome

Despite the extensive research and coverage dedicated to the ancient Roman era, the subject remains perennially captivating. The following pages retrieve traditional scholarly researchers' main contributions about the period, blended with insights derived from the latest archaeological findings and historical research, ensuring up-to-date and accurate information. In addition to this, the book is a springboard for more in-depth exploration, with curated recommendations for further reading.

The team at Aeon History has a vast appreciation for ancient history and classical archaeology and it believes in the power of history as a tool to shape the present and build a better future. This book is an invitation to discover engaging and accurate insights into a period that seems so distant and, at the same time, is hidden in the little things of the modern world.

Whether you are a history buff who constantly seeks out new books or this is your first approach to studying the past independently, we invite you on a fascinating journey over 2,500 years to vividly revive the days of Roman gladiators, emperors, philosophers, artists, and soldiers. Embark on this adventure of conquests, dominating the *Mare*

Nostrum ("Our Sea" – The Mediterranean), fighting against the Barbarians, and building the foundations of Western civilization. *Omnes Salvete!* (Welcome, Everyone!)

Note: All translations from ancient sources are by Aeon History.

Part 1: Prehistoric Italy to the Fall of the Roman Monarchy

(ca. 753 B.C.E. – 509 B.C.E.)

Chapter 1: Italian Prehistory and the Bronze Age

Humans dwelt on the Italian landscape long before Rome existed. Its fertile soil, pleasant climate, and central location ensured that all inhabitants had an opportunity to thrive.

The Geographic Landscape of Prehistoric Italy

Italy is a boot-shaped peninsula measuring 600 miles long and 150 miles wide that juts out into the Mediterranean basin. It is surrounded by the Adriatic

Sea to the east and the Tyrrhenian Sea to the west. The northwest side limits the Ligurian Sea, and the Ionian Sea separates Italy from Greece. Italy also includes two large Mediterranean islands, Sicily and Sardinia.

Italy is crossed from north to south by the Apennine Mountain range, the backbone of the peninsula. While in ancient Greece, mountains served to divide the city-states, or *poleis*, in the Italian Peninsula, the Apennines facilitated trade and connected communities. Italy is enclosed in the north by the highest peaks of Europe, the Alps. At present, they are Italy's natural border with France, Switzerland, Austria, and Slovenia.

Prehistoric Italy didn't have the same political boundaries as in the present, but the native prehistoric people settled in the plains at the bottom of both major mountain ranges. During the last Ice Age, people sheltered in the natural refuges provided by rocky caves on the slopes of the mountains.

Then, after the climate warmed and agricultural knowledge arrived, they searched for lands near the rivers. This process mirrored events in Mesopotamia, along the Tigris and the Euphrates, near the Ganges and Indus Rivers in India, and by the Nile in Egypt. In Italy, the most fertile lands were the basins of key rivers like the Tiber, in central Italy, and the Po, in the north.

The Tiber is the most important river in prehistoric Italy. It is the second longest on the peninsula, behind the Po. The Tiber begins in the

Apennine Mountains and runs southwest into the Tyrrhenian Sea. It divides the peninsula into two parts, and it was a source of fresh water for the population that settled in its basin.

Moreover, the river was an important means of transportation that allowed the evolution of trading because of its direct connection with the Mediterranean Sea. It was used to link the peninsula with people from Greece and Northern Africa, like the Phoenicians (*The Geography of Ancient Rome*, n.d.). The river was also a natural frontier, useful in case of attack when the first urban settlements were established in the region.

At a bend in the Tiber River, a system of hills created the perfect landscape to build a city. The hills protected the inhabitants from attack and allowed them to control commerce between the north and south. The weather—hot and dry summers and wet and mild winters—was perfect for animals, crops, and the blossom of a new civilization. It was the perfect place for the Eternal City.

Defining History

Historians have divided the past into periods to facilitate the study and comprehension of humankind's evolution. The concept of "prehistory" refers to everything before the invention of the written word. This is certainly a modern, "Eurocentrist" designation. Even at present, many cultures don't use the written word either to register their present or to study their past, and that definitely doesn't mean they lack a vibrant and meaningful past. Likewise, the so-called "prehistoric" cultures of the ancient world faced the same trials, tribulations, and (often) triumphs of later peoples. Nevertheless, without writing, most of their narrative remains hidden from us.

"History," therefore, starts with the invention of the written word about 6,000 years ago in Mesopotamia. Historians divide it into ages or eras considering relevant events as landmarks that represent the transition from one to another. On the other hand, "prehistory" is divided in regard to the elements human beings mastered to attend to their needs.

About 12,000 years ago, people began to develop techniques for cultivating the land - agriculture. Being able to raise their food allowed and motivated people to settle in river basins. The invention of agriculture marks the beginning of the Neolithic, or New Stone Age. Agriculture and its attendant advancements are often called the Neolithic Revolution.

When people settled and became sedentary, more complex societies emerged. They developed a division of labor and social hierarchies based on the roles people performed or the properties they owned. They learned to cultivate crops, grow livestock, and master metals. Therefore, the Neolithic isn't divided by counting years, but by the stages of humankind's evolution regarding the metals they used to manufacture weapons and tools.

The Deepest Prehistory of Italy

During the Paleolithic and Mesolithic periods (Old and Middle Stone Ages), people lived in nomadic hunter-gatherer tribes. In Italy, the first early human presence can be traced back to 850,000 years ago. According to recent archaeological findings, *Homo erectus* lived 700,000 years ago in the La Pineta district, and it is the oldest human settlement found in Europe. There is also evidence of human presence in the Balzi Rossi caves in Liguria. These were inhabited between 350,000 and 300,000 B.C.E.

The earliest permanent settlements on the peninsula, dating to the Stone Age, belonged to *Homo neanderthalensis* – Neanderthals, who lived in Europe and Southwestern Asia. In Italy, they were at the Saccopastore site by about 250,000 B.C.E.

Homo sapiens sapiens (modern humans) appeared in the region about 34,000 years ago, and their first settlements were found in the Grotta *di Furmane*, Sardinia, Lombardy, and Liguria (Ancos, 2018). Modern humans spread across Europe in the Paleolithic period when a Glacial Era enlarged the polar caps.

While there is still controversy about how or why the Neanderthals disappeared, it is now known that they coexisted with modern humans and even mixed with them. The first modern humans in Europe had dark hair and dark skin, and Neanderthals had red hair. It is believed that the species interacted, and some current modern human populations have genes from both (Carr, 2017), although *Homo sapiens sapiens* predominated.

Archeological remains suggest that the first modern humans who arrived in Italy came from West Asia about 10,000 B.C.E., roughly in the Middle of the Mesolithic period in Europe (Carr, 2017). This was also near the end of the Last Ice Age. Several theories explain the migratory flows. Since they were hunter-gatherers, they probably moved from one place to another, following the animals they hunted for food and their skin and bones. They must have also sought more temperate climates and placed their temporary settlements in places with enough resources, including water and shelter.

During the Last Ice Age, people (Neanderthals and modern humans) sheltered in caves and left paintings on the rocks. The most important remains in Italy are the rock carvings and paintings in Valcamonica. Archeologists have found some remains of that early population, such as stone tools and paintings of animals, probably reflecting what they hunted or part of their rituals to ensure success in the hunt.

Nonetheless, those remains are significantly fewer than at other archaeological sites on the continent, for instance, in France and Spain. This suggests that the region wasn't densely inhabited if compared to other regions of the continent (Carr, 2017).

The Neolithic Revolution in Italy

In Italy, the earliest farmer communities settled between 7,000 and 5,000 B.C.E. (Carr, 2017; Shaw, 2015) in the period called the Neolithic or New Stone Age. These people weren't the same nomadic groups that sheltered in the caves. Instead, it is believed that they came from Greece in boats, sailing along the coasts.

These people had already developed agriculture and sedentary settlements, and the colonization of new lands was due to the depletion of natural resources in their homeland. Colonization processes were a response to social pressure when the distribution of resources wasn't enough to sustain parts of the population.

It doesn't mean that there weren't any native social groups on the peninsula by the time eastern migrants colonized the coastal areas. The central lands of the peninsula were indeed inhabited by the natives, who also developed agriculture and entered the Neolithic period sometime after the arrival of people from Greece and the Balkans.

Even though there were very limited means of communication, prehistoric peoples interacted much more than is usually imagined. They exchanged goods and traded, but, more importantly, they taught and learned from each other. Therefore, agricultural communities inspired hunter-gatherer nomadic groups to introduce new economic and social practices.

One of the key pieces of evidence to prove the passage from nomadic to sedentary life is burial sites. People might have had burial rituals and beliefs regarding the passage from life to death, but burial sites reveal the intention to keep the deceased close by. It is a sign of evolution in the development of a sense of belonging and social identity.

In Italy, archeologists found the oldest burial site in Europe. They found the bones of at least 22 human beings, many of them children, who died between 7,500 and 7,200 years ago. The bodies were buried in Scaloria Cave in the Tavoliere region (Southern Italy) (Shaw, 2015) and became the first documented remains of the first farmer community in the area. According to the reports, the bodies underwent the process of defleshing: "When people died, villagers stripped their bones bare, pulled them apart, and mingled them with animal remains in a nearby cave. The practice was meant to separate the dead from the living" (Shaw, 2015, para. 1).

The Italian Bronze Age

The Bronze Age was a stage of technological growth that developed out of the Neolithic and implied the use of bronze. This metal is obtained by alloying tin and copper at about 1742 °F. Then, artisans would mold the new metal and use it to manufacture weapons and tools instead of stone. It is associated with early European civilizations that lived in the 4th and 3rd millennia B.C.E. (Knowles, n.d.).

In Italy, the Bronze Age is dated between 2,300 and 950 B.C.E., and it concentrated in the wetland locations along the Alpine margin. It is believed that former communities inhabited the area, but there is no evidence. The oldest artifacts found in the area are axes, which were stored in a separate place from the settlement. These people also used amber and faience (glazed ceramics) to manufacture prestige artifacts, which revealed different social statuses.

Later, settlements in the Po Valley region increased. These banked and ditched settlements are called *Terramare*. The demographic density increased throughout the period, and the complex drainage works and the pile-built dwellings are signs of a highly organized society mainly dedicated to metal production (*The Italian Bronze Age*, n.d.).

In the central plains and the upper lands of the Apennines, the period is usually referred to as the Apennine Bronze Age (*The Italian Bronze Age*, n.d.). The remains show pastoralist communities. They also had levels of social status revealed by the burial rituals. According to the archeological findings, the warriors were at the top of the social pyramid. The evolution of the use of bronze is linked to trade with the cultures in the Aegean Sea – early Greeks.

Traders from the Aegean reached the southern coasts of Sicily and Sardinia. However, they also reached the north-central region of the Terramare by sea. There are Aegean pottery remains in northern Italy, and they reveal a vibrant trade relationship in the 13th and 12th centuries B.C.E.

The Nuragic Civilization: An Example of Indigenous Tribes

There were many prehistoric Italian cultures, each with its own distinctive styles of pottery, architecture, jewelry, weapons, and other artifacts. A survey of every group would be massive, but a short description of one culture might give the reader an impression of the richness of many ancient societies that are now lost to time.

Between the early Bronze Age and the 2nd century B.C.E., Nuragic civilization flourished on the islands of Corsica and Sardinia. These "prehistoric" people evolved before and during the Romans' hegemony in Italy.

This civilization owes its name to the towers they built, known as Nuraghe. They are examples of megalithic remains (monuments of stone with different meanings depending on the period and culture). Some theories suggest that these towers were used as fortresses, prisons, temples, or tombs (Ancos, 2018).

During the Bronze Age, Nuragic art depicted animals from Africa and weapons from the Aegean, which suggests contact with people from other lands. They were in touch with the Mycenaean Greeks, the Egyptians of the New Kingdom, and later with the Phoenician and Greek colonial settlements around the Mediterranean (*Nuragic Monuments of Sardinia*, n.d.).

The Dawn of the Iron Age

The passage from one age into another didn't happen in a short period of time and in all regions simultaneously. Around the 13th century B.C.E., while many civilizations were still developing the use of bronze in Scandinavia and other areas of Europe, some discovered how to refine a new metal that was found in nature - iron. It was easier to find than copper but required kilns capable of much higher heat than those used for making bronze.

Once human beings mastered the metal, a true technological revolution started with significant consequences. The process of manufacturing weapons and tools became faster and cheaper; therefore, the number of products quickly increased. New and more sophisticated tools enabled an improvement in the production of everything and better infrastructure for towns.

Increased production capacity led to a rapid demographic increase, and that implied a higher pressure on the environment. More crops were needed to feed an increasing population; therefore, more trees were cut down to widen the farmland and to provide more wood to fuel the furnaces used to melt and shape iron. Wood was also used to manufacture weapons and tools, and the circle continued.

In the long term, the Bronze and Iron Ages witnessed an unprecedented demographic expansion and a large-scale technological revolution. Societies changed, and the emergent states began to fight each other to conquer lands and obtain resources that became progressively scarce.

The shift from bronze to iron introduced many changes in warfare. Its evolution coincides with the collapse of several important civilizations in the Bronze Age: the Egyptian, Mycenaean Greek, and Hittite cultures were in crisis caused by the so-called Sea People. This meant a reshaping of the Mediterranean world's balance of power.

Moreover, the discovery of iron changed the trading networks. The coastal settlements of Italy traded for bronze and iron with the Middle East, India, and the lands in between. Then, over the centuries, other goods were incorporated into a far-reaching network of trade routes (Sherry & Zamechek, n.d.).

The Iron Age in Italy

Between the 12th and 8th centuries B.C.E., different West Indo-European tribes entered and settled the Italian peninsula from the Po valley through the plains at the feet of the Apennines to the southern coasts. They interacted with the native tribes of Italy, including the Etruscans, whom we will discuss in depth in the following section.

The Indo-European tribes originated from the Balkan Peninsula and likely migrated there from the Pontic steppe, located on the northern coast of the Black Sea. They may have entered Italy from the northeast (Kessler & Dawson, 2019).

Many Indo-European groups arrived in Italy in the late Bronze and early Iron ages. The three most important for our purposes here are the Iapyges, Italics, and Greeks. The first group settled primarily in the southeast, in modern Apulia – the heel of Italy's boot. The Italics arrived about two centuries later and settled in the central plains at the foot of the Apennines (Kessler & Dawson, 2019).

Starting in the 8th century B.C.E., Greeks began to colonize the western Mediterranean. Their presence in the southern half of Italy was so widespread that the later Romans called southern Italy *Magna Graecia* – "Greater Greece." All three groups intermingled with the native population. Therefore, the tribes that lived in Italy during the early Iron Age were a mixture of immigrants and natives.

Finally, in the late Iron Age, another tribe coming from central Europe entered the peninsula through the Alps and pressured the populations living in the Po valley. They represent the Golasecca culture, and some of their descendants were known to the Romans as Ligurians. They remained present in the northwest of the peninsula and controlled the northern plains for several centuries (Kessler, n.d.).

The Iron Age includes all of ancient Roman history. For the duration of the Roman Monarchy and most of the Republic, the peninsula was a patchwork of many different cultures that exchanged ideas, goods, and resources – all mutually shaping one another. And they just as often went to war, eventually losing to, and being absorbed by, Rome. As one scholar has put it, "Politically, many of these people were fiercely inclined towards independence. At the same time, however, the diffusion of Hellenistic (Greek) ideas, fashions, and styles created a range of 'hybrid' cultures that were only unified by Rome" (Kamash et al., 2013, p. 336).

The Etruscans

One of the most important civilizations that lived on the Italian Peninsula during the early Iron Age was the Etruscans. Their origin was different from the other tribes described before, and there is no certainty about where they came from. They had unique practices, although they interacted with and received influence from the Greek colonists. For scholars, the origins and early history of the Etruscans remain a mystery.

This ancient civilization thrived in central Italy between the 11th and 9th centuries. After a long, slow decline in influence, they were eventually supplanted by the Romans in the 3rd century B.C.E. Genetic samples gathered by researchers indicate that the civilization flourished mostly in Etruria, modern Tuscany, and the island of Corsica.

Herodotus, the ancient Greek historian, argued that these people, who called themselves Rasenna, invaded Etruria from Anatolia before 800 B.C.E. and displaced the native population of the region. Other historians, instead, believed that they were native to the peninsula and that they were even the Sea People who caused the collapse of other ancient empires, including the Mycenaean Greeks and the Hittites (Comunale, 2022).

One of the greatest mysteries surrounding the Etruscans is related to their language. In the historical period, they were surrounded by Indo-European languages: the Greeks in the south, the Celtic Gauls in the north, and the Italic Umbrians, Samnites, Sabines, and Latins to the southeast (Comunale, 2022). Nonetheless, the Etruscan language didn't share the same Indo-European roots, and (if the prevalent modern theories are correct) it may have formed as a distinct member of the "Tyrsenian" language group by the 13th century B.C.E. Unfortunately, the Tyrsenian languages are all poorly attested, and the earliest Etruscan inscription dates from about 700 B.C.E.

One major theory hypothesizes that, during the late Bronze Age, they arrived from across the sea and established themselves in Tuscany, where they founded important cities such as Pisa, Bologna, and Capua. But the large number of Etruscan inscriptions isn't helpful. We cannot translate them with much certainty, and the language had largely fallen out of use by the 2nd century B.C.E., when Rome had absorbed the Etruscan people.

However, they had a large and long-lasting influence on other emerging civilizations in Italy: "It was from the Etruscans that the Romans inherited many of their own cultural and artistic traditions, from the spectacle of gladiatorial combat to hydraulic engineering, temple design, and religious ritual, among many other things" (Taylor & Brenan, n.d., para. 10).

Essential Highlights

Civilization on the Italian Peninsula started several centuries before the Romans emerged. Early Indo-European peoples reached these lands during the Bronze Age from the Aegean and Balkans by land and sea. They developed agriculture and animal husbandry, built the first large settlements, and formed the first complex societies.

Many of the original tribes would merge to form a new civilization: the Romans, who began as Latins, dominated their Italic neighbors, and eventually controlled all of Italy. The Etruscans, on the other hand, remained a distinct linguistic group that was later subdued by Rome.

Throughout this chapter, we outlined how different tribes interacted with each other through trade and cultural exchange. Technological evolution impacted demographics, influencing migration waves and human settlement patterns. It also strained natural resources. The shift in materials and strategies used for survival paved the way for Western civilization.

However, all the aspects covered in this chapter are what archeologists and scholars have taught us about prehistoric Italy. There is another history about the time when Rome still didn't exist—the history created and held by tradition. Roman mythology.

While prehistoric tribes intermingled and paved their paths, a legend was born. Two twins, abandoned to die in the wild, were raised by a she-wolf, the totem animal of Mars, god of war. Later, they laid the foundations of the city that would conquer and rule this landscape. In the next chapter, we will discuss the earliest legends of Rome - how Romulus and Remus founded Rome and established the monarchy.

Chapter 2: The Founding of Rome

Rome was not built in a day. –Marcus Tullius
Cicero

Rome, the city, and its civilization weren't the
products of an overnight process. It was the outcome
of a complex of tradition, myths, and cultural
integration among people with different
backgrounds.

Nations' identities are a combination of historical
facts, reliable evidence, and a sense of belonging that
is usually based on a mythical origin. The legend of
Romulus and Remus explains the origins of not only
Rome but all the Latin tribes (of which the Romans
were a part). Early Roman identity was a mix of
native and imported cultures, formed over centuries
of migration waves, and consisting (mainly) of
Etruscan, Italic, and Aegean influences.

The Founding Myth

The Romans traced their ancestry back to
Aeneas, one of the many heroes of Homer's *Iliad*, one
of the two great epics of Greece's most important poet
(~8th century B.C.E.). Aeneas fought for Troy
(modern Hissarlik, Turkey) against invading Greeks.
After a ten-year siege, the Greeks stormed, pillaged,
and torched the city.

The image of Aeneas carrying his elderly father and the statues of their family gods out of the inferno has inspired artists for millennia, and greatly impressed the Romans. If factual, the Trojan War likely occurred between 1,200 and 1,150 B.C.E. – the archaeology of the site preserves scorch marks and possible evidence of attack.

Many centuries later, the Roman historians Livy (Titus Livius, 59 B.C.E. – 17 C.E.) and Dionysius of Halicarnassus (ca. 60 – 7 B.C.E.) tied Aeneas to Rome's founding with slight variations. Dionysius offers more detail. However, the elegance and drama of Livy's prose helped define Golden Age Latin literature. The following excerpts from Livy trace Aeneas' adventures in Italy and the foundation of Rome by his descendants, Romulus and Remus. They are edited for brevity.

Aeneas Arrives in Italy

"The consensus is that most Trojans met a savage end after their city was captured. However, the Greeks showed mercy to Aeneas. Ultimately, the Fates led him to greater deeds. First, he came to Macedonia (north of Greece), then to Sicily, looking for a home. Finally, he reached Laurentum with his fleet (an early Latin coastal town).

With nothing left after their wandering but their weapons and ships, Aeneas' men plundered the fields. But King Latinus and the Aborigines who occupied the land rushed from their city and crops and armed themselves to fend off the violent invaders. The opposing armies formed up for battle; however, before sounding the charge, Latinus advanced with his nobles and called the leader of the invaders to a meeting.

He asked who they were, from where or for what reason they had left home, and what they sought in the land of Laurentum. He learned that they were Trojans, that Aeneas, son of Anchises and Venus (the Greek Aphrodite), was their leader, and that they had fled their devastated homeland and now wanted to found a city. Amazed by Aeneas and his divine parent, and how he seemed equally disposed to war or peace, Latinus offered his right hand in friendship.

Aeneas became a guest in Latinus' house, and the king forged a family alliance by giving Aeneas his daughter Lavinia in marriage. The Trojans founded a town, and Aeneas named it Lavinium in honor of his wife. Soon, a child was born whom they named Ascanius.

Turnus, king of the Rutulians, waged war upon both Aeneas and Latinus, for Lavinia had been promised to him before Aeneas' arrival. The Rutulians were defeated, but the Aborigines and Trojans lost Latinus, their king.

The demoralized Rutulians fled with Turnus to the rich and powerful Etruscans and their king, Mezentius who then ruled the wealthy port city of Caere (modern Cerveteri, 35 miles north-northwest of Rome). The Etruscan leader had not been pleased by the birth of Aeneas' new city, and he felt Trojans were growing too quickly and endangering their neighbors. Therefore, he willingly forged an alliance with the Rutulians.

To overcome the Aborigines' fear of such a war, and to give them the same name, Aeneas called upon Trojans and Aborigines both as Latins. Thereafter, the Aborigines matched the Trojans in fondness of and faith in Aeneas.

The Trojan hero led forth his army even though the reputation of Etruria's power filled the length and breadth of Italy from the Alps to the Sicilian Strait. The outcome favored the Latins, but it was the last of Aeneas' mortal deeds. He lies by the river Numicus.

Ascanius left Lavinium to his mother when its population grew too large – it was already a flourishing and wealthy city – and he founded a new settlement near Mount Albanus called Alba Longa. Peace prevailed between the Latins and Etruscans, with the river Albula, which we now call the Tiber, forming the border." (Livy, 1.1-2 abridged)

Romulus, Remus, and the Founding of Rome

"[Eleven generations passed before violence grew] more powerful than family duty or respect for seniority (cf. Whelan, 2020; García, 2018). Amulius ruled Alba Longa after he expelled his elder brother, Numitor, from the city. He heaped crime upon crime, first murdering his nephew, then depriving his niece Rhea Silvia of the hope of motherhood (*Romulus and Remus: The Story of the Founding of Rome*, 2016).

He enforced her chastity by making her a Vestal Virgin, a pretext rather than an honor.

The Vestal was ravished by force, and after she gave birth to twins, she claimed Mars was the father. Amulius ordered the priestess to be chained up in prison and the children thrown into the river. But, when the slow-moving water stranded the floating basket that held the boys on a dry patch, a thirsty she-wolf from the surrounding mountains turned to their plaintive cries. She nursed them so tenderly that the master of the royal flock, Faustulus, found her caressing the infants with her tongue.

He brought them to the house he shared with his wife, Larentia. As soon as they were able, they wandered the woods to hunt, but they neglected neither their homestead nor its flocks. In addition to wild animals, they attacked bandits carrying loot and shared it with neighboring shepherds – the youthful band of Romulus and Remus grew day by day.

Angry because of their lost loot, some bandits ambushed the brothers. Romulus fought them off by force, but they captured Remus and handed him over to King Amulius. The main crime, they claimed, was that the brothers attacked Numitor's fields, pillaging them with a band of young men as if they were an enemy army. Therefore, Remus was sent to Numitor for punishment.

Now, Faustulus knew that a pair of infants had been exposed by order of the king. Moreover, the time he himself rescued the twins corresponded exactly. Therefore, he fearfully told Romulus the truth of the matter. Numitor, too, was reminded of his grandsons when he held Remus in custody and heard he had a twin brother. He drew the same conclusion as Faustulus, and thus King Amulius' misdeeds now surrounded him on both sides.

Romulus was not in favor of open war, so he did not assemble his entire band. Instead, he chose a select few to make their way covertly to the palace at an appointed time and attack the king. Remus supported him with another force he had gathered from the house of Numitor, and thus Romulus slew his great uncle, Amulius.

Numitor called a council and laid out his brother's crimes against him, the lineage of his grandsons, and how they were born, raised, and revealed. When the youths pushed through the council with their band and saluted Numitor as king, the shout of agreement from the crowd confirmed his title and power.

Thereafter, Romulus and Remus were seized by the desire to found a city near where they were exposed and raised. However, since they were twins and respect for seniority was unable to make a distinction between them, they agreed that the gods should dictate through bird signs who would name the new city and rule it. Romulus took the Palatine hill as his place to perform the auguries (a ritual to interpret bird signs), Remus the Aventine.

A sign first came to Remus – six vultures. Yet, as soon as this was reported, twice as many revealed themselves to Romulus. Each twin's followers proclaimed him king - Remus claimed kingship based on when his sign appeared, Romulus on the number of birds. They fought first with words before turning to violence, and Remus fell, struck down in the melee.

A more common report is that Remus vaulted over the city's new wall in mockery of his brother. The enraged Romulus killed him as he shouted, '*Thus shall die anyone who should leap over my walls!*' Romulus alone took power, and the new city took the name of its founder." (Livy, 1.3-7 abridged)

Later Roman tradition dated the founding to 753 B.C.E. (Encyclopaedia Britannica, 2023).

Proximity to Contemporary Greek Culture

It is unknown when this story was told for the first time. However, it reveals the deep influence of the ancient Greeks on Roman culture. The god Mars is the Roman version of the Greek god of war, Ares, and their mother, Rhea, shares the name of a Greek Titan, the mother of Zeus and the other gods.

It isn't coincidental that a she-wolf was the animal that saved Rome's founder. The she-wolf represented one of Mars' (Ares') sacred animals. Somehow, it symbolized that Rome—and therefore, Romans—were Mars' people. Their entire history bears this out.

The myth explains the origins of the political community and provides it with legitimacy. The destiny and the actions of the twins, and therefore their people, were ordained by the gods. It played an important role in the constitution of political power and, later, in the establishment of the Republic and Empire.

In addition to Livy, this legend and the origins of Rome were linked to Hellenistic (Greek) culture by the Roman poet Virgil. Like Homer, Virgil wrote poetry that helped define the identity of his society. Among other poems, he wrote the *Aeneid*, an epic that tells Aeneas' story, consciously tying it to the social and political structures of the early Roman Empire.

The Aeneid was written by order of Rome's first emperor, Augustus, at an inflection point in Roman history when the Empire was being built. This fact illustrates two important aspects of Rome's founding mythology. First, the story that blended Italic, Etruscan, and Greek elements was an integral part of Roman identity by the 1st century B.C.E., if not long before – it was the Romans' national story.

Second, the tradition was so fundamental that, at least in Augustus' mind, manipulating it had the power to permanently reshape Roman society. The third part of this book analyzes how history, popular culture, and oral tradition blend to shape a nation's identity, often influenced by political and social motivations (Vandiver, n.d.).

The Roman Kingdom

The Historical Foundation of Rome

While we can't settle on a precise foundation date for the city, most scholars accept the Roman calculation of 753 B.C.E. as an acceptable ballpark figure, if too precise. Nevertheless, archeological findings reveal that the first political regime at Rome was a monarchy. Most civilizations in the early first millennium B.C.E. developed around a principal city and had concentrated power – a city-state. Most city-states initially formed under the centralized power of a king.

In Italy, several excavations have exposed the ruins of the Regia, the king's house. In addition, archeologists have found a cup with the word *rex* (king in Latin) inscribed on it, and it was dated to the 7th century. There was also an inscription on the *Lapis Niger* (the Black Rock), a shrine in the Roman Forum, with the word *recei* (an archaic form of *rex*). The inscription is difficult to interpret, but many scholars believe it was probably a law (*Ancient Roman Monarchy*, n.d.).

According to the tradition, after founding Rome, Romulus invited merchants and men from all walks of life to join his new community. He recognized them all as citizens with equal rights, and all of them agreed to appoint him as their king. That is how the monarchy was established in Rome.

Unlike many other ancient civilizations, Roman kings didn't necessarily belong to a hereditary nobility, nor did they rely on a military caste that supported them. People elected them, and they served as kings for the rest of their lives. Twelve bodyguards called lictors accompanied the king. They each bore a bundle of wooden rods surrounding an axe – the *fasces*. These were stark visual symbols of the king's *imperium*, his power to command obedience. The rods could compel; the axe could execute. The later Roman magistrates vested with *imperium*, were similarly accompanied, though their power of command was limited to a specific task or geographical region – a *provincia*, or province. The term *Imperium Roman* came to denote the regions subject to the commands of a Roman magistrate. Its direct English equivalent – Roman Empire.

Roman kings sat in a curule (usually foldable) chair and wore the purple *toga picta* (colored toga) and red shoes. Instead of a metal crown, they wore a white diadem made of wool or linen around their heads (*The Roman Kingdom*, n.d.). These physical objects symbolized their royal authority and sovereignty. Their origin seems to have been Etruscan.

Social Hierarchical Organization

The growing city was organized as a monarchy. Its founder, Romulus, gave citizenship to all the people who joined him, and, in turn, they elected him as the first monarch. It set the basis for the monarchy going forward: "The kingdom was established by unanimous acclaim with him at the helm when Romulus called the citizenry to a council to determine their government" (*The Roman Kingdom*, n.d., para. 5).

Roman society organized itself as a fixed hierarchy that reflected its values and ensured its political unity. Hierarchies rank people according to their power, status, or privileges. This inequality was accepted by Roman society.

The nuclear unit of ancient Roman society was the family, and it influenced all the other institutions of the political system. It was the cornerstone of the whole social pyramid and was also hierarchically organized (Schultz, 2019).

Even though the word "family" comes from the Latin word *familia* they carry slightly different meanings. The Roman *familia* was a complete social and political unit led by the *paterfamilias* ("the father of the family," a head of the household); thus, it was patriarchal. He formally owned the family's property and was the source of family law.

There were three types of familial bonds (Schultz, 2019):

- the agnates (*agnati*): Relatives by blood or adoption through the father's line, the *paternum gens.*

- the cognates (*cognati*): All relatives, including the *maternum genus*, that is through the mother's line.
- and *affines/adfines*: Those related by marriage, like brothers-in-law.

Each category had a particular political role within the family and society. The agnates could inherit property and, in this capacity, enjoyed the full benefits of Roman citizenship. They were the only ones who could inherit the *paterfamilias'* power, called *patria potestas*. It allowed them to celebrate contracts, lend, mortgage, and interact with other families through their respective *patresfamilias*.

A *familia* was self-sufficient, and each *paterfamilias* had full authority over its members, including the power of life and death. Yet, tradition imposed the moral imperative to provide for and protect the welfare of the *familia* upon the *paterfamilias*. An unduly tyrannical (by Roman standards) head of the household would face social and religious blowback for failing to look after his responsibilities. Therefore, Roman society was a complex network of extended families, each ruled by a head. This patriarchal organization defined relationships between families as well.

Often, the heads of weaker, poorer, or less illustrious households would ally themselves with the heads of more powerful families. The more powerful *paterfamilias* would become a *patronus* (patron – note the shared root *pat-* denoting the superior role) of the weaker, who would be called a *cliens* (client) of his superior. For most of Roman history, *clientes* were expected to support their *patrones* politically, electorally, or even physically, while the patrons would protect their clients from legal action or otherwise promote their welfare. The relationship was fundamental, and relied on *fides*, or faithfulness. This critical value was religiously grounded, and failing to maintain *fides* was generally considered a serious taboo.

This patriarchal structure permeated the Roman worldview. As a result, and as later chapters will show, it extended to Roman foreign policy. To the Roman mind, Rome was always the *patronus*. As a rule, it would form treaties with individual city-states or tribes as a powerful head of household would pledge to protect a weaker client. Of course, the arrangement always favored Rome, but the client states often enjoyed more safety, stability, and prosperity as tributaries. Besides, the *fides* of the Romans often made them reliable friends. However, the idea is abstract, and many tribes and city-states found themselves the subjects of Roman anger when they may have followed a treaty to the letter, but did not satisfy the Roman definition of *fides*.

At the bottom of the social scale, there were slaves and freedmen. Slavery was a common practice in antiquity. Slaves were former war prisoners or people with unpaid debts. At the early stage of the Roman civilization, slaves weren't massively exploited. However, they were considered part of the *paterfamilias'* property (Schultz, 2019).

Slaves could achieve manumission and become freedmen or freedwomen. They became free, able to vote, and otherwise participate in Roman society. However, they could not hold political office beyond low-level local magistracies. Moreover, they would immediately become a client of their former owner. (Schultz, 2019).

Fundamental Roman Values

For Romans, social order was closely linked to their moral background, which was rooted in traditions. This first stage of the life of Rome was mainly based on customary law. They followed the rules of traditions: It was good because it had been used before. They used the term *mos maiorum*, or "the customs of the ancestors" (Jasiński, 2020).

As explained before, *fides* was an essential value for ancient Romans. A citizen's word was enough to create a formal obligation or institute a contract. However, *fides* also applied to informal promises that should be held and fulfilled.

Another core value was bravery. It was considered a virtue, a concept that originally came from the word *vir* (husband, man, or hero), thus it was associated with masculinity. It meant having the ability to distinguish good from bad and fight against evil. In war, it was considered a virtue to fight bravely against Rome's enemies.

Women weren't excluded from this value, but for them, being brave implied remaining attached to Roman traditions and being an exemplary wife and mother. That was her role within a patriarchy (Jasiński, 2020). Women had an assigned role within this patriarchy. The mother of the family was the *materfamilias,* and along with their husband and other free adult members of the household, they were the family council (*concilium*) (Schultz, 2019).

Piety, *pietas,* was another foundational value. It encompassed the worship of Roman deities, strict attachment to their traditions, and dedication to family, which had to instruct future generations in those traditions. Consider, again, how powerfully the image of Aeneas carrying his father and the statues of their family gods out of burning Troy struct the Romans.

Seriousness, or *gravitas,* was self-control as a means of respect for social conventions and morality. Romans repressed their emotions in public, for instance, expressions of anger or affection. Those were preserved in the private realm.

Then, they valued respect and worthiness: *dignitas.* Women had to bear their husbands' children and carry with dignity all their responsibilities as mothers and wives. Men, on their end, held the position they had within a hierarchical society: they had to show that position and honor it, respecting others while also demanding respect from their subordinates. Often, the number and power of a man's clients was a measure of his *dignitas*.

Last but not least, authority: *auctoritas* was of utmost importance in a hierarchical society. It came along with *dignitas* in the case of men, who had the power to give orders and be obeyed. It was associated with personal relationships and honor rather than formal laws.

Rome's Unique Inclusivity

Early Roman society was quite small and interacted freely with the neighboring tribes. As explained earlier, different communities interacted with each other and not only exchanged and traded goods but also shared knowledge. They shaped each other's culture and cooperated in development.

Many early Romans were former people from other tribes who gathered to create a new political community. According to the foundational myth, Rome was founded by Romulus, a refugee, and the people who accompanied him after killing the king. Therefore, they had a unique perception of the foreigner. This conception made Romans more welcoming to foreigners and allowed many newcomers to achieve the status of a Roman citizen, which wasn't common in many other ancient civilizations (Beard, 2018).

Since the earliest Romans were a handful of families who settled among the hills near the Tiber, they needed others to make the community grow.

Therefore, they developed an inclusive foreign affairs management system. They interacted with other cultures and later conquered many of them, but they didn't destroy their institutions or forbid their traditions. The Romans were devoted to traditions. Instead, they blended. When Rome became more powerful, Latin culture eventually became predominant throughout Italy, but this policy of inclusivity was one of the pillars of Rome's power and stability.

Inclusivity was crucial for the early Roman kingdom's development. It enabled foreigners to become citizens, which is important not only to support demographic expansion but also for economic and military reasons. The Romans were open enough to accept the idea of a foreigner as ruler – they may even have had a Greek king. According to legend, in the 6th century, Lucius Tarquinius Priscus became the 5th king of Rome. His original name was Tarquin, and his father was a Greek who had migrated to Tarquinii, an Etruscan city. The family moved to Rome, and Tarquin, who changed his name to Lucius Tarquinius (a Latin name), became the guardian of the sons of King Ancus Marcius. Later, Tarquin became king of Rome although he was a Greco-Etruscan immigrant. The story may belong in part to mythology, but there is some archeological evidence supporting the existence of the Tarquins during the period (Encyclopaedia Britannica, 1998).

Early Sabine Integration

Despite this inclusive nature of the Romans, we should not downplay their tendency to assert their patriarchal worldview by force. A controversial episode at the earliest stage of Roman history serves as a colorful illustration. It involved a neighboring tribe, the Sabines. The legendary Rape of the Sabine Women, as the event is called, took place around 750 B.C.E., shortly after the city was founded.

The Sabines lived on the Italian peninsula, on the east bank of the Tiber River, along the Apennine ridge. There is limited evidence of their original language, which was probably Oscan, but only some of their dialect survived and many of the words were adopted by Latin speakers (Tikkanen, 2022). Scholars believe the Sabines belonged to the same ethnic group as the Samnites and Sabellians. They were Italic, and distantly related to the Latins since they all shared Indo-European roots (*The Sabines: A Glimpse into an Ancient Italic Tribe*, 2023).

The Greek biographer Plutarch told the story of a strategy deployed by Romulus to provide the men of his kingdom with wives since there were no women in their community. Without women, the community was doomed.

Plutarch wrote that Romulus invited the Sabines to a banquet in Rome during a festival of the god Neptune Equester. During the feast, the Romans dashed in and kidnapped the women. Then, the

Sabine women were kept as captives and forced to take Romans as husbands (David, 2013).

Livy also wrote about the abduction of the Sabines. According to him, Romulus was concerned about the decline in the birth rate within the young community and attempted to make arrangements with neighboring tribes to make women marry Roman men. Since their neighbors refused to accept the deal, they were compelled to plan the abduction of the Sabine women (Sal, 2020).

Both authors Plutarch and Livy, agreed in pointing out that after the abduction of the Sabine women, a war was started between both communities, but the women interceded to stop the attacks.

The Sabine influence can be found in two of the first four kings of Rome, Numa Pompilius and Ancus Marcius, and also in one of the three names of the original tribes of Rome: the *Tities*. The other two tribes, the *Ramnes* and *Luceres*, supposedly represented the early city's other two predominant ethnic groups, the Latins and Etruscans, respectively.

Furthermore, many Sabine family names appear in prominent positions throughout Roman history. Many Roman families had traditional connections going back centuries, presumably to a theoretical common ancestor. A group of families connected in this way was called a *gens*, or clan. Several influential Roman *gentes* had a Sabine origin: *gens Curtia, gens Pompilia, gens Marcia,* and *gens Claudia* (*The Sabines: A Glimpse into an Ancient Italic Tribe,*

2023). The first dynasty of Roman emperors bears the name Julio-Claudian because the emperor Augustus' successor, his adopted son Tiberius, belonged to the *gens Claudia*.

The Sabine cities didn't disappear after many Sabines inhabited Rome, and the tense relationship continued through the 5th and the 3rd centuries B.C.E. (*The Sabines: A Glimpse into an Ancient Italic Tribe*, 2023). There were many battles between both societies, but the interaction between them became regular over time, and the Sabines were eventually fully absorbed by the Romans by 290 B.C.E. (Tikkanen, 2022). At that point, they all became full Roman citizens.

Essential Highlights

Legend and historical evidence blend to explain the origins of the Eternal City. The strength of both components reveals the power of tradition and heritage within ancient Roman society. The attachment to their mythical origin and the cultural legacy that made them what they became is rooted in the backbone of their society.

The new city became a monarchy, but one based on strong values that ensured unity. As a kingdom, it relied on the solid bonds of the most important institution: family. Then, it evolved into a powerful civilization capable of conquering and subjugating neighboring tribes, not to destroy them but to incorporate them into their growing society.

Romulus was the first king, the founder, and the one accountable for setting the foundations of the monarchy, but... who were the subsequent rulers that helmed the burgeoning empire? In the next chapter, we'll delve deep into the reigns and realms of the 7 Kings of Rome.

Chapter 3: The 7 Kings of Rome

*History is filled with the sound of silken
slippers going downstairs and wooden shoes
coming up.* –Voltaire

Unraveling Myth from History

The study of ancient history poses certain challenges
to historians. Ancient civilizations at their early
stages, like the moment of the foundation of Rome,
didn't have a systematized procedure to record facts
and events. The concepts of history and science
hadn't been developed yet. Therefore, historians rely
upon archeological findings and attempt to rebuild

that part of history by interpreting those findings (*Online Ancient History Undergraduate Tutors Spires*, n.d.).

On some occasions, what is known about the distant past with no written records is based on what later writers from those societies told about their past. That is the case of Homer and his *Iliad* and *Odyssey* in ancient Greece, or the works of Virgil and Plutarch in ancient Rome. It is almost impossible to distinguish between what happened and what was created by popular imagination.

For those societies, there was a blurry line between historical facts and popular beliefs transmitted through oral traditions. Reality blended with myths and mystical explanations, and it was part of their daily lives. Therefore, it can be accepted that ancient history is a combination of what history as a modern discipline can prove and what is taken from ancient people's own perceptions of their past (*Online Ancient History Undergraduate Tutors Spires*, n.d.). Moreover, their perception can be shaped by cultural or political bias. Even so, it is still a valuable source of information about the past because it gives us insight into their cultural, intellectual, and literary history.

The legend of Romulus and Remus hasn't been proven with empirical evidence. It "probably originated in the 4th century B.C.E and was set down in coherent form at the end of the 3rd century B.C.E. It contains a mixture of Greek and Roman elements" (Encyclopaedia Britannica, 2023, para. 5). Although there is no empirical evidence of Romulus and Remus' existence or their relationship with a she-wolf, it is still part of Rome's history. Indeed, it would be difficult to argue that the idea of Romulus had less far-reaching consequences for Roman society than, say, a historical figure like Pompey the Great – as important as he was.

The two centuries following Rome's foundation present these complexities. There is little evidence about the monarchy and the first rulers. However, we tend to include Romulus as the first of the seven ancient kings. There is enough evidence to assert the final three were likely historical, and many historians also believe the first three after Romulus existed (*Ancient Roman Monarchy*, n.d.). Most of them appear in literature from different periods of Rome's history, and archeological remains sometimes seem to support their existence (Marta, 2021).

Having said this, let's proceed into what historians have learned about the first rulers of the civilization that grew to dominate the known world. It is inevitably the result of blending historical facts discovered by historians and archeologists with myths and legends from the Romans' self-reflections on their own past (Marta, 2021).

The First Kings of Rome

Most historians agree to mention seven kings: "Romulus (753–716 BC), Numa Pompilius (715–673

BC), Tullus Hostilius (673–641 BC), Ancus Marcius (641–616 BC), Tarquinius Priscus (616–579 BC), Servius Tullius (578–535 BC) and Tarquinius Superbus (535–509 BC)" (The Roman Kingdom, n.d., para. 3). The number seven had a special symbolism for ancient Romans since it is also present in the seven hills where Rome was founded (Gill, 2019).

Other historians include an eighth king, Titus Tatius. He was the Sabine ruler when the Romans kidnapped the Sabine women. According to some scholars, the conflict between both communities was resolved with a dual monarchy: Romulus and Titus Tatius. This regime lasted a few years until Titus Tatius was killed by a mob, but it further supports the early integration of the Sabines with the Romans (Encyclopaedia Britannica, 1998). Even though Titus Tatius is usually left off the list of Roman monarchs, he is credited by tradition for establishing altars to many Sabine deities that were later included in Roman religion.

Romulus

His arrival to power was framed by bloodshed and hate, and he emerged as a single leader after killing his brother Remus. As a ruler, he "kept his guards close, and his enemies closer—after all, founding a culture on the blood of your twin brother does not give the people you are ruling any sort of comfort" (Winters, 2019, para. 3).

His first acts of government were focused on ensuring the growth and stability of the city's population. He came back to his birthplace and gathered men to join him. Later, he arranged the episode with the Sabines that secured wives for the male population – albeit by force. He may have shared power for a while with the Sabine king, Tits Tatius, until he was assassinated, and Romulus became the sole ruler again.

Besides establishing the fundamental political institutions of Rome, like the Senate (see below), he led the first expansion of the city through war and conquest. After Numitor's death, Romulus incorporated Alba Longa, the semi-legendary Latin city founded by his ancestor Ascanius, son of Aeneas. In addition, he formed alliances with neighboring settlements like Lavinium, the town founded by Aeneas himself (Garcia, 2018).

The end of Romulus' reign remains shrouded in mystery. Some people claimed to have witnessed how he was lifted to heaven and became a god. Another hypothesis poses he was killed by a senatorial conspiracy. It is known that "Romulus disappeared in 717 B.C.E., as reported by Plutarch, at the age of 53, but Dionysius of Halicarnassus reports that he died at the age of 55" (García, 2018, para. 9).

Numa Pompilius

After Romulus' death, there was an *interregnum* of a year. During that time "between the reigns," an *interrex* would hold power for 5 days. Their mandate was to oversee the election of a new king and, if they were unable to do so, another *interrex* would be appointed. The process repeated until the election of a new king by the Senate. The extraordinary office of *interrex* survived down to the end of the Republic, and kept the state functioning in times of turmoil. Eventually, the Senate chose Numa Pompilius. He was a Sabine man who at first was reluctant to accept the offer but eventually agreed to it after consulting with the goddess Egeria (Vučkovič, 2023).

He was a strict and wise ruler who introduced several political, religious, and social reforms. He formulated a calendar of 12 months based on the moon's cycle and established the Vestal Virgins, and cults of Mars, Jupiter, and the deified Romulus (Quirinus). Unlike his predecessor, he advocated for peace.

He is credited with writing the first laws of Rome based on justice and equity and creating the concept of private property. He founded religious colleges and built many temples (Gill, 2019). His kingdom was one of splendor and prosperity.

Whether Numa actually lived is a matter of debate. He is mentioned by Plutarch and Livy, and his figure is exalted as a great and virtuous king who contributed to the greatness of Rome. According to these historians' versions, he reigned for over 40 years and died at the age of 81 (Vučkovič, 2023).

Tullus Hostilius

Very little is known about Tullus Hostilius. His existence is also open to debate. Historians assume he was elected by the Senate after Numa's death and that by then, the population of Rome had doubled.

Tullus is remembered as a warrior king, like Romulus. He destroyed Alba Longa and several other neighboring cities like Fidenae and Veii. He also compelled more Sabines to integrate into Rome. He is credited with building the first Senate House, initially called the *Curia Hostilia*, where the Roman Forum stands at present (Winters, 2019).

Unlike his predecessor, he neglected proper worship of the Roman gods. Livy said that at the end of his reign, Tullus grew very ill and begged for help from the gods. Jupiter, instead, threw a bolt of lightning that burned the king and his house to ashes (*The Seven Kings*, n.d.).

Ancus Marcius

There is also little historical evidence of his existence or of his reign beyond what ancient Roman historians tell us. However, he was an influential figure in the Roman consciousness at least until the late Republic. There is a reference to his name, for instance, in a silver denarius found in archeological excavations, dated from 57 B.C.E.

Ancus Marcius was Numa Pompilius's grandson and is credited for publishing his grandfather's religious works. However, Ancus was a warrior king who promoted the kingdom's expansion by conquering the Latin cities nearby and forcing their population to move into Rome (Winters, 2019).

Reforms During the Monarchy

The first rulers shaped the formal institutions of the Monarchy and set the foundations of a growing city-state. Their mandates were characterized by their contributions to the institutional organization of the government and the buildings constructed under their rule.

Unlike contemporary monarchies, these kings didn't belong to or establish a dynasty. Each of them was elected by the people. Romulus was directly elected by the people of Rome; the others were elected by deliberative or legislative bodies like the Senate and Curiate Assembly (see below, Chapter 5) (*The Seven Kings*, nd.). The hereditary nature of the throne was only established after the 5th king.

Once elected, kings had near absolute power and had the authority to pass laws, control the army, and be the supreme judges (Johnson, n.d.). However, Romans soon developed representative institutions and established a source of popular participation. The Senate and the Curiate Assembly were created during the first decades of the monarchy and although they had limited powers, it was a counterbalance to the king's supreme power. Despite his near-complete control, the king needed the assembly's support to declare war. When necessary, the Senate proposed the new king and the Curiate Assembly voted - these institutions were the ultimate source of the king's power (Winters, 2019).

The Senate

This institution is almost as ancient as Rome, since Romulus created it from the first citizens after being appointed king. It is also the most permanent element throughout Roman history, although its power, influence, and function changed throughout the different periods, and its essence has survived until the present. The word senate derives from the Latin word *senex*, which means old man. Therefore, the Senate was the assembly of the more experienced members of the community, a tradition inherited from the ancient Indo-European tribes, which were ruled by aristocratic groups of the oldest and (presumably) wisest men (Vermeulen, 2020).

Romulus chose 100 men to act as his advisory council. Each was a *paterfamilias*, and members of their families were thereafter called patricians, the privileged class (Vermeulen, 2020). Observe again the *pat-* root, denoting fatherhood. Indeed, later senators were often addressed as *patres*, fathers on the Senate floor. They represented their ancient tribes and held their power until they died (Encyclopaedia Britannica, 2023).

The Senate's power was indefinite and mainly consisted of providing advice to the king, but they had the last word to select the new ruler. After Romulus' death, the power reverted to the community embodied in the Senate, and their primary responsibility became keeping the state stable during the *interregnum* (Vermeulen, 2020).

Later, king Lucius Tarquinius Priscus (see below) chose 100 more senators from non-patrician families, and the number of senators increased. By 509 B.C.E., the Senate was composed of 300 members, patricians, and men from lesser families. Lucius Tarquinius Superbus, the last of the seven kings, executed many of the senators and didn't replace them with new members (Winters, 2019). This ushered in the decline of the Monarchy. After the Monarchy was replaced by the Republic, the Senate changed in composition and political role within the Roman system.

The Three Etruscan Kings

The Etruscans were introduced in Chapter 1 as people with uncertain origins who reached the Italian Peninsula before Rome's foundation and established themselves in central-western Italy (present-day Tuscany) and the island of Corsica. Their culture flourished between 700 and 500 B.C.E. which coincides with Rome's monarchical period.

For about 150 years, the Etruscans were raided by Celtic tribes from the north and engaged in several wars with the Romans. Both cultures coexisted and interacted intensely as the Romans acquired many of the Etruscans' institutions and cultural features. In fact, many of the patrician families of early Rome were Etruscan: "Examples include the *gens Herminia*, the *gens Lartia*, the *gens Tarquitia*, the *gens Verginia,* and the *gens Volumnia*" (Howells, 2023, para. 3). This phenomenon further reinforces the open nature of early Roman society – Rome may have had a Latin core, but the Sabine and Etruscan elements were strong from the earliest period.

By the middle of the 7th century B.C.E., Rome still had a small population with a citizen militia army, mainly composed of shepherds and farmers. However, its tendency to absorb people from among its neighbors meant that grew quickly. Nevertheless, some historians believe that the Etruscans eventually took control of the Roman population, moved by their interest in the resources in and around the Roman hills. Rome was attractive because it was near the Tiber, it was easy to defend, and there were salt works nearby. In the ancient world, salt was a tremendously valuable commodity. The Etruscans were warriors, much like the Romans, and they also raided other tribes to expand their territory or take plunder.

At the end of the 7th century, the Etruscans had consolidated their place in Roman society. According to ancient Roman sources, the last three of the seven kings were Etruscan and played a key role in shaping Roman culture. Whether this represents a hostile takeover of Rome or is merely more evidence of Rome's tendency to be free with its citizenship is an ongoing debate.

Lucius Tarquinius Priscus

His Latin name was Lucius Tarquinus Priscus, though his Etruscan name was likely Lucomo; however, this may have been a title instead of a name. He is accepted as the 5th king of Rome and was in power between 616 and 578 B.C.E. As noted above in chapter 2, Tarquin was a Greek man's son who lived in Etruria and moved to Rome on his wife's urging. He was appointed as a royal guard, and when the king died, he lobbied the Senate, securing election over the former king Ancus Marcius' sons.

During his reign, the kingdom expanded its lands, and he added 100 senators. He was the first king to establish circus games as public entertainment. He is credited for some early monumental buildings such as the Temple of Jupiter Capitolinus and the *Cloaca Maxima*, Rome's massive sewer system (Gill, 2019).

Servius Tullius

Tarquinius Priscus was eventually killed by the sons of Ancus Marcius, and he was followed in office by his son-in-law, Servius Tullius. The 6th king of Rome carried out successful military campaigns that provided him with the resources to build the first stone fortification of the city: walls that encompassed the 7 hills of the early city. Remains of the so-called "Servian Wall" have been uncovered, but their construction likely dates from the early 4th century B.C.E., two centuries after Tullius' reign.

Later Romans attributed several important reforms to Servius Tullius. He instituted the first census, reformed the tribal system, and fixed the military obligations of 5 census-determined economic classes. (Gill, 2019). He set the basis for a new constitution with different rights for citizens regarding social classes: "Servius's reforms brought about a major change in Roman life—voting rights were now based on socioeconomic status, transferring much of the power into the hands of the Roman elite" (*The Seven Kings*, 2020, para. 19).

He reigned for 44 years and was murdered in a conspiracy. It was carried out by his daughter Tullia and her husband Lucius Tarquinius Superbus who wanted to seize power for himself (*The Seven Kings*, 2020).

Lucius Tarquinius Superbus

Tarquinius seized power after killing his father-in-law. He also made efforts to extend the kingdom's lands and continued to fight against neighboring tribes. Even though he carried out a few important public works, his reign is remembered for corruption and violence. He turned his back on the Senate and the Roman traditions, concentrating all the power in his hands.

In 509 B.C.E., a revolution led by Lucius Junius Brutus compelled Tarquinius and his family to flee from Rome. The trigger was the rape of Lucretia, by Tarquinius' son. She was the wife of Tarquinius' own nephew, Lucius Tarquinius Collatinus. After the king's expulsion, Brutus and Collatinus became the first consuls, the chief executives of the Republic (*The Seven Kings*, 2020).

Tarquinius' terrible reign left Rome with a negative view of monarchy and, for many generations, the Romans would avoid any semblance of one-man rule. Indeed, accusing a Roman politician of aiming at *regnum* was a serious charge.

The Etruscan Heritage of Rome

The Etruscans were skilled engineers, and they left a significant heritage in Roman architecture. The Colosseum, aqueducts, and other buildings were possible thanks to the design knowledge the Etruscans taught the Romans. They made the city cleaner and safer: "One example of the Etruscan impact on early Rome was the *cuniculus*, a type of drainage channel that the Etruscans used extensively. Notably, the earliest piece of hydraulic engineering in Rome was a sewer system, the *Cloaca Maxima*" (Howells, 2023, para.11).

The Roman architectural style was significantly influenced by the Etruscans. They adopted the use of what is known as the "Tuscan column," and the earliest monumental buildings in Rome were supposedly commissioned by the Etruscan kings (Howells, 2023).

The Etruscan kings also expanded the arable lands by draining the marshes that filled the valley in the midst of the seven hills. The area would later become the Forum Romanum, the beating heart of the Republic and Empire. The Etruscans also improved the production capacity and enlarged the city. They built walls around the city to protect the population. They also introduced the gladiatorial contests during the reigns of the Tarquins. This was a funerary practice when a noble or king died. Men were forced to fight to the death, and the bloodshed was a sacrifice to the underworld deities (*How Did the Etruscans Shape Roman History and Society*, n.d.).

Essential Highlights

Like most of its contemporary civilizations, Rome established a monarchy as a political regime. Soon, the young new state created institutions to organize the election of their monarch. Despite the king's absolute power, the Romans developed representative institutions, particularly the Senate, that functioned as a counterbalance for that power. This was an enduring and stable institution throughout all Roman History.

As explained in the previous chapter, the Romans were a mixture of people from different tribes who soon merged to give birth to a unique Roman culture. This blending allowed immigrants and men from conquered tribes to become kings.

Nonetheless, this population was divided regarding its ethnic origin. That division was transferred to the distribution of power and privileges within society. The descendants of the earliest citizens at the time of the founding became the patricians, the class with a higher status and power. The rest of the population were the plebeians, who would play a key role in the next stage of the evolution of the state.

As the last king was expelled and the Roman Kingdom came to an end, the seeds for the next phase in Rome's history were sown. A period where the people would reign supreme and where the ideals of the Republic took root.

Part 2: The Republic
(509 B.C.E. - 27 B.C.E.)

Chapter 4: The Early Republic

In the aftermath of the monarchy, Rome forged a new identity—one of the people, by the people, for an empire. The last king and the tyranny he established weakened the foundations of the Monarchy, but by then, Rome was a mature political community. The other institutions and the strong tradition of order and hierarchical organization had prepared them to create a new political system that would unleash Rome's greatness.

That political system was the Republic, and it entails a period in Roman history that spans between 509 B.C.E. and 27 B.C.E. It is one of the earliest and most enduring political forms based on popular representation and self-governance. The first two centuries of the Republic are poorly recorded, and most that is known about the period was written by the historian Livy and others from the 1st centuries B.C.E. and C.E. Written history didn't start in Rome until the 3rd century B.C.E.

The early stage of the Republic lasted until 275 B.C.E., when Rome wrested control of southern Italy from Italic natives and Greeks. During this period, Romans fought wars against other Latins, the Etruscans, Gauls, and Samnites, achieving limited unity over the whole territory (*Ancient Rome*—Early Republic, n.d.).

The Structure and Function of the Republican Government

The republican system is based on two main principles. First, the ultimate source of power is the people. The Latin name for this system was *res publica* – literally, public welfare, commonwealth, or (in American terms) a republic. Second, power must be exercised by magistrates who represent popular sovereignty. The arrangement entails a balance of power between different institutions that aims to prevent one from gaining too much control while avoiding stagnation. In modern terms: checks and balances.

The Roman Republic developed a mechanism of control to prevent the return to a monarchy, even in times of crisis. The fundamental principle was collegiality – magistracies had an even number of posts at any given time, with almost no exception. The exercise of power was divided into different functions. There were legislative bodies, executive offices, and magistrates to administer justice. Except for the Senate, magistrates served a specific term in office, usually one year, and there were often restrictions on consecutive terms.

Citizenship in Rome

Citizenship is a key concept for understanding the Roman republican system of representation and popular participation in political affairs. The scope of the concept changed throughout the republic, but in general terms, full citizenship was restricted to adult men.

Only a full male citizen was considered *optimo jure* (a citizen with the greatest rights): they had full civil and political rights to get married, appear at trial, make an appeal, vote in elections, enter into contracts, and own property. Women were also citizens but didn't have the right to vote or hold public office.

As noted above, Rome's population was divided between patricians (the founders' descendants) and the plebeians (the rest of the people, descendants of immigrants and conquered tribes) and they had different political rights. The Latin word for the entire class of plebeians was the collective singular, *plebs*.

Early in the Republic, intermarriage may have been prohibited, and plebeians faced many restrictions. However, by the mid-Republic, there was political, if not social, equality between the classes. This nominal equality was won after many years of hard-fought struggle.

The Senate

This institution was created almost at the same time as Rome was founded. Originally, it was composed of 100 patricians, direct descendants from the founder families, and their main function during the monarchy was to advise the king and select the candidates to take the throne.

When the Republic was established in 509 B.C.E., the Senate became the advisory council to the two main magistrates that had executive functions, the consuls. The Senate only gathered when these magistrates requested it. However, it was the institution that ensured stability. While the other magistrates had a limited period to hold office, the Senate was life tenure.

Although there are no precise sources, it is believed that during the early Republic, the Senate was composed of 300 members, the *patres et conscripti* ("the fathers and the enrolled"). This suggests not only that the patricians were included but also the plebeians, although the groups remained separate. Even though the Senate didn't have executive power, decisions approved by the Senate were mainly followed by the magistrates and enacted as law (Vermeule et al., 2023). After all, if a consul made enemies in the Senate, what sort of political career could they possibly have after their term in office?

Roman Magistrates

The executive magistrates traditionally followed the *cursus honorum*, a series of offices to which an aspiring Roman could be elected. All of them derived their power from the popular assemblies that elected them, and the terms of office were one year.

The highest office consisted of two consuls. They were the chief executives of the state and commanded the army in war. The consuls were followed by the praetors who administered justice, presided over the courts, and (later) were the commanders of provincial armies.

The aediles managed domestic issues such as the public market or street spectacles. This office may not have been a required step, but it offered Roman politicians an opportunity to impress the Roman people with lavish games and festivals. The electorate remembered them vividly, and electoral success to higher offices often followed noteworthy performances. Finally, the quaestors were accountants for the treasury and frequently served under consuls and praetors in the army to manage logistics.

Several offices existed outside the *cursus honorum*. Plebeians elected 10 tribunes of the plebs each year, who had the power of vetoing any other magistrate's actions. Their bodies were sacrosanct, meaning that anyone who harmed a plebeian tribune could be killed with impunity. An ongoing bone of contention throughout the Republic was the power of the tribunate, with some senators trying to restrict their authority, and others trying to expand it.

The censors served 18-month terms. While in office, they were responsible for conducting the Roman census, appraising the value of every citizen's property, and assigning them to the appropriate economic class. In addition, they controlled the list of senators. They could remove members who did not meet the property qualifications or who failed to uphold traditional Roman values. Finally, the censors often oversaw large public works projects and negotiated contracts on behalf of the state. Elections for the censorship were held once every five years.

Another irregular office was created in 501 B.C.E., the dictator. According to tradition, its main role was to replace the consuls in times of crisis when the circumstances demanded a strong and centralized military command. A dictator lasted in office for six months and was "also termed the master of the army (*magister populi*), and he appointed a subordinate cavalry commander, the master of horses (*magister equitum*)" (Seller et al., 2023). It was a constitutional resource to sustain the system's stability in times of great turmoil. Indeed, some dictators were appointed to ensure the integrity of elections for regular magistracies.

Roman Assemblies

Popular assemblies were the cornerstone of the whole republican system, as they represented the ability of the *Populus Romanus*, the Roman People as a collective unit, to govern itself. Each citizen was a member of several different assemblies, each organized according to how the people would meet to perform a given function.

The Curiate Assembly

The *comitia curiata* dates back to the Monarchy. There were 30 *curiae*, each representing one of Rome's 30 original patrician families. In the earliest years of the Republic, the Curiate Assembly could pass legislation, try judicial cases, and elect consuls. Since it was originally a patrician assembly, plebeians could not vote in it, but they could participate. Moreover, tribunes of the plebs could veto the decrees of the consul who presided over the Curiate Assembly. Over the course of the Republic, the *comitia curiata* declined in importance, eventually able only to confirm the investment of higher magistrates with *imperium* and ratify wills.

The Centuriate Assembly

The *comitia centuriata* originally divided the citizenry into groups of 100 based on their military role. As Roman society developed distinct economic classes, the determining factor became wealth. This dovetailed nicely with a citizen militia-style army, since the centuries of the highest classes would be the men able to afford the best arms and armor.

During the first half of the Republic, there were 193 centuries. The number increased later to 373. Arranged on the battlefield, they always had an equal paper strength. However, on the electoral field, poorer centuries grew to have more members, and thus the votes of the wealthy carried more weight than the poor. Conversely, the wealthy stood to lose far more resources in the case of a military reverse.

When voting, each century had a single vote. The simple majority within each century determined which way the century as a whole voted. During a vote, the centuries would vote one at a time, starting with the wealthiest. Once a simple majority of centuries voted in a certain direction, the vote was finished. The lowest centuries rarely voted.

The Centuriate Assembly inherited some powers from the Curiate Assembly after the first few decades of the Republic. Ultimately, it elected consuls and praetors and invested them with *imperium*. Likewise, it elected the censors and gave them the power to conduct the census. As the *Populus Romanus* in its military capacity, the *comitia centuriata* was the only instrument of the Roman state able to declare war. Finally, it was the court of final appeal for treason trials.

The Tribal Assembly

The *comitia tributa* represented the Roman people in its tribal capacity. Unlike the Curiate Assembly, where the distinction was ethnic, and the Centuriate Assembly, where it was economic, the Tribal Assembly was geographic. There were 35 Roman tribes – four urban, and 31 rural. They were somewhat analogous to U.S. congressional districts and were just as prone to gerrymandering. Like the Centuriate Assembly, each tribe had one vote, and it was cast according to a simple majority of its members. The Tribal Assembly elected lower magistrates like quaestors and aediles, and it presided over non-capital trials.

Roman Heroes of the Early Republic

The consolidation of a new political system can only be achieved with the participation of large parts of the community. However, any process of change requires leaders to inspire and guide the masses. Later Romans would look back on semi-legendary figures who embodied traditional Roman values as heroes of the Republic. These important figures are closely associated with the emergence of Republican institutions. Several of them remain symbolic of true patriotism to this day. The following figures represent a small sample of Roman heroes from the early Republic.

Agrippa Menenius Lanatus

Menenius was appointed consul of the Republic and had to deal with the plebeians who complained about their lack of rights and impoverished living conditions. In 494 B.C.E., Rome was under enemy attack, and the *plebs* rebelled and walked out of the city, refusing to fight for Rome. Instead, they camped on the Sacred Mount, roughly three miles from the city. The episode became known as the first "Secession of the Plebs." Menenius took on the mission of negotiating with the rebels and convincing them to rejoin their compatriots.

He prevailed upon the crowd with a fable. The story was about a time when a man's limbs got angry with his belly because they had to work hard for it while the belly didn't do anything for them. The limbs agreed not to work anymore. Since the belly didn't obtain any food or water, the body started to starve, including the limbs. Then, the limbs understood that every part of the body was important for the survival of the whole (*Menenius Agrippa's Fable*, B.C. 494, n.d.).

According to tradition, the fable told by Agrippa Menenius persuaded the plebeians to stop the riot and return to Rome's defense.

Gnaeus Marcius Coriolanus

Coriolanus was a Roman soldier who earned the nickname "Coriolanus" after his distinguished performance during the siege of Corioli (493 BC). By then, Rome was at war with the Volsci, an Italic tribe to the southeast of Rome. The Volsci launched a sneak attack on Rome to weaken the siege of Corioli. However, Coriolanus led his troops to the gates of Corioli and set fire to the neighboring houses. When news reached the Volscian troops marching on Rome, they turned back in dismay.

However, Coriolanus was later sent into exile because of a dispute with the *plebs*. He went to live among his former enemy, the Volsci, and offered to guide their army against Rome. When he was about to attack his former city, his mother, Veturia, and his wife, Volumnia, were brought to the camp to persuade him to abandon his decision (Britannica Encyclopaedia, 2019). They convinced him to withdraw. In honor of these women, the Romans dedicated a temple to *Fortuna*, goddess of luck and good fortune.

The Gens Fabia

The *Fabii* were one of the ancient patrician families of Rome, and they were the wealthiest and most powerful. Between 485 and 479 B.C.E., a Fabius held the consulship seven consecutive times. At first, they were hated by the plebeians as much as the rest of the patricians, but at one point, one of the Fabian consuls started advocating for plebeian rights. That earned the family the sympathy of the plebeians and the rage of the patricians, who called the *Fabii* traitors.

In 479 B.C.E., Rome was at war with Veii, the most powerful Etruscan city. Kaeso Fabius spoke in front of the Senate on behalf of the whole *gens Fabia* and asked for the honor of confronting the enemies on their own. The Senate accepted, and the following day, the family left the city to camp by the small

Cremera River between Rome and Veii. No other patrician family offered to join them.

The entire *gens Fabia* and all of their clients went to the camp at Cremera. They resisted for two years, successfully repelling the Veientines ,until one day they were ambushed and destroyed. Of the 306 members of the *Gens Fabia*, only one boy was left alive and returned to Rome (Harding, n.d.). The specifics of the story are legendary, and they closely resemble the last stand of the 300 Spartans at Thermopylae. Moreover, the *gens Fabia* remained one of the most distinguished patrician families of the Roman Republic, so it is unlikely that the 306 *Fabii* at the battle comprised the entire *gens*. Yet the battle may well have occurred, and there is evidence that the *Fabii* held country estates around the Cremera River.

Lucius Quinctius Cincinnatus

In 458, B.C.E., a Roman army was surrounded by enemies on Mount Algidus, and Cincinnatus, a farmer, was appointed dictator by the Senate to save it. Cincinnatus was not the first Roman dictator, but he may have been the most symbolic of the office when performed properly.

Cincinnatus is remembered for having kept the title of dictator only for the 16 days that it took him to save the trapped army and ensure Rome's safety. It is uncertain if his story is real or if it has been adorned by tradition. However, his figure was praised by the

Romans because he represented the value of republican institutions above personal ambitions: "He knew that his duty as a Roman dictator was to ameliorate the situation as quickly as possible. When order had been restored, his job was to allow the state to return to its normal operations—one without a dictator" (Burns, 2022, para. 4).

Verginia

In 454 B.C.E., the Romans elected a board of 10 legislators to help smooth the tensions between patricians and plebeians. Among the *decemviri* or "board of 10" was the powerful patrician Appius Claudius Crassus Inregillensis Sabinus. The board traveled to Athens, seeking inspiration from the law code of the great Athenian lawgiver Solon. They returned after two years debates continued over how to compile just legislation.

Verginia was the daughter of a plebeian centurion named Lucius Verginius. She was very beautiful, and in 452 B.C.E., the powerful patrician *decemvir* Appius Claudius wanted to possess her, but the girl was already engaged. Making use of his superior power, Appius Claudius kidnapped the girl and claimed she was, in fact, a slave.

The plebeians were outraged, and Lucius Verginius took a knife and killed his daughter in the public market to save her from such dishonor. The event triggered the second secession of the plebs that ended with the overthrow of Appius Claudius and his henchmen and restored Republican values (Virginia, n.d.).

In 449 B.C.E. the Twelve Tables were published based on the work of the *decemviri*. They were Rome's first written laws, defining terms and procedures. Most importantly, they clearly expressed the rights and responsibilities of patricians and plebeians. Ultimately, they did not completely resolve Rome's social problems, but they eased some of the tension between the two major classes. And though they might not constitute a fully articulated law code, the Twelve Tables formed the basis of Roman law until the fall of the Western Empire in C.E. 476.

Appius Claudius Caecus

Appius Claudius was a member of the patrician class, appointed censor in 312 B.C.E. During his censorship, he started a series of reforms to allow sons of freedmen into the Senate and other measures to improve land distribution among the lower classes. This earned him the resentment of the other patricians and he was accused of being a demagogue who only launched those reforms to gain popular support and concentrate power.

Nonetheless, his most important legacy was the many building projects he carried out during his mandate. The most remarkable were the *Aqua Appia*, the first aqueduct in Rome that brought water to the city, and the Appian Way, or *Via Appia*. It was the first road used to transport military supplies across Italy and enable trade between Rome and Capua, an important city in southern Italy. It originally ran the 132 miles to Capua, but it was extended to 230 miles over many years, eventually connecting Rome with Brundisium, an important port on the heel of Italy's boot (Hoffman, n.d.).

The Struggle of the Orders

As explained, Roman society was divided into patricians and plebeians based on their ethnic origin, which was linked to the foundation of Rome. They had significant differences regarding civil and political rights. This distinction wasn't supported by a legal frame but by tradition, status, and mutual recognition as the founders' descendants or later immigrants.

Status was the main factor that determined the hierarchical organization of Roman society (*The Struggle of the Orders: Plebeians and Patricians*, 2016). The strength of tradition in shaping every aspect of daily life and social order created a stable system that survived almost unchanged for nearly four centuries. During the Monarchy and the early Republic, there were some reforms to extend plebeians rights and access to high magistracies, but the essence of the system prevailed.

Even though the division wasn't based on economic criteria, patrician families were generally wealthier and more powerful than plebeians. The patricians were the nobility, while the plebeians were the farmers and workers of the lower classes. Both classes were considered citizens and could own lands and slaves.

Eventually, the differences in economic and political rights incited a conflict within the Republic: The Struggle of the Orders. The tension boiled over in 494 B.C.E., with the first secession of the plebs, and spanned until 287 B.C.E. During the 200 years of social friction, some wealthy members of the plebeian class reached higher office, gaining them entrance into Senate. This allied them with the patricians. The nobility of Rome, defined by having an ancestor who had held high office in the family tree, now extended to certain wealthy plebeian families.

However, although some plebeians became even wealthier than many of their patrician counterparts, the vast majority of the population remained poor farmers and laborers, nearly all of them plebeians. Their demands were for structural changes in the legal framework of the Republic. Even after they received legal equality, the tensions between the urban poor and the nobility contributed to the growing difficulty of the republican system to govern a growing empire effectively (*The Struggle of the Orders: Plebeians Unite to Lift their Shackles*, n.d.).

The Twelve Tables

The stories of Menenius and Verginia above developed out of the early Struggle of the Orders. Appius Claudius Crassus was one of ten men appointed to compile the basic laws that would define and ensure the civil rights of Roman society. It was the Romans' first attempt to solve the conflict between the classes. After the overthrow of the last king, the imbalance of powers led to the plebeian secession to the Sacred Mount, leaving the aristocracy without the productive class and the bulk of the army. Therefore, the patricians searched for a peaceful way to solve the conflict (Kershaw, 2023).

Whether Menenius' fable or Verginia's heinous murder are true is debatable. Beyond debate is the existence of the Twelve Tables. The document, first carved on wood and later copper, is the earliest source of Roman written law and the most ancient evidence of written legislation defining a republican form of government (Kershaw, 2023). The laws of the Twelve Tables set the basis of civil equality in Rome, a civilizational value that endures in contemporary Western societies. This principle implies that all citizens must be treated equally under the law, even those in power.

Written and public laws are the foundations of the republican system, along with periodical and elective public magistrates. The Twelve Tables were placed in the middle of the city, where every citizen could read them.

Before the Twelve Tables, the patricians held political and religious power to create and modify the rules and to interpret and enforce them. As religious authorities, the priests (known as pontifices), played a role in judicial procedures. Therefore, the plebeians were at their mercy. The Twelve Tables prevented the abuse of power by the aristocracy and made every citizen aware of their civil rights (Kershaw, 2023).

Before the Twelve Tables, the plebeians only had the tribunes of the plebs as magistrates to represent them in front of the patricians. The legal system was shaped by a patriarchal and patrilineal society, and the conflicts between parties were solved by the *paterfamilias* in any family, whether they were plebeians or patricians. But if it was a major issue, the conflict fell under the jurisdiction of the patrician pontifices. Plebeians were always under the influence or protection of a patrician family, and it was ultimately the latter who decided upon the conflicts.

Some of the major subjects addressed by the Twelve Tables were:

- A pre-established procedure to conduct a trial.
- Common sentences and punishments.
- The rights of the *patresfamilias* regarding inheritance through the masculine line and the right to divorce their wives. It was also allowed to euthanize disabled children, similar to the Spartan system.
- Women's restrictive rights and their conceptualization as citizens with similar rights to minors.
- Property ownership.
- The prohibition of capital punishment without a trial.
- Religious law and burial procedures.
- The prohibition of marriage between members of different orders.

The Struggle of the Orders brought profound changes to the Republic; however, even after the conflict subsided, its embers helped stoke the fire of the civil wars that would end with the decline of the Republic.

Roman Expansion in Italy

The early expansion of Rome began almost immediately after its foundation. Romulus and the other warrior kings fought against the neighboring tribes to incorporate the population into the new state and conquer territories to expand the arable lands. By the 6th century B.C.E., the Etruscan kings controlled the Latin communities that lived to the south of the Tiber River.

In 509 B.C.E., Rome centered into a treaty with the city-state of Carthage (present-day Tunisia). Rome accepted Carthage's commercial monopoly across the Mediterranean in exchange for continued Carthaginian hostility toward Rome's Greek and Etruscan adversaries. Carthage sought to prevent Rome from expanding into Sicily and North Africa (Kinder & Hilgemann, 1996).

When the last Etruscan king fell, Rome's hegemony was weakened, and the villages that occupied the region of Latium rebelled against the city. Their alliance, which Rome had dominated during the Monarchy, was called the Latin League, and the Latin War unfolded between 498 and 493 B.C.E. (Kinder & Hilgemann, 1996). Rome fought and defeated its neighbors in the battle of Lake Regillus in 496. Legend holds that the twin gods Castor and Pollux aided the patrician cavalry in the battle, inspiring them to victory. Rome and the Latin League signed the treaty of Cassius in 494 B.C.E.

This treaty not only put the war to an end but also ensured the Latin cities' autonomy, although the treaty set Rome itself as equal to the entire rest of the League. It was a defensive alliance, but any forces raised against external adversaries would fall under Roman control. This system of Rome calling upon the manpower of neighbors and former adversaries allowed a single city-state to punch far above its weight, militarily. And the arrangement had significant consequences for Italy and beyond as the Republic matured.

Both sides conquered territory and founded joint Latin colonies. The treaty ensured the same rights and obligations for all citizens and established freedom to trade. Nonetheless, the League didn't dissolve as it protected Latium from the attacks of the Aequi and the Volsci.

During the early 4th century, Rome had to resist attacks from the Gauls from the north, who settled in the plains of the Po River. The Gauls were a fearsome foe to the Romans, and a warband led by Brennus swept through northern Italy around 387 B.C.E. The Gauls annihilated a Roman army at the Battle of the Allia, about 10 miles north of Rome. Brennus then plundered the city.

The episode became a great source of shame for the Romans and left a near-permanent imprint on their psychology. We have no definitive knowledge of any previous occupation of Rome by a foreign power, and it would be about 800 years before another foreign army succeeded. Later Roman literature presents an almost complete destruction of the city, similar to the razing of Troy. However, the more likely outcome is that the Romans bought off the barbarian warband after an embarrassing defeat, and slowly regained steam over the next several decades. But their fear of the Gauls remained a defining characteristic of many foreign policy decisions in the late Republic and early Empire.

The Romans later also allied with the Samnites, people who may have been an offshoot of the earlier Sabine population that had not Romanized under the Monarchy (Kinder & Hilgemann, 1996).

Despite the peace heralded by the Treaty of Cassius, Rome became a threat to the Latin colonies when it resumed expansion after its humiliation by the Gauls. A second Latin War broke out a century and a half after the first, and it ended in disaster for the Latins and their allies. The conflict started in 341 and ended in 338 B.C.E., when Rome conquered some Latin and Volscian cities, and the League was finally dissolved. People from the conquered cities were integrated as Roman citizens of various degrees, and they preserved relative autonomy. The conquered city-states had direct relationships with Rome but not with each other (*Latins*, n.d.).

After the end of the Latin War, the Romans started a colonization campaign beyond the lands of Latium. Latins spread in the colonies throughout the peninsula, and the word "Latin" (*latii*) no longer referred to ethnolinguistic criteria. Rather, it became a legal category that came with some of the rights and privileges of roman citizenship (*Latins*, n.d.).

Essential Highlights

The Republic replaced the Monarchy after the last tyrannical king was overthrown. The new system attempted to prevent absolute power from being concentrated in one person. It created institutions to enable the balance and control of power. The hierarchical Roman society based on principle was modified by several reforms that ensured more representation and rights for the plebeians. The concept of citizenship as the basis for the whole system evolved and expanded throughout the process.

Having laid its foundation firmly on the Italian Peninsula, the Roman Republic eyed horizons further afield. With growth, however, came both opportunity and challenge.

Chapter 5: Expansion and Conflict

As Rome's territories expanded, so did its internal conflicts, a byproduct of ambition and avarice. The new state grew, as did pressure on a population in need of more resources, and tensions driven by inequality. This forced Rome to expand its territories to solve internal crises, but it also caused new conflicts with its neighbors. The balance of power in the surrounding areas of the Mediterranean Sea changed, with consequences for Rome, its allies, and its enemies.

All these changes directly impacted the internal organization. While the Republic expanded, social changes led to new struggles for wealth and power among the traditional classes and among many new citizens who were integrated as Rome expanded the franchise to neighboring cities. Rome also allowed many conquered city-states to keep their cultures and institutions. The only requirement was to provide Rome with soldiers and military support when needed. Offering the defeated a part of the future victory was a great incentive for Rome's enemies to become its allies (*The Roman Republic*, n.d.).

However, it created a new challenge for the Roman Republic: to build a Roman identity that enabled stability and a sense of belonging. This identity developed loyalty to Rome, which would become a solid basis first for the Republic and later for the greatest empire of antiquity.

The Effects of Rome's Territorial Expansion

The Annexed Territories

Rome was under constant aggression by neighboring tribes and other people who came from outside the peninsula. War was, on occasion, defensive to repel its enemies and, on other occasions, offensive to gain allies and strengthen its position. Roman expansion wasn't a peaceful colonization process. Instead, it was a sequence of wars that eventually provided Rome with the identity needed to strengthen the state.

During the 3rd century B.C.E., the Romans fought and subjugated most of the people living on the Italian peninsula. Their greatest concern was the heavy Greek presence in the South, particularly the vast port of Tarentum. Later, the Romans directed their attention to the Po Valley, the islands of Sardinia and Sicily, and the southern region of Hispania (present-day Spain).

In the early 3rd century B.C.E., the Greeks of Thurii were under constant attack by the Lucani, a southern Italic tribe, and they asked for Rome's military intervention. Tarentum, the most powerful Greek colony in Italy, felt that Thurii should have tuned to fellow Greeks instead of the Romans. After all, Roman intervention would increase their influence in the south. In 282 B.C.E., the Romans saved Thurii from a siege by the Lucani, Samnites, and Bruttians, spreading Rome's control farther out from Latium and into Southern Italy. This alerted the Tarentines, who attacked Roman ships near the coast and sacked Thurii. Tarentum took Roman soldiers as prisoners, and in response, Rome declared war.

The Pyrrhic War

Tarentum engaged mainland Greece's participation. King Pyrrhus of Epirus, one of the most remarkable military leaders of the age, commanded a force of Greek mercenaries and invaded Italy from the south in 280 B.C.E. He brought 25,000 soldiers and 20 war elephants, a strategy that would later be used by other enemies of Rome.

Rome's first battle against a sophisticated Hellenistic Greek army did not go well. Pyrrhus quickly defeated them at Heraclea and enlisted the help of the Samnites. The king of Epirus offered peace to Rome, but it entailed confining their influence to central Italy. The now elderly Appius Claudius Caecus (see above, Chapter 4) persuaded the Senate to keep fighting, since peace would be perceived as a weakness if the terms were not favorable to Rome.

Appius' sentiment evoked long-held Roman tradition. Rome was always a patron, never a client.

Roman commanders held *imperium* over their troops – they could, and often did, execute any legionnaire who left his position in the battle line. Moreover, the Roman approach to war differed greatly from that of the city-states in the Hellenistic East. For Rome, it was definitional. The word "peace" essentially meant a favorable treaty for the *Populus Romanus*. A favorable treaty, by definition, was one that relegated the opponent to permanent client status. It was all or nothing – once war started, it did not end until the enemy became a client. In contrast, Hellenistic states would often make peace after a slight gain or loss of treasure or territory and reopen hostilities a few years later to try their luck again. Enemy societies rarely appreciated the misalignment of victory conditions between themselves and the Romans.

Pyrrhus attacked Rome again at Asculum in 279 B.C.E. However, he suffered many casualties against the ferocious legionnaires. Our sources conflict on who actually won the battle – both sides suffered significant losses. According to Plutarch, who claimed that Pyrrhus came away victorious, the king of Epirus felt that "another such [victory] would utterly undo him." His successes against an implacable Rome coined the expression "Pyrrhic Victory," any win purchased at too high a cost (Badian et al., 2023, para. 13). Just one year after the loss at Heraclea, Rome fought Pyrrhus to a standstill.

Pyrrhus left Italy to fight against the Carthaginians in Sicily. In 275 B.C.E., he returned and attacked Rome again, but this time, the Romans defeated him at the battle of Beneventum. This was a key victory for Rome not only because it proved the power of its army to repel a foreign invasion and control the tribes in Southern Italy, but because it validated the Roman system against a powerful opponent. The Pyrrhic War illustrated that Rome's arrangement with its allies could allow a single city-state to draw upon the manpower reserves of an entire geographic region. This meant that Roman forces could sustain horrific losses and keep fighting when any other society would have capitulated long before.

The Punic Wars

Carthage was a 9th century B.C.E. colony of the Phoenician city Tyre, in modern Lebanon. The Phoenicians founded several trade colonies in the Western Mediterranean in the early 1st millennium B.C.E., and Carthage was well-positioned on the coast of modern Tunisia. In time, Carthage grew into an independent city-state, and then a mercantile empire that dominated trade in the Western Mediterranean. Rome's expansion proved a threat, and diplomatic relations ran hot and cold from the very founding of the Republic in 509 B.C.E.

The conflicts reached their peak during the 3rd century B.C.E., in the three Punic Wars. *Punicus* was the Latin adjective for "Phoenician." For Rome,

Carthage was a threat to Roman hegemony on the peninsula due to its alliances with rebel tribes and its presence in nearby Sicily. The first objective Rome pursued was to limit Carthaginian influence on the peninsula, but the Carthaginian Empire sought to hamper the growth of a city-state it considered an upstart.

The First Punic War

The First Punic War (264–241 B.C.E.) started after the eruption of a military and diplomatic conflict in Sicily. About 288 B.C.E., a roving band of Italic mercenaries took over the port of Messina in the northeast corner of the island. It sat opposite Rhegium on the toe of Italy's boot, and the two cities controlled the crossing from the island to the mainland. The mercenary group called itself the Mamertines after Mamers, an Italic war god. For 20 years they raided and plundered the areas around Messina.

Eventually, in 264 B.C.E., King Hiero II of Syracuse moved to destroy them, but the Mamertines appealed to Carthage for help. A Carthaginian fleet arrived to help, and the Syracusans withdrew, but the Mamertines soon chafed under Carthaginian control – they now appealed to Rome. The Romans had misgivings about helping a mercenary group that had unjustly conquered a city, but they feared Carthaginian proximity to Italy even more. grew worried about Carthaginian proximity to Italy. Rome allied itself to the Mamertines, and Syracuse to Carthage. The defining wars of the Republic had begun.

Rome sent an army of 40,000 to Sicily. The Romans quickly subdued Syracuse, which received no aid from Carthage. The Syracusans were forced to agree to supply Roman troops in the Sicilian theater. Although a great naval power, the Carthaginians did not feel confident about engaging such a large Roman force on the rugged Sicilian terrain. Nevertheless, they recruited a mercenary army of over 50,000 infantry, including warriors from African tribes, Iberians from Spain, and Celts from France and Britain. The ground war in Sicily was a slog, but the Romans generally outperformed Carthage.

But Carthage ruled the seas and was able to supply its forces in Sicily and raid the Italian coastline with impunity. The ground war became a stalemate. Rome had never engaged in large-scale naval warfare, but it needed to hit Carthage where it hurt. Exhibiting the Roman tendency to absorb rather than exclude, the Romans built a fleet using a wrecked Carthaginian warship as a model. Of course, the inexperienced Roman crews were no match for their opponents, which they learned in several small engagements. The Carthaginian ships were too maneuverable and could easily ram and sink the Roman vessels.

However, the Romans developed a device they called the *corvus* or "raven." It was a movable gangplank with a spike on the end that, when dropped, would penetrate the deck of the opposing ship, building an immovable bridge from one ship to another. A handful of heavily armed Roman marines could overwhelm the lightly defended Carthaginian sailors. At the Battle of Mylae in 260 B.C.E., the *corvus* helped the Romans overcome a large Carthaginian fleet.

The Romans now felt confident enough in their navy to press Carthage. They brought together considerable resources to assemble a fleet of over 300 warships with many more transports and ancillary vessels. Aboard the transports was an invasion force of 26,000 veteran soldiers. They planned to invade Carthage itself. However, the Carthaginians assembled their entire navy to defend the homeland, and the forces met off Cape Ecnomus in southern Sicily in 256 B.C.E. Scholars debate whether it is the largest naval battle in human history, but largest or not, the resources of human and material capital spent are staggering – perhaps 50,000 men killed, and 50 ships sunk in a single engagement.

The Roman invasion of Africa was only partially successful. The Romans defeated Carthage in 255 B.C.E., but they tried to impose terms so harsh that the Carthaginians soon regained their will to fight. They pushed the Romans back, but the fleet sent to evacuate the legions from Africa defeated another Carthaginian fleet at the Battle of Cape Hermaeum. But the entire successful Roman fleet was sunk in a violent storm off the south coast of Sicily. The losses may have exceeded 100,000 soldiers and crewmen and 350 warships.

Yet the Roman system could withstand such staggering losses and continue. They built and crewed another fleet quickly, renewing the war in Sicily. But it dragged on, with the Romans winning some victories on land and at sea, but the Carthaginians holding their own in Sicily under the leadership of General Hamilcar Barca. In 253 B.C.E., the Romans lost another fleet of 150 ships in a massive storm.

The toll on both great civilizations continued to rise, with the Carthaginians seeking massive loans from Egypt, and Roman nobles donating personal finances to the bankrupt state. Eventually, in 241 B.C.E., after 23 years of atrocious bloodshed, the Carthaginians sued for peace. The settlement required Carthage to abandon all its territory in Sicily, Sardinia, and Corsica, and pay massive reparations to Rome to recoup the cost of the war. The Carthaginian Empire in Africa and Spain remained intact. For the next 20 years, Hamilcar Barca would expand Carthaginian territory in Spain. Rome would add Sicily to the *Imperium Romanum* as the first province outside the Italian peninsula. Corsica and Sardinia soon followed. To govern these provinces, the Senate would appoint a praetor who had just finished his term of office. Such a governor was called a propraetor.

The Second Punic War

Despite the victory and peace treaty, Rome was determined to destroy the Carthaginian Empire and prepared a double attack on Spain and Africa, departing from Sicily. However, those plans were delayed due to the emergence of a new military leader, Hannibal Barca, son of Hamilcar Barca. The hero of the first Punic War had ruled Hispania like a private kingdom, and after Hamilcar's death in 228 B.C.E., Hannibal grew in influence.

Hannibal planned to attack Rome directly. Instead of reaching through the south or from the islands, which were predictable moves and guarded by the now-dominant Roman fleet, he outlined a bold plan. He would reach Rome from the north. He gathered an army of 50,000 men, including many native Iberians, and 9,000 cavalry. He included 37 elephants on his trek across the Pyrenees and the Alps.

The Romans had no defensive positions in the Alps and didn't expect an attack from the north, so Hannibal reached the Po Valley in 218 B.C.E., counting on the support of the Gauls. After the first victories, Hannibal consolidated his position in the north but decided not to attack Rome directly until he could erode support from its allies.

The Roman legions confronted Hannibal's army on the battlefield several times and suffered repeated disasters – Trebia in 218 and Lake Trasimene in 217. The Battle of Cannae in 216 B.C.E. was the worst. An army of over 80,000 Romans and allies was almost completely annihilated by an inferior force of 50,000. Hannibal employed the first well-attested double envelopment or "pincer" attack in Western warfare to devastating effect.

Hannibal was able to hold his position and extend his influence across much of Italy, but it was difficult to obtain supplies, manage allies and mercenaries of many different ethnicities, and keep his army loyal. The fact that he managed to do so while sitting in enemy territory for 14 years places him among the greatest strategic and logistic generals in history.

On the other side, Rome struggled to repel an invader of such genius, but the same system that absorbed catastrophic losses in the previous generation managed to field enough men to keep the Carthaginian terror away from the walls of Rome. Moreover, they conducted the war in several theaters, including Spain and, in 204, Africa itself.

By 203 B.C.E., the Romans had long known not to attack Hannibal head on. Instead, they maneuvered in a strategic dance to take and defend strongholds and threaten supply lines. At that point, with the brilliant Roman general Publius Cornelius Scipio Africanus devastating the African countryside, the Carthaginian Senate recalled their greatest general, and Hannibal withdrew back to Africa.

In 202 B.C.E., Hannibal confronted the Romans in the Battle of Zama. The Romans, led by Scipio, fielded 30,000 men, many of the survivors of the disaster at Cannae 14 years before. He received help from Masinissa, a Numidian king who had defected from the Carthaginians. Hannibal commanded a force of 50,000, including 80 war elephants. The Romans won a terribly hard-fought but complete victory that "effectively ended both Hannibal's command of Carthaginian forces and also Carthage's chances to significantly oppose Rome" (Hunt, 2018, para. 1). The Carthaginian Senate exiled Hannibal and sued for peace. They lost all their overseas territory, some of their African territory, and had to pay Rome a massive amount in reparations. Most importantly, the treaty stipulated that Carthage could not wage war without Rome's permission.

The Third Punic War

Despite the success in the battle of Zama, many Romans felt the Carthaginian threat was not gone. Cato the Elder and other prominent senators advocated for war. In 149 B.C.E., the Roman Senate secured a good reason to attack Carthage, when the latter attacked Numidia, still led by a now elderly Masinissa, who was mercilessly raiding Carthaginian territory. He knew the Romans would intervene if Carthage retaliated (The Punic Wars vs. Carthage, n.d.).

Rome prepared its troops to besiege Carthage, but with no positive outcomes for two years. Eventually, in 146, a new military leader entered the scene: Scipio Aemilianus. He succeeded in successfully blockading Carthage itself. Scipio's army breached the walls and captured the city house by house until 50,000 Carthaginian people surrendered. The city was destroyed, and the survivors were sold as slaves. The Carthaginian Empire had disappeared, and it became the Roman province of Africa (Ray, 2023). However, the Romans left the city empty for the next century, when they rebuilt it as a Roman colony.

The Macedonian and Seleucid Wars

The fact that Rome could field (and lose) massive armies time and time again through the 3rd century B.C.E. while fighting Carthage is noteworthy. But the Romans also operated in other theaters against other opponents at the same time. The struggles between Rome and several Hellenistic Greek states are known as the Macedonian Wars. Four conflicts during the 3rd and 2nd centuries B.C.E. spread Rome's influence in the East.

By 214 B.C.E., the successors of Alexander the Great's empire had been fighting one another for over a century. The three major players were Antigonid Macedonia, Ptolemaic Egypt, and the Seleucid Empire from the Middle East to India. Under the rule of Philip V, the Macedonian Empire was a threat to Rome since it had allied with Hannibal. The

Macedonian Wars took place in the context of the Punic Wars. Therefore, Rome sought allies among various leagues of Hellenistic Greek city-states primarily to stop Philip from sending aid to Hannibal in Italy. They were successful in doing so.

After the Second Punic War ended, the Romans were fairly disinterested in Greek affairs. However, when tensions between the three great Hellenistic empires flared and threatened to impact the free leagues of Greek city-states, they had nowhere to turn but Rome for help – diplomatic or otherwise. As happened so often in Roman history, once the Greek cities became clients of Rome in 200 B.C.E., the Romans took their job of patron seriously.

Over the following decades, Rome sought to stabilize the political atmosphere in the East. Roman and allied forces defeated Macedonian armies in Greece at Cynoscephalae in 197 B.C.E. and at Pydna in 168. These victories illustrated the superiority of the versatile Roman legions over the inflexible (but nearly unstoppable) Macedonian phalanx. They also ended Macedonia as an independent entity – the Romans divided it into four client states.

Almost simultaneously, the Romans entered into conflict with the vast Seleucid Empire, entering Asia for the first time. Antiochus III ruled the territory from modern Turkey to the Hindu Kush mountains. Nevertheless, Lucius Cornelius Scipio Asiaticus, the younger brother of Hannibal's nemesis Scipio Africanus, smashed Antiochus' superior force at Magnesia in 190. The Romans withdrew, but relieved

Antiochus of all his territory in Europe (Chaliakopoulos, 2022). The Seleucid Empire dwindled over the next century until, eventually, its last few cities in Syria fell to Gnaeus Pompeius Magnus in 63 B.C.E.

In the meantime, Rome wrestled with the unruly Macedonians and Greek city-states to maintain peace. After the Romans defeated a Macedonian uprising at a second Battle of Pydna in 148 B.C.E., a league of Greek city-states declared war on Rome. As former allies, the Romans perceived this as a client refusing to meet their obligations. The Romans utterly destroyed Corinth, one of the most culturally advanced city-states in Greece. In the same year that Rome destroyed its greatest enemy, Carthage, it brutally subdued Greece. The Romans plundered all treasure and artistic works from Corinth, and turned Macedonia and Greece into the new provinces of Epirus and Achaea (Kinder & Hilgemann, 1996).

Rome in the West: Expansion in Europe

After the war against Hannibal ended in 202 B.C.E., the Romans also operated widely in the north of Italy and Spain. There, Carthage allied with the tribes that resisted Roman influence, such as the Boii, the Insubres, and the Gallic tribes in the Po Valley. The Gauls, who came from present-day France, joined forces with the Ligurians and attacked the Latin colony of Placentia in 198 B.C.E. However, by 197, the Romans had pacified the entire Mediterranean coast of Spain, dividing it into two new provinces, Nearer and Further Spain.

The Republic also fought many battles against the Gauls living both north and south of the Alps, and by the end of the period, Rome conquered some of their lands. In 194 B.C.E., Lucius Valerius Flaccus launched a campaign that consolidated Roman hegemony in Italy after defeating the Insubres and the Boii. Peace was established and the Romans built new colonies at Bononia and Aquileia (Saller et al., 2023).

The Romans also built a new road, the *Via Emilia,* to establish trading connections with the northern tribes of Europe. It implied an expansion of the Roman commercial scope. The French territory near the Mediterranean became the Roman province of Gallia Narbonensis in 121 B.C.E., with its capital at modern Narbonne. (*The Roman Republic*, n.d.).

Structural Changes in the High Republic

Impact on Citizenship and a New Balance of Political Power

The role of citizenship was key throughout the whole history of Rome, from the earliest moment of its foundation. The status and rights encompassed in Roman citizenship were progressively transformed and reached more people. During the first stages of expansion, citizenship was framed by land, military service, and political levels of participation: "Because a person had to be physically present in Rome to vote, the extension of voting rights beyond the population of the city itself did not drastically alter the political situation in Rome" (*The Roman Republic*, n.d., para. 13).

After the expansion, there were three types of citizens in Rome (Kinder & Hilgemann, 1996):

- Citizens of the city and the surrounding rural areas. This category included civil and political rights which meant that they could own land and also take part in assemblies and vote. They were the *cives optimo jure,* citizens with full rights.

- Communities with citizenship rights: usually conquered populations who were considered Roman citizens but lacked voting rights at Rome (*civitates sine suffragio*).

- Confederates: These were autonomous city-states that recognized Rome's hegemony – clients, essentially. These cities were *civitates foederatae*, allied states. Their citizens could trade with Rome and even marry full Roman citizens.

It was important for Rome to build a stable and balanced relationship with the new populations and simultaneously avoid risking internal stability. Rome needed soldiers and military support, but that couldn't be achieved without making them part of the political unit. It is difficult to measure how much power should be allowed to a conquered city-state. It had to be enough to develop loyalty to Rome but not so excessive as to hamper Roman hegemony. The right to vote was the main feature that regulated that participation: "The offer of citizenship did help to build a sense of shared identity around loyalty to Rome" (*The Roman Republic*, n.d., para. 13).

Political Organization of the New Territories

Wars cost money and demand resources. Mobilizing an army wasn't an easy task. Since soldiers were Roman citizens, sending troops away on a long military campaign entailed preventing them from working their lands and producing food. Once victory was ensured, there was a second task to address: keeping power. However, relying solely on military forces would be excessively costly for the state, even threatening the food supply.

By the end of the 3rd century B.C.E., the territory of the Roman Republic was nearly 50,200 square miles, and it was inhabited by about 292,000 citizens (Kinder & Hilgemann, 1996). The enlarged territory and population demanded effective political organization and administration. The Republic created formal provinces: "In 241 Sicily became Rome's first province, followed by Sardinia-Corsica in 238, and Spain, divided into two provinces, in 197. After a 50-year hiatus, Macedonia and Africa were annexed in 146, and the province of Asia (northwestern Turkey) in 133" (Hornblower et al., 2023, para. 10).

The Senate appointed officeholders called governors (usually an ex-consul or praetor), a *quaestor*, and three lieutenants called *legati* to govern a province. Their power was limited to the territory of the province. The Republican government found a balance between giving governors enough power to keep the provinces under control but not so much that it would challenge Rome's central power (*The Roman Republic*, n.d.). However, the relative autonomy of the provinces was a temptation for governors who, far away from Rome, abused their power over the provinces' inhabitants to enrich themselves (Encyclopedia Britannica, 2023).

Economic Changes in the Republic

Economic evolution facilitated territorial expansion and simultaneously led to an even greater expansion. Besides the increase in population and, therefore, their military forces, the Republic enlarged its vast network of roads. This made the transportation of goods, weapons, and soldiers easier and safer.

Pacifying the surrounding city-states allowed Rome to expand its arable lands, and that led to an increase in overall production capacity. After conquering more lands and communities, Rome's public finances gained new sources of income. The Republic established two types of taxes: war taxes (*tributum*), and indirect taxes linked to trading (*portoria*, or customs) (Kinder & Hilgemann, 1996).

Higher incomes spread the demand for greater supplies produced in the field. The production rose but also diversified. With the annexation of territory, some upper-class Romans obtained large plantations called *latifundia* to cultivate crops and grow livestock, not only for survival as in the earliest stages of state, but also for high profit. Many farmers stopped producing grains to dedicate their lands to producing high-value crops like olives and grapes for wine. This process deepened the social division between the classes since those changes were only available for large farms, and the new goods were destined for high-class consumers.

This led to the evolution of trading within the Roman territory and with people beyond its borders. The defeat of the Gauls in the North and the building of the *Via Emilia* enabled trading with Northern Europe. And after the annexation of the Macedonian Empire the Roman marketplace became the entire Mediterranean world. The basis of the Roman economy was agriculture, but trading also gained importance. It led to the development of currency to facilitate the trading of different goods with different cultures in regions outside Roman territories. The Romans started minting coins of copper and alloys until, in 296 B.C.E., they established silver coins (Kinder & Hilgemann, 1996).

The Role of Slavery

The evil of slavery was ubiquitous in the ancient world. A slave wasn't considered a person but property and, therefore, could be sold and bought. According to the law, a slave was defined as a *res* (thing). Even though they lacked most of the common rights free people enjoyed, they had a few to preserve their lives. Slaves remained in the same condition for the rest of their lives, and that place within society was inherited by their offspring.

Many societies allowed slavery, but not all of them developed slavery as the basis of production. Rome's Monarchy is an example of this – Romans employed slaves when they could get them, either in domestic or agricultural service. Acquiring slaves was another element of social status. On the other hand, the massive influx of slaves and new citizens during the Republic meant that slaves became the dominant workforce (Hellie, 2023). Moreover, the inclusion of highly cultured Greek slaves meant that wealthy Romans could outsource education, medicine, engineering, and many other fields to slave labor.

Before the 3rd century B.C.E., slavery wasn't widespread. The increase of slaves in Rome coincides with the years of the greatest expansion of the territories of the Republic: "In 225 B.C., there were an estimated 600,000 slaves in Roman Italy, but only 194 years later that number grew to approximately two million" (Burks, 2008. p. 9).

Unlike more recent civilizations, slavery in Rome (and throughout most of human history) wasn't based on ethnic or racial differences. Instead, stronger populations enslaved vulnerable ones, while trying not to become vulnerable themselves. Greeks enslaved as many Greeks as they did others, likewise with Romans, Africans, Asians, and Middle Easterners. In Rome, slaves "include prisoners of war, sailors captured and sold by pirates, or slaves bought outside Roman territory. In hard times, it was not uncommon for desperate Roman citizens to raise money by selling their children into slavery" (PBS, n.d., para. 3).

The war on the borders of the state was one of the most important sources of slaves because prices were lower. Kidnapping was another common way to take slaves to sell them in the Roman market.

Slaves worked everywhere: On farms, mines, factories, as domestic service in the houses of the *paterfamilias*, and even on public works. Beside them, free people also worked in the Roman system. However, the great expansion of the Republic's citizen population created a huge demand for production that only an equal increase in available slave labor could meet.

Internal Conflict and Social Change

The development of the *latifundia* and the increase in the number of slaves widened the gulf between the rich and poor. Only the wealthiest families could hope to obtain a *latifundium* and dedicate their lands to high-value crops. So, the wealthy were the ones who benefited the most from imperial expansion and the changes it brought.

On the other hand, the massive arrival of slaves to work on the large farms displaced most of the free labor. It was less costly to have slaves; they produced more, and purchasing them was an investment.

Rome struggled to integrate the conquered population, expand public finance, and keep a delicate balance of power. The system that governed a city-state failed to find equilibrium in the economic and demographic growth of an empire. All these changes and their consequences led to social unrest – the free urban poor resented the wealthy and the slaves; the slaves wanted freedom. Between 132 and 103 B.C.E., two slave wars, also called Servile Wars, further destabilized the system.

Riots happened in Sicily, where there was a higher concentration of slaves. These lands were obtained in the war with Carthage and given to wealthy landowners. The slaves' living conditions were often much worse in greater *latifundia*.

The first riot was led by a slave named Eunus, who organized guerilla tactics to confront the Roman army sent to suppress him. Some slaves escaped or roamed the countryside, stealing what they could to survive. The second followed the same strategy, and although it spanned a few years, it was beaten by the Roman forces.

However, some Republican visionary leaders attempted to make reforms by enacting laws that could prevent the runaway disparity between rich and poor from growing further. Two of them were the Gracchus brothers, both elected as plebeian tribunes.

Tiberius Gracchus' reforms didn't attempt to destroy private property. Instead, he proposed to establish a limit for a *latifundium*, which was already legally set at 500 *iugera* (309 acres). Gracchus suggested that land over the limit should be redistributed to landless citizens to ensure their survival (Ferguson et al., 2023).

His proposition had wide support in the Plebeian Assembly, a subset of the Tribal Assembly without the participation of patricians. However, it was strongly resisted in the Senate, which was mainly composed of large landowners of both classes. The following year, Tiberius tried to be re-elected as Tribune, which was beyond the constitution, although he had enough votes. The election unleashed a violent conflict in the Senate, and Tiberius was killed (Gill, 2019). This was a momentous introduction of violence into the Roman political system.

Ten years later, Gaius Gracchus took Tiberius' place and continued with similar proposals for land reform. In 123 B.C.E., a plague ravaged the crops in the south of Italy, and Gaius ordered the construction of state granaries to ensure food supplies for the entire population. He tried to found colonies in Sicily and Carthage, and humanized laws regarding military conscription. He also advocated for full Roman citizenship for everyone in Italy.

Like Tiberius, Gaius had the common people's support but the Senate's opposition. Violence broke out again, this time with Gaius' supporters killing an opponent. The Senate immediately convened and issued a new type of senatorial decree – the *senatus consultum ultimum*, or ultimate decree of the Senate. It gave the presiding consuls permission to preserve the state by any means necessary, even in violation of civil rights. It was a last ditch measure to quell political and social tension by force, and its introduction was the most visible institutional symptom of an ailing Republic. Gaius knew he was doomed like his brother, and he committed suicide by falling on the sword of a slave. After his death, the Senate ordered the execution of many of Gaius' supporters and the confiscation of their property (Gill, 2019). The Senate asserted control, but the quickly growing free population of Rome was becoming more disaffected, and more likely to be roused by strong politicians taking a populist approach.

Essential Highlights

In the 3rd and 2nd centuries B.C.E., Roman territory expanded and dominated much of Western Europe, Northern Africa, and the ruins of the Macedonian Empire in Greece and Asia Minor. Through several wars, Rome consolidated its supremacy over the Mediterranean Sea and the surrounding areas. This expansion was enabled by economic and political evolution, and at the same time, the annexation of lands and the acquisition of slaves triggered a large-scale strain on Republican institutions.

As a counterpart, all these changes brought internal conflicts, and the system revealed contradictions and inconsistencies that led Rome down a path of decline for the Republic.

After a string of miraculous successes, it stood unchallenged in its raw might for several centuries. Yet, every entity, no matter how powerful, has its breaking point. The next chapter will explore how, while the power of Rome over its empire grew, the institutions of the Republic would be shaken to dust.

Chapter 6: The Fall of the Republic

In times of war, the law falls silent. –Cicero.

The Crisis of the Late Republic

The crisis of the Republic was a consequence of multiple causes that evolved and remained underappreciated for decades. One of them was the hierarchical nature of Roman social organization. It had given stability to the early society and was supported by the strength of tradition, but it became the main source of rampant economic inequalities. The differences between the patricians and the plebeians during the monarchy or even the early

Republic were mainly a matter of status. It certainly manifested in their political rights and the expansion of their wealth, but as there was little to share and a lot of trouble to deal with (external war, for instance), those differences were set aside. Moreover, the patron-client relationship offered protection and stability to many poorer free Romans.

When the Republic expanded, there was wealth and land to distribute. On the one hand, it was used to encourage people to support military campaigns, and on the other hand, the rewards weren't equally assigned (*Crises of the Republic*, n.d.). The creation of *latifundia* and the establishment of slaves as the primary workforce led many people (mostly plebeians) to impoverishment. Duncan explains (Boissoneault, 2017. para. 6):

> After Rome conquers Carthage, and after they decide to annex Greece, and after they conquer Spain and acquire all the silver mines, you have wealth on an unprecedented scale coming into Rome. The flood of wealth was making the richest of the rich Romans wealthier.

All that wealth was concentrated in the hands of the senatorial elite, consuls, and generals. Meanwhile, the plebeians were forced to leave their lands to fight for Rome and received very little in return.

Economic inequality and the living conditions of large parts of the plebeian population and the enslaved people led to social unrest. Revolts became more frequent, and the once-essential values of being Roman, such as *fides*, *gravitas*, and *dignitas*, slowly lost meaning for many citizens.

These conflicts didn't boil over every day, and there were several attempts to reduce the turmoil and appease the citizens. These initiatives often repurposed the institutions that encompassed the Republic. They implied building a whole new equilibrium of power and a system of new checks and balances. While the lower classes gained rights, constant crises slowly pushed the government toward centralized power. The Senate's authority diminished while a small number of politicians, many of whom followed a populist agenda, accrued tremendous influence.

The Republic had created the institutions to prevent drastic political changes in times of crisis and to avoid a return to monarchy. However, as the internal conflicts increased and the external threats rose, crises became the norm instead of the exception. Neither the Senate or the assemblies were able to solve people's needs, and that led to the discredit of the state (Boissoneault, 2017).

The Social War

As the Republic reinforced its supremacy in the Mediterranean and subjugated other powers, the policy toward the conquered people also changed. In the past, conquered tribes kept their autonomy and became Roman allies. When the Republic expanded during the 4th and 3rd centuries, these people often sought Roman citizenship to enjoy the benefits of the expansion. However, the growing population of citizens without voting rights became a source of conflict as these people lacked any sense of identity with Rome.

During the expansion phase, Italy was a confederation. Italians had the same economic inequalities as Roman citizens but didn't have the right to vote. A civil war broke out in 90–89 B.C.E. between Rome and the Italian allies or *socii*, hence the term Social War. The Italians organized their confederacy and gathered an army to confront the Roman troops.

The rebels were successful in the North and the South, and to appease the conflict, the Consul Lucius Julius Caesar passed a law to extend Roman citizenship to the Italians. Some tribes, like the Samnites, resisted but were fiercely repressed. However, peace was ensured by establishing new rights for the *socii* and the creation of the municipal organization of the communities as part of the Roman state (Encyclopedia Britannica, 2018).

The Rise of Popular Leaders

The Failure of the Gracchan Reforms

As discussed in the last chapter, Tiberius and Gaius Gracchus had attempted to implement land reform to limit the concentration of land in the hands of the super-rich. As plebeian tribunes, the bills they passed through the Plebeian Assembly carried the force of law, but they had almost no senatorial support. Indeed, both brothers were killed for their efforts to threaten the traditional order (*10000 years of economy*, n.d.).

The general aftermath of Gracchan attempts at reform was negative. The plebeians didn't derive any long-lasting benefit from them, and social unrest increased. In the end, the failure of this attempt contributed to weakening the loyalty of citizens to the state. Until then, in the conflict of interest between individual and collective, the solution always leaned toward the state. The Gracchi posed a disruptive question: "Who was to govern Rome, the Senate or the People?" (Henderson, 1968, p. 1). The Gracchan reforms pushed the Senate to a defensive position in front of the citizens, and that undermined its power and the soul of the Republican system.

The Military in Politics

In times of the monarchy, the army was closely linked to the social organization of Roman society. One's role in the army was associated with status, and that status was determined by wealth. The lowest groups were excluded from the army and, therefore, lacked rights. If they couldn't afford military equipment, they couldn't be part of the army.

During the Republic, the army was organized into legions. They were the backbone of Roman identity in lands far away from the capital. The sense of belonging to the army was the main source of loyalty to Rome, fighting in distant places for little reward. The generals played a key role in the legions, but it was difficult for the Republic to keep a balance between allowing enough power to control the troops but not enough to challenge central authority.

Things began to change when seasonal campaigns were replaced by lengthy tours of duty, sometimes for years on end. Then, the generals slowly became the patrons of their soldiers, paying them in the form of booty captured from the enemy, since the soldiers could not support their families at home otherwise. The loyalty of the soldiers moved from the state to the commander. In a way, it was a fundamentally Roman reflex, for a client to be loyal to their patron – but it conflicted with the administrative apparatus of a growing empire.

Gaius Marius

As the Republic faced military challenges, more troops were needed. In that context, Gaius Marius was elected consul in 107 B.C.E. He was not a native Roman, but a man from Arpinum, about 60 miles southeast of Rome. Arpinum had received full citizenship earlier in the century, and Marius pursued a political career as an outsider. He became the first person in his family to become consul, a rarity. The consulship was generally held by the traditional nobility, and they called anyone who joined the consular ranks a *novus homo*, a new man – a term of derision. Nevertheless, Marius introduced several military reforms. He allowed people from the lower classes with no property to enlist in the army. The state provided them with armor and weapons (Lloyd, 2013).

While this was part of a necessary solution to deal with a campaigns against African rebels and a massive invasion of Germans into northern Italy, Marius' plan created its own issues. The problem was what to do when soldiers retired. He passed a law that assigned a plot of land to each of his retired soldiers. This created a new source of power used by the generals to manipulate people and increase their political power (White, 2011). Marius ended up being elected consul 7 times, remaining popular among the plebeians for many generations after his death. After Marius, a politician who pursued popular policies to further their career was called a *popularis*.

Sulla's Civil War

Lucius Cornelius Sulla was from an illustrious Roman noble family. Although he was originally one of Marius' lieutenants, he became a staunch defender of the rights of the traditional senatorial class. In this period, politicians who sought to further their careers by endearing themselves to the Senate and traditional nobility were called *optimates*, the "best men." He was a brilliant general who won against the rebels during the Social War.

In 88 B.C.E., he became consul. After a falling out with Marius, Sulla marched on Rome with the army he was preparing for a campaign in Asia. He drove Marius out of Italy and repealed many pieces of *popularis* legislation. This deeply disturbed a vast majority of the population of Rome and Italy. Then, he left for Asia.

Lucius Cornelius Cinna served as consul in 87, and he recalled Marius from exile. Together, they instituted a bloody purge of Sulla's supporters in the Senate, confiscating property, murdering, and driving many into exile. When Marius died of illness, Cinna assumed leadership and monopolized the consulship for the next three years. He enacted some popular social and economic reforms but died in a mutiny in 84 B.C.E. (Encyclopedia Britannica, 2008). Left without a clear leader, many old allies of Marius and Cinna defected to Sulla in fear of repercussions upon his return from Asia. Others allied with rebel Italian bands of Samnites and

Lucanians who resented Sulla's victory in the Social War.

Sulla returned to Italy in 84 B.C.E. and fought a bloody campaign to retake Rome. He was victorious at the Battle of the Colline Gate just outside the city in 82. Between 82 and 80, he was appointed dictator in consecutive terms, extending the time he could stay in office.

As a dictator, Sulla introduced a series of reforms, trying to strengthen the power of the Senate and reduce the that of the plebeian tribunes. His reforms as a dictator eventually led to the further weakening of the Republic and ignited individual ambitions (White, 2011). Even though Sulla fought to strengthen the nobility, he (much like Marius before him) was the focus of loyalty, not the state. Nevertheless, after enacting his optimate reforms, Sulla laid down his dictatorship and retired to private life until he died in 78 B.C.E.

Pompey, Crassus, Caesar: The First Triumvirate

By the middle of the 1st century, the Republic was plunged into a deep crisis. Violent ambitious figures raised and claimed power for themselves, and the Senate was divided into petty factions. Some, like Sulla, were *optimates*, who advocated for power to reside in the Senate. Others followed Marius and

Cinna as *populares* who advocated for the plebeians. First, with Marius, then Sulla, these mentalities held power alternately, but by 60 B.C.E., the *populares* had increased their influence again.

Most of the Senate remained staunchly opposed. Therefore, three powerful populares made an informal alliance that historians have called the First Triumvirate.

Pompey the Great

Gnaeus Pompeius Magnus was a military leader who had a remarkable performance in Spain during the Social War and helped overcome the famous slave revolt led by Spartacus from 73 to 71 B.C.E. He also went on a brilliant campaign to Greece and Asia, putting an end to the Seleucid Empire and pacifying the region. He returned to Rome with his troops professing loyalty to him, which alerted the Senate. In addition, the sheer amount of wealth his conquests brought in made him the most successful conqueror in roman history to that point. The population at large adored him for it.

However, he didn't march on Rome like Sulla. Instead, he shared his reward for the military victories with his soldiers and common people, providing money for public buildings. His popularity continued to rise. However, the main problem was that Pompey had promised the veterans under his command to receive farmlands after their retirement, a measure the Senate denied (*How the First*

Triumvirate Changed Ancient Rome, n.d.). In 60 B.C.E., Pompey found himself in need of allies to deliver the promises he had made to his troops.

Crassus

Marcus Licinius Crassus was an ex-Sullan who was rumored to be the wealthiest man in Rome. He came from a wealthy plebeian family and augmented his riches by compelling people to sell their properties at lower prices and forming political connections with important businessmen. Many of them were from the *equites*, the knights. They were traditionally wealthy families who were not part of the nobility – that is, they had enjoyed no success in elections for higher office. Others were tax collectors (*How the First Triumvirate Changed Ancient Rome*, n.d.).

Unlike Pompey, Crassus was not hugely popular – many people remembered he helped Sulla win the Battle of the Colline Gate, but some viewed this as a victory against Rome's enemies, others an assault on popular sovereignty. Nevertheless, Crassus had many clients who had used him as a powerful financier. In this way, he was also a threat to the Senate. In 60 B.C.E., Crassus needed help to assist many of the Roman tax collectors in Asia who were his clients.

Caesar

Gaius Julius Caesar (about whom see more below) cut quite a figure in the Senate. His patrician family traced itself back to the Monarchy, and legend held that the Julii were descended from Aeneas' son Ascanius, whose alternate name was Iulus. Yet, recent generations of the family had worked closely with Gaius Marius, Caesar's uncle, and Cinna, Caesar's father-in-law. 60 B.C.E. was the first year Caesar was eligible to run for the consulship, but he needed money and massive support. Crassus could foot the bill. Pompey and his veterans could all vote.

Caesar and Crassus had worked together for years, but Crassus and Pompey hated each other. To bring Pompey around, Caesar offered his daughter Julia in marriage. She was 17, and Pompey was about 47 – six years older than Caesar. Nevertheless, by all accounts Julia and Pompey were devoted to one another.

The Failure of the Triumvirate

Thus, the First Triumvirate was created, and in 59 B.C.E. Caesar became consul. In office, he railroaded popular legislation through the Assemblies, making many (admittedly, much-needed) reforms. Caesar knew that his bullying of the Senate could lead to prosecution when he left office. So, he enlisted Pompey and Crassus' help to get him assigned as the governor of the two provinces in Gaul, and Illyricum in modern Albania.

However, the triumvirate didn't last because there were deep differences among the triumvirs. However, Caesar called the others to a Council at

Luca in 56 B.C.E. They pooled their resources to get Pompey and Crassus elected consuls for 55, despite rampant mob violence in Rome. Pompey received Spain for his governorship after his term as consul, and Crassus received Syria (Gray, 2023).

For a while, the agreement worked, but everything changed when Crassus died in 53 B.C.E. in the Battle of Carrhae against the Parthians – a terrible blow to Roman prestige. As a result, Pompey searched for more allies in the Senate in fear of Caesar's growing reputation. Meanwhile, Caesar enlarged his power, and the *Imperium Romanum*, through breathtakingly savage military campaigns in Gaul. That was the end of the Triumvirate (Burns, 2023).

Cicero

Neither a member of the *populares* or *optimates*, Marcus Tullius Cicero was a prominent figure in the late Republic. Like Marius, he was from Arpinum and a new man. He was a remarkable oratorical genius with influence both in the Senate and among the people. He could evoke the audience's emotions, no matter if they were plebeians or patricians. He mastered the art of public speaking and implemented innovative strategies that came to be known as Ciceronian rhetoric (Ferguson & Balsdon, 2023). For many, he represents the greatest public speaker in the history of the West. Moreover, he may also be the greatest of all Latin prose stylists.

He had a brief military career, but he stood out for his performance as a politician. He completed the *cursus honorum* holding office as a quaestor, praetor, consul, and proconsul. He was a strong advocate of the Republic, promoting law and order. Because of his influence in the Senate, Caesar called upon him to join the Triumvirate, but he didn't accept.

He was famous for his loyalty to institutions and laws. However, when he was elected consul for 63 B.C.E., he won the election against Catiline, a powerful and greedy patrician who wanted to pass reforms to benefit himself and hide many crimes that he had committed. After his defeat, Catiline prepared a conspiracy to kill Cicero and several senators. Cicero found out about the conspiracy and arrested five of the conspirators (*Teach Democracy*, n.d.).

When Cicero decided to execute the conspirators to save the Republic, Caesar advocated against the death penalty. Cicero thereafter admired Caesar's intellect and cultural refinement but always distrusted his ambition. However, the Senate supported Cicero's decision. Catiline died in battle and several conspirators were executed. Cicero was credited with saving the Republic. After Cicero's finest hour, politicians on all sides sought Cicero's support. Even the *optimates* who looked down on him as a new man recognized his influence. Caesar, in particular, wanted Cicero's support, but the orator's heart was given to the traditional values of Rome.

When the civil war between Caesar and Pompey flared up in 49 B.C.E., Cicero joined Pompey, but lamented the civil strife. Later, in 44, he was accused of taking part in the conspiracy to kill Caesar; but he wasn't at the Senate when it occurred. He didn't want the civil strife to continue and promoted a law of amnesty to Caesar's assassins to restore the Republic, but it was too late. The Second Triumvirate ordered his execution in 43, and his head and hands were displayed on the *rostra,* the public place for the speakers in the Roman Forum (Ferguson & Balsdon, 2023).

Caesar's Civil War

Julius Caesar was born on July 12 or 13, 100 B.C.E. His family had deep roots in Roman history, but recent generations had been less influential. He proved himself a dashing military officer in his youth, winning the Civic Crown at the Siege of Mytilene on the Greek island of Lesbos in 81. The prestigious award was given to a Roman who saved the life of a fellow citizen in battle. He returned to Rome and established himself as a brilliant speaker – second only to Cicero. He was also a successful governor of Further Spain in 61, subduing native tribes and expanding Roman (and his own) influence.

After allying with Pompey and Crassus, his star rose sharply due to his impressive achievements in the Gallic Wars. The Gauls beyond the Alps had always been a problem for Rome since the time of the monarchy. In 58 B.C.E., Caesar led a campaign into Gaul to support allied Celtic tribes that lived there and were under attack from Germans who were moving across the Rhine River into modern France.

While pacifying all of Gaul, he consolidated Roman control and became a popular leader among the people, bringing in many more slaves and much treasure to the tottering Republic. Inspired by Sulla, he was determined to use his power within the army to promote his political career. In 50 B.C.E., Caesar marched with his troops to northern Italy and stopped at the Rubicon River, the border of his province and Italy. According to the law, he wasn't allowed to take his army south of the river.

However, he talked to his men and told them that the Senate was after him and that if he was removed from his position, he wouldn't be able to fulfill his promise to give them lands and wealth, which had been customary since Marius' reforms.

His speech was convincing, and his people proved to be loyal to him rather than Rome. In January of 49 B.C.E., he crossed the river and entered Italy as a victorious commander. By then, the Triumvirate had already vanished, and Pompey and part of the Senate had departed for Greece. Pompey felt that the hastily raised legions of Italy stood no chance against Caesar's battle-hardened veterans of eight years. However, Pompey had many clients in Greece and Asia from his time there in the 60s. He hired mercenaries and began to train troops to confront Caesar.

In Rome, Caesar didn't find any opposition to seizing power. The civil war between the two popular leaders had begun. While Pompey was training his army in the East, Caesar left for Spain and confronted Pompey's many supporters there – clients tied to him since the Social War. After defeating them, Caesar moved to attack Pompey in Greece. When the two armies confronted each other at Pharsalus in 48, Caesar defeated Pompey and scattered his forces. Pompey had been hailed as the greatest commander in Roman history. Caesar beat him in less than two years. Pompey fled to Egypt where he was assassinated. Caesar mopped up remnants of the Pompeian faction in wars in Africa and Spain.

Back in Rome, he had himself appointed dictator and enacted several reforms to widen and consolidate his power. At the same time, he enlarged the Senate, decreased the state debt, sponsored a large building program, broke ground on the *Forum Iulium* adjacent to the Roman Forum, and ordered the reconstruction of Carthage and Corinth. To gain popular support, he gave full rights as Roman citizens to foreigners who lived within the territory of the Republic (Stanfield, n.d.).

In 44 B.C.E., Caesar made one more move beyond the law: he appointed himself as dictator for life and claimed absolute power (Stanfield, n.d.).

Caesar's Assassination: The Ides of March

By 44 B.C.E., little remained of the Republic. During the celebration of Lupercalia, a religious festival, Julius Caesar, "seated in a gilded chair at the front of the *rostra*, publicly refused the diadem of kingship presented to him by (Mark) Antony. He already exercised the power of a dictator, and many regarded the gesture as nothing more than pretense" (*Ides of March: The Death of Caesar*, n.d., para 1).

Despite this gesture of rejecting absolute monarchical power, the senators were already persuaded of Caesar's limitless ambition. He already had full control over the state. He didn't accept a crown as king; he passed decrees sitting on an ivory and gold throne; he established as national festivals the anniversaries of his most important victories; he put under his power priests and Vestal Virgins; and last but not least, he forbade magistrates to oppose any of his orders and decrees (*Ides of March: The Death of Caesar*, n.d.). He didn't hold the title of king, but he was one *de facto*. The Senate started to conspire to get rid of him.

The conspirators called themselves "the liberators," and they plotted the assassination of Caesar before his departure to fight against the Parthians, a growing Empire in the East. Among the conspirators, Cassius and Marcus Brutus were the masterminds behind the plan and the ones who would execute it. Marcus Brutus was a man of Caesar's confidence who was the son of Caesar's longtime lover, Servilia.

The day set for the attack was the Ides of March, the 15th. It was a deadline for settling debts and a day of religious celebrations. That day, Caesar went to the Senate for the last time before his military campaign was set to begin. It was meeting that day, ironically enough, in the Theater of Pompey while the Senate house underwent renovations. Cassius, Brutus, and up to 60 other conspiring senators waited for him. At the given signal, they attacked, stabbing Caesar 23 times.

The seasoned warrior fought back unarmed, but finally succumbed, sinking to the floor at the foot of Pompey's statue and pulling his toga over his head in shame. The scene has been immortalized in literature and film. Shakespeare has him fall after recognizing Brutus and uttering the famous words, "*et tu, Brute*?" – the global expression of betrayal. Suetonius, the Roman biographer suggests he said in Greek, "*kai su, teknon*?" In either case, Caesar's last words heralded the end of the Republic.

Essential Highlights

After centuries of expansion, internal struggles and external threats undermined the Republic. While common people fought to expand their rights and improve their economic lot, the upper classes concentrated more and more power and wealth. The *Imperium Romanum* expanded. Keeping the conquered lands under control presented unbeatable challenges to a government designed to run a city-state. Meanwhile, traditional institutions and values perished due to individual greed and a thirst for personal power.

The Republic, once a beacon of democratic ideals, was overshadowed by the looming silhouette of one-man rule. The age of emperors had arrived.

Part 3: The Roman Empire
(27 B.C.E.—476 C.E.)

Chapter 7: The Rise of the Empire

I found Rome a city of bricks and left it a city of marble. –Augustus.

The greatest empire of antiquity was built on the ruins of the Republic. However, there is a continuity. Many structures of the dead system that became the basis of the new one. In this chapter, we are going to explore the audacious journey of Rome's first emperor and the birth of an empire.

The Transition from Republic to Empire

It is difficult to establish exactly when the Roman Republic truly died. However, the turning point was indeed Julius Caesar's assassination. Even though he had already assumed absolute power, a few institutions of the Republic remained. The Senate and the consuls had lost political power over the previous 150 years. However, most military campaigns were still led by the consuls, with a few exceptions. Sulla and Caesar became dictators, but they had led imperial military campaigns as proconsuls and, along with Marius, Pompey, and Crassus, used traditional republican institutions. Of course, they did it to benefit themselves and eventually destroyed the system.

As dictator, Caesar held a legitimate title created by the Republic – he refused to be called king. Even though he ruled as an autocrat, the fact that he used the trappings of republican institutions had consequences. Dictatorship as a republican office meant that there was a time limit. Yes, a powerful tyrant could force others to extend the term, but the power of the dictatorship was not transferable. This left an open question after Caesar's death – who would wield power, and from where would the power be derived?

Caesar he was the only one of the 66 dictators in Roman history who was declared dictator for life. While it is unlikely that he would have resigned, his premature death leaves that question unanswered. But the most powerful men in Rome after the assassination rejected the office. (Bellomo, 2022, para. 14):

> The dictatorship as an office was banned by (Mark) Antony, who probably wanted to dissociate himself from the office of dictator. However, it was not forgotten. Augustus was offered the dictatorship in 22, and the reason why he rejected it was that Caesar's heir had found new ways to acquire absolute rulership of the empire.

How did Antony try to accrue power to himself without using the office? And how did Augustus succeed?

The Political Aftermath of Caesar's Assassination

The crisis in the Republic deepened sharply after the assassination of Caesar. The Senate didn't have the power it once held, and people had lost confidence in the institutions. The patrician leaders who feared Caesar had been concerned about the emergence of popular leaders who could concentrate all power by appealing to the masses. By the time of the conspiracy, it was already too late.

Even though there were many other political leaders assassinated in Rome, the Ides of March was the only one that caused a complete shift in the political system, not only because Caesar held a position as a perpetual dictator but because his successor, Octavian, would reshape the state within a short time (*What was the Impact of Julius Caesar's Murder?* 2023).

The conspirators had planned the assassination well but didn't calculate the repercussions. They believed that with Caesar, the problems of the Republic died too. On the contrary, the moments after the crime proved them wrong. After Caesar fell dead at the feet of Pompey's statue, Marcus Brutus went to the Temple of Jupiter to speak to the crowd. He believed people would consider it a heroic act of liberation from a despot, but instead, the crowd was furious at him. The original plan was for the Senate to pass an amnesty law to exonerate the conspirators, but considering the situation of social unrest, they were forced to flee from the city (Wasson, 2016).

The Ides of March left a power vacuum, and many ambitious leaders were ready to claim it. The Senate couldn't fill it because it lacked legitimacy and real power. Instead, two men from Caesar's closest circle claimed to be the legitimate heirs to Caesar's position at the top of the Roman order: Marc Antony, one of Julius Caesar's most important generals, and Gaius Julius Caesar Octavianus, Caesar's grand-nephew and adopted son.

Caesar had a son with Cleopatra, the Pharaoh of Ptolemaic Egypt. His name was Ptolemy Caesar, known as Caesarion, but neither he nor his mother were liked in Rome. Moreover, Roman law did not recognize Caesarion as legitimate. After Caesar's death, they both fled to Egypt. Nobody in Rome considered him a real heir, and Cleopatra would never find enough support to impose him. However, she wouldn't give up on her son's right to a throne. She eventually allied with Mark Antony and lent him Egyptian forces to invade Rome as part of his army.

Mark Antony had been a close ally of Caesar and had the support of many of Caesar's followers. He counted on all his troops to take revenge for Caesar's death and establish himself as preeminent. He tried to assert himself, but he faced fierce opposition from the Senate, which saw in Mark Antony the same threat as in Caesar.

On the other hand, Octavian was ready to take his adopted father's place in power and take vengeance on his killers. At first, he allied with Mark Antony, but their partnership was doomed to failure.

The Second Triumvirate

The Republic would have one last chance to survive with the establishment of a Second Triumvirate. However, internal conflicts would hamper the last attempt to avoid going back to a monarchical system. The Second Triumvirate was the attempt of Mark Antony, Octavian, and a third ally, Marcus Aemilius Lepidus, to form a government that could bend the Senate. However, each of them brought, along with their troops and strength, their ambitions.

The alliance was unstable from the beginning because Antony and Octavian both believed they had the legitimate right to follow Caesar. The Senate, particularly prominent figures like Cicero, were more worried about Antony as they saw him as a potential tyrant – he was notoriously bloodthirsty. Lepidus was a powerful old ally of Ceasar's who had formal control of several legions in Italy as well as the city. However, he was not as volatile as Antony – he could perhaps be reasoned with. Octavian was 18 years old and had no military or political experience. Therefore, he wasn't considered a threat by the Senate.

The Second Triumvirate arranged legislation to give it the power to make laws and appoint magistrates for period of five years. They used their power to implement a series of extreme measures (Lendering, 2019; *The Second Triumvirate*, n.d.):

- executed 4,700 opponents, including Cicero, some other senators, and wealthy knights – confiscating all their property.
- gave farms to Caesar's veterans from confiscated land.
- declared war against the conspirators and defeated them at the Battle of Philippi.
- introduced measures to reduce the Senate's influence, such as depriving it of the power to appoint magistrates and enact laws independently.

The victory of Philippi in 42 B.C.E. was a landmark moment for the Triumvirate, but soon the differences between the two major leaders increased. After the Triumvirate's victory at Philippi, the three Triumvirs divided their areas of influence: Lepidus ruled in Africa, Antony was appointed to the territories in the East and Egypt, and Octavian remained in Rome, controlling Europe. Internal tensions would erode the Triumvirate for the following 10 years.

In 36, Octavian accused Lepidus of plotting against Rome because he attempted to enlarge his influence in other territories. Lepidus was removed from his office. The stage was set for conflict between Antony and Octavian. The winner would control the whole Mediterranean world.

The Pivotal Battle of Actium

Octavian and Antony first divided the empire into equal parts, but their rivalry increased. Antony had married Octavian's sister, Octavia, in 40, but it didn't help smooth the tensions. Instead, Antony centered his attention on the Egyptian queen Cleopatra, believing her money and troops would help him conquer Rome. His idea was to move the capital to Alexandria – he even gifted Roman territory to her in 34, enraging the Roman populace and further antagonizing Octavian.

Aware of Antony's plan, Octavian played a strategic card. He stirred up public and senatorial opinion against Antony all through 32, arguing that he didn't represent the traditional Roman values and became an ally of foreign countries. However, Octavian framed the conflict as a battle against eastern decadence and meddling - he persuaded the Senate to declare war not on Antony, but on Cleopatra.

In 31 B.C.E., Antony's camp was at Actium, on the western coast of Greece. He had the support of the Egyptian navy led by Cleopatra herself. The couple had 500 ships and 70,000 infantry to offer battle against the Roman army (Encyclopedia Britannica, 2023).

When Octavian arrived in Greece with 400 ships and 80,000 infantry, he landed at Patrae and Corinth, and cut Anthony's connection with Egypt (Encyclopedia Britannica, 2023). Antony and Cleopatra were isolated, and the supplies they required expected never arrived. They needed to fight before they ran out. In a massive sea engagement, Octavian's fleet demolished the combined forces of Antony and Cleopatra, who both fled back to Egypt.

In 30, Octavian invaded. Both Antony and Cleopatra committed suicide. Octavian returned to Rome as a hero, and the Senate recognized his leadership, voting him a new title: Augustus. The word *imperator* was added after his name. It was the traditional title that victorious legions would give to their general. Its meaning in the Republic was something like "commander." But from Augustus forward the direct cognate is more appropriate. Emperor. Over the following decades, Augustus reformed the Roman state into the form of the Roman Empire we call the Principate (Wegen, 2012).

The Principate and the Role of Augustus

Augustus was 19 years old when Caesar was assassinated, and he was immediately thrust into a military and political role. He needed to be capable of dealing with two experienced and powerful opponents (Antony and Lepidus) and of manipulating the senators to act in his favor. He proved equal to the task. In hindsight, the rise and reign of Augustus may be the greatest example of political genius in history, certainly in the West.

He had been formally adopted by Caesar only six months before the assassination. Before the Ides of March, nobody was concerned about him. When Caesar died and his executioners fled, he wasn't considered a threat, and instead, Cicero and the other senators focused on Antony and his ambitions. Two months after March 15, 44 B.C.E., Octavian appeared on the Roman political scene to claim his place as Caesar's heir.

His first victory against Marc Antony was when he imposed on the Senate his decision to go to war against Caesar's executioners. Antony was an advocate for amnesty. Then, he was wily enough to frame his initiatives as a rebuilding of traditional Roman institutions. He played the patriotism card better than anyone; and, as Caesar's heir, he inherited tremendous wealth and the loyalty of many thousands of Caesar's veterans.

Once he put public opinion and the senators on his side to build legitimacy, he used the re-energized republican apparatus to strike. At first, Antony was the successor. After the Battle of Actium, the Senate welcomed Octavian as the hero who saved Rome.

The Principate

Octavian started using the title appointed by the Senate: Augustus, and in 27 B.C.E., he was named princeps, "first citizen." He was *primus inter pares,* "first among equals." The principate finds legitimacy in the *consensus universorum,* the agreement of all. It represents a collaboration between the Republic and the *princeps.* This collaboration is achieved by the power of the Senate to represent the will of the people (Kinder & Hilgemann, 1996).

Augustus rarely used the title of *imperator,* emperor, during his reign because he sought to avoid connotations of military enforcement of his regime. He veiled his power and made a show of restoring the forms of the Republic. Thus, between 27 and 23 B.C.E., he obtained the consulate and had the power of *imperium* over the territories under Roman influence. This meant he had ultimate *auctoritas* - executive power - supreme command over the army, the power to lead foreign policy, and control of the army.

In 23 B.C.E., he took on the *tribuncia potestas,* the power of a plebeian tribune, most importantly, the power to veto any governmental procedure. During the following two years, he continued to concentrate power and functions in his hands over almost every aspect of the political and economic life of Rome. In 19 B.C.E., he was granted *imperium* for life, and later, he was also appointed *Pontifex Maximus,* chief priest of Rome (Kinder & Hilgemann,

1996). Then, he also obtained the title of *pater patriae*, the father of his country, in 2 B.C.E.

While he concentrated all the political power, he was wise and astute enough to keep part of the republican structure: "The traditional magistracies that distributed power and state responsibilities were maintained, as were elections. Theoretically, nothing changed, except that they became essentially an ineffective formality, and Augustus assumed for himself a number of these powers for life" (Fernandes, 2022, para. 7).

Rome was a vast empire, and it needed more and better management, which was centered on the *princeps*. Augustus maintained the Senate, the bastion of the higher classes. However, he changed some of its traditional functions. To ensure his control over the Senate, he reduced it from 900 to 600 members and declared himself *princeps senatus*, "first man of the Senate." It continued to debate and pass laws, but he had the last say.

Augustus divided the provinces of the Empire into two groups: Senatorial and Imperial. The former were thoroughly Romanized and peaceful provinces, unlikely to rebel or be invaded by external threats. The Senate maintained the right to govern senatorial provinces just as it had governed them under the Republic – with proconsuls and propraetors. Imperial provinces, on the other hand, were on the frontiers and required large armies for defense or expansion. Augustus personally appointed legates as governors, usually experienced commanders. The system gave Augustus control of most of the army, but the Senate controlled the wealthiest and most stable territories.

Last but not least, the Senate lost the power to choose the consuls. Augustus would design his successor. Regardless of the institutions that were preserved, the power became inherited, and therefore, the Republic didn't exist any longer.

Other Reforms

Once the political realm was stabilized and his power was ensured, Augustus launched a series of additional reforms. First, he had to take certain measures to improve the defense, government, and administration of a vast territory. Therefore, he introduced a series of military changes:

- He created a permanent standing army and raised the number of legions to 28.
- The fixed term of service for soldiers was set at 16 years and later increased to 20 years.
- He created a fund under his control to pay the soldiers' salaries, taking that power from the Senate and avoiding the misguided loyalty allowed by Marius' reforms.
- All those who enrolled as soldiers were considered Roman citizens with full rights and gained exemption from certain taxes.

Augustus' reforms helped separate the military from politics. The importance of the legions for the long-term stability of the Empire is part of the following chapter. Suffice it to say here that the Empire needed soldiers who would be loyal only to Rome and were eager to give their lives for it. Augustus' military changes ensured this.

In addition to military reform, Augustus installed a series of social initiatives to promote traditional Roman values:

- He promoted marriage by taxing single people and giving tax breaks for families with more children. He also criminalized adultery.
- He repaired old temples and dedicated new ones. As Pontifex Maximus, he revived many ancient rituals and sacrifices to present himself as a religious and moral leader.
- He sponsored a massive building and beautification program for Rome and other cities throughout the Empire.
- He reformed education and became a great patron of the arts, ushering the Golden Age of Latin literature.
- Instituted social welfare for the urban poor and promoted games and festivals to foster Roman identity.

Augustus encouraged religious festivities and the worship of traditional Roman deities. However, he simultaneously created the imperial cult. Even though he declined the Senate's attempt to declare him a living god, Caesar was proclaimed Divus Iulius – "the Divine Julius." Augustus often included *Divi Filius* - "the son of God" – on official coinage and proclamations. However, the imperial cult was encouraged but not imposed, and at first the Roman citizens were reluctant to adopt such a deep transformation of their cherished traditions.

The Savior of Rome

Augustus was capable of creating a new political unit, pacified and stabilized, from the ruins of a Republic after a century of civil strife. His greatest accomplishment, however, wasn't to become an emperor without any significant opposition either from the people or from the traditional ruling elites. He was capable of persuading people that he was the best solution to save Rome from chaos. He ruled every aspect of the citizenry, and they didn't complain; on the contrary, the ruler became someone they could feel personally linked to. Augustus developed a new concept of political and popular leadership.

He dedicated himself to building an empire and also to his public image as the emperor the people needed. The greatest proof of his achievement is the *Res Gestae*, the inscription he spread across the territory of the *Imperium Romanum* celebrating his accomplishments: "he subjected the whole wide earth to the rule of the Roman people" (Fernandes, 2022, para. 23). The text was completed after the emperor's death and carved on the walls of the Mausoleum of Augustus.

Essential Highlights

Even though the Ides of March were a turning point in the final dissolution of the Roman Republic, the old order's death warrant was signed as early as the murders of the Gracchi. Amid the chaos, a man paved his way to power, fighting against other men's ambitions and the reactionary power of the corrupted institutions of the moribund Republic. He was Augustus, the first emperor of Rome.

He laid the foundations of a new era in Rome and created from out of nowhere a completely innovative conception of politics. The Republic as a political regime ended, but he created a new *res publica* to take its place.

As Augustus meticulously laid the Empire's cornerstones, he heralded not just a new era of governance but a golden age of peace and prosperity – the *Pax Romana*.

Chapter 8: The Pax Romana and the Height of the Empire

Give therefore your love and respect to the cause of peace, and to that capital in which we, conquerors and conquered, claim an equal right. –Tacitus

Two centuries, and not a single major conflict within Rome's borders. The *Pax Romana* – Roman Peace - wasn't just an era; it was Rome's magnum opus. It represents the age when Rome was the heartbeat of the known world.

This was a period of outstanding achievements in every realm: The Empire ensured the boundaries of its territory, and internal peace allowed unprecedented economic growth. Most of what is depicted about Rome in pop culture, and therefore, what is commonly known, comes from this period of high culture. Monumental buildings like the Roman amphitheaters and forums blend public spectacle with a political purpose to strengthen loyalty to Rome - and to the embodiment of Roman identity: The Emperor.

The *Pax Romana* also supported the emergence of the greatest names in Roman literature and philosophy. Arts and science flourish when society has solved its essential needs and can dedicate time and resources to the abstractions of human existence.

The Empire at Its Height

The *Pax Romana* is a period that covers the foundation of the Roman imperial system under Augustus Caesar in 27 B.C.E. to around 180 C.E., when Emperor Marcus Aurelius died (Campbell, 2022).

For a period of slightly over 200 years, 16 emperors ruled Rome. After Augustus' death in 14 C.E., the Julio-Claudian dynasty followed him on the throne: Tiberius, Caligula, Claudius, and Nero. Then, the Julio-Claudian family was replaced in 69 C.E., in a brief, one-year period of instability – The Year of the Four Emperors: Galba, Otho, Vitellius, and Vespasian. Vespasian was the first of the Flavian

Emperors, and was followed by Titus and Domitian (Beauchamp, n.d.). Then, the Five Good Emperors abandoned a dynasty based on bloodline. Rather, they chose successors through adoption (Encyclopedia Britannica, 2023). The Five Good Emperors were Nerva, Trajan, Hadrian, Antoninus Pius, and Marcus Aurelius (Beauchamp, n.d.).

The emperors of the *Pax Romana* continued to expand the boundaries of the *Imperium Romanum*, which reached its largest geographic area in 117 under Trajan. After his death, part of the conquered lands in Mesopotamia were soon lost, while the remaining frontiers were stable for the rest of the period.

At its peak, the territory of the empire reached 2.75 million square miles (Zhou, 2015). It spanned from England, Portugal, and Morocco in the West to the Persian Gulf, Caspian Sea, and western Iran in the East (Vulic, 2023). Nearly 30 countries occupy that territory today.

The challenge wasn't limited to defending the boundaries from external enemies. It was a multiethnic empire with different languages, customs, and religious beliefs that needed to be either integrated or subjugated by the Romans to ensure peace and stability.

Pax Romana

The *Pax Romana* was much more than a period in the Empire's history: "It was above all an ideal. A cultural notion that fundamentally shaped the Roman Empire and even our modern conception of what ordered living is" (Campbell, 2022, para. 3).

The *Pax Romana* didn't just happen; instead, it was the result of a series of policies intelligently implemented by Augustus. There were three potential flashpoints where Augustus needed to ensure peace. He had to enforce the borders and stability of an extensive and heterogeneous territory. He also needed to defend the empire from foreign threats and prevent local rebellions. Finally, he had to be wary of the emergence of individual powers among the representatives of Rome within the confines of the state.

In Rome, Augustus had to consolidate his authority and control the traditional ruling class. Simultaneously, he had to create new sources of legitimacy for the government to appease social unrest. Historians have highlighted how Augustus was capable of taming the ambitions of the traditional ruling class while concentrating all power in the figure of the *princeps* - not as an autocrat but as the embodiment of the Roman *Res Publica*.

The *cursus honorum* survived, but only in name. Augustus created a new type of ruler, which was described by Tacitus in these terms: "Rome is not like primitive countries with their kings. Here, we have no ruling caste dominating a nation of slaves. You [the emperor] are called to be the leader of men who can tolerate neither total slavery nor total liberty" (Campbell, 2022, para. 18).

It's true Augustus continued the violent history of the last period of the Republic. He killed many of his rivals and eventually succeeded in putting the civil war to an end through a bloody victory. But once in power, he ensured the continuity of the Roman system. The *Pax Romana* was officially celebrated with the building of the *Ara Pacis Augustae* – the Altar of Augustan Peace.

Besides, the empire pursued creating a "Roman style of life" imposed across the territory, from Hispania and West Africa to the Near East. Augustus and his successors installed a "civilizing" agenda over all the conquered people. While this was a direct benefit for Rome, it also brought prosperity and peace to the provinces and the inhabitants of the Empire. This view is open to criticism as being Romanocentric or Eurocentric. Indeed, the subject peoples of the Empire, particularly in the East and Africa had a long history of advanced culture – some longer than the Romans. Nevertheless, the standard of living under the Empire was higher for its subjects than for those who lived outside the *Imperium Romanum*.

Administrative Reforms

The previous chapter described many of the reforms Augustus carried out to transform Rome into a new political order that coalesced around the figure of the *princeps*. It wasn't a reformation of the state, but the creation of a new conception of politics where the individual power of the ruler isn't dissociated from the common interest.

Augustus implemented security measures in Rome and Italy. He instituted *vigils*, or "watchmen," and urban legionary cohorts to patrol the streets with commanders under his direct orders. This extended the police power to around one per 100 inhabitants - far higher than in modern cities (Fuhrmann, 2011). This policy was extended to Italy, where he ordered the installation of military posts to discourage banditry and social upheavals. He also employed praetorian cohorts as personal bodyguards under his command, not that of the Senate.

However, he didn't always use direct intervention in the provinces, even those he was responsible for governing. This preserved a sense of autonomy. Instead, Augustus acted through intermediaries who eventually depended on him to remain in their positions and were thus compelled to obey his orders.

Besides increasing police presence in the provinces and the city, Augustus developed a system of post offices to enhance and accelerate communication within the empire. It was called the *cursus publicus* and it transported official messages and tax revenues from one province to another. It used single messengers equipped with fast horses and light carriages called *rhedae*. The land speed average of the imperial courier service was about 50 miles per day (*The Cursus Publicus*, n.d.).

The Legions

The army always played a key role in the Roman society. It was closely connected with citizenship; it was a source of political participation in the form of the *comitia centuriata* that dated back to the Monarchy. It was a reflection of the hierarchical organization of society according to status. During the Republic, it had become a dangerous resource for growing individual power and hampering the state's stability.

However, during the *Pax Romana*, the period of expansion that started with the Republic continued until reaching its highest point with Trajan. And the larger and more heterogeneous the territory of the state was, the bigger the challenges faced by the emperors to preserve the empire's cohesion. The Legions became the backbone of Roman identity in the Empire, especially for provincials. The legionaries represented the pinnacle of military power in the ancient world and the cornerstone of the Empire's stability and security.

The Roman legions evolved throughout Roman history. At all periods, they developed discipline, commitment, and loyalty. The loyalty might not have always been directed at the state, but it was loyalty nonetheless. A legion was formed of around 4,500 men, and then the number was raised to 5,200 and 6,000 at the peak of the Empire. This was paper strength, and when the Empire entered a deep crisis, attrition could lower the force of a legion to 1,000. The legion was divided into 10 cohorts of 480 men, each organized into six centuries, each in turn led by a centurion.

Each century was divided into a *contubernium*: a group of eight soldiers who shared the same tent and responsibilities. Then they fought together, side by side, on the battlefield. This routine lasted for the entire 16, 20, or 24-year term of service for a legionnaire, depending on the current requirements (Bileta, 2023). It was an effective way to create strong bonds among the soldiers. Rome might have been too far away for them, or they could have felt their loyalty to their emperor faint, but on the battlefield, they fought to protect the band of brothers they belonged to.

Despite the discipline and superb strategies deployed by the Roman army, the legions weren't unbeatable: "The legion also suffered horrendous defeats. The most notable ones are the catastrophes at Cannae in 216 BC, Carrhae in 53 BC, and the Teutoburg Forest in 9 AD. In the latter, three legions were annihilated, never to be restored" (Bileta, 2023, para. 3).

The legions were feared and respected because they knew how to fight on the battlefield. The main goal for every soldier was to survive, and the best way to do it was through discipline. The general strategy of a legion in battle was to avoid casualties instead of killing more enemies. Victory was achieved by the capability of maintaining the battle line until the enemy was compelled to surrender (Zhou, 2015).

Roman equipment was well-suited to the task. It generally included a large semi-cylindrical shield called a *scutum*, a well-made helmet of bronze or iron, and metal armor, also of bronze or iron. The most common armor through the Republic and Empire was chain mail, *lorica hamata*, probably copied from the Gauls in the early 3rd century B.C.E. The most iconic Roman armor throughout the *Pax Romana* was the distinctive cuirass of segmented metal bands that we call *lorica segmentata*. It was incredibly durable and could defend against almost any weapon commonly in use at the time. But it was heavy.

Offensively, imperial Roman soldiers usually carried a heavy throwing spear called a *pilum*. A *pilum* was generally longer and heavier than most ancient javelins, but could also be used as a proper spear to ward off cavalry. Republican soldiers had carried two of slightly different sizes. The main weapon of the Roman legionary was his short sword, usually called a *gladius*. There were several different styles, but the *gladius* was mostly around 18 inches long, slightly waisted, and with a tapered point.

While it was likely a thrusting weapon, the entire length of the blade was sharp on both sides. The Romans adopted the *gladius*, as they adopted most of their equipment, from their enemies. Early Roman historians use the term *gladius Hispaniensis* – the Spanish Sword.

Another core element of the legions' strategy was the multi-line formation and the organization of the soldiers into different cohorts that didn't attack at the same time. This avoided exposing all the troops to danger at the same time. It allowed Roman armies a tactical reserve, meaning they could bring in fresh reinforcements when needed during a battle.

The vast Roman Empire wasn't static, and the key to keeping it safe was to have a versatile and flexible strategy. Between Augustus' institution of the *principate* in 27 B.C.E. and Marcus Aurelius' death in 180 C.E., emperors developed different management styles of the legions and balanced expansionist military expeditions with the use of defensive forces to keep internal peace.

The Legions demanded the mobilization of the population and the expenditure of resources, which translated to a tax burden on the citizens. Therefore, emperors had to set priorities. Some emperors led more aggressive and expansionist strategies, moving the legions from one province to another wherever they were needed.

This entailed the risk of leaving a province unprotected in case of internal social unrest. Therefore, other emperors prioritized stability and left permanent garrisons in every province to ensure peace and keep the population under control (Zhou, 2015). Augustus had moved the legions out of Rome and placed them on the frontiers to reduce the risk of a plot against him. He used the Praetorian Guard instead to ensure his security. Nonetheless, in the future, the Praetorians became a mechanism to remove and install new emperors.

Economic Prosperity and the Role of Infrastructure

During the almost 200 years of the *Pax Romana*, the empire reached unprecedented prosperity. The territory reached the peak of its expansion, and that meant an increase in arable land. Production rose and diversified, which was a boost for trading. On the other hand, the population of about 70 million people (*The Pax Romana*, n.d.) led to a higher demand for goods and a larger workforce to increase and accelerate production.

The Empire was divided into three economic regions. Europe included the lands of Great Britain, Italy, the Gauls (present-day France), the western region of Germany, and the Alps. The second region encompassed the provinces of Hispania (present-day Spain and Portugal) and northern Africa. The third region covered Greece, Egypt, and Asia Minor, including Palestine and Mesopotamia (Kinder & Hilgemann, 1996).

Besides keeping peace within and beyond the borders, the state played a key role in economic expansion. The increase in trading was enabled not only by the expanded demand and availability of diverse goods but also by the infrastructure. Augustus and the other emperors made significant investments to develop a network of roads and paved ways to connect all the corners of the empire, and they all led to Rome. These roads and paths were used to transport goods for trading and to facilitate the movement of the army.

Even though the land routes were important, the state also promoted the use of sea transportation. To encourage this, the Romans built lighthouses and harbors in the main coastal cities. Since many goods were regional, the development of trading routes across the sea facilitated interregional trading. For instance, the oil produced in Egypt was taken to the south of Hispania. Furthermore, trading across the Mediterranean and the Black Sea intensified with regions outside the empire, such as India, China, and southeastern Asia (Cartwright, 2018).

In addition to these public works, the Romans carried out monumental engineering works. They built bridges to connect the roads, aqueducts to provide cities and farms with water, and walls to protect the population from foreign invaders. The best example is Hadrian's Wall, built in 122 C.E. in the province of Britannia. The wall was finished in six years and crosses the island from side to side. It was built to prevent an invasion of the Picts from modern Scotland (Montoya, 2022).

Even though the large population demanded a lot of goods, it didn't imply the development of industrial production. Indeed, the landowners increased their incomes by selling their crops, including luxury goods (such as olives and wine), but there wasn't a massive interest among the aristocrats in investing in industry or commercial development. Instead, they wasted their fortunes on trivial expenditures. In the long term, the economy stagnated (Malvasi, 2023).

As in earlier periods, the wealth was concentrated in a few hands, and the number of poor and unemployed increased, in part due to the lack of jobs and the use of slave labor on plantations. To ensure food and avoid social turmoil, the state kept the price of grains artificially low and often distributed part of the harvest for free. While this avoided starvation for large parts of the population, it discouraged farmers and landlords from improving production as it didn't result in larger incomes (Malvasi, 2023).

Achievements of the Principate

Monumental Buildings

The economic splendor of the early Empire led to higher tax revenue, and this was used by the emperors to construct monumental buildings that didn't have a direct economic purpose but impacted the Romans' lives. When societies reach a high level of stability and economic development, citizens and the state can dedicate resources to leisure and non-productive activities.

During the *Pax Romana*, the Romans built public baths and amphitheaters in many important cities to provide the citizens with spaces to entertain themselves. Besides being a symbol of the Empire's greatness, these places were also used to enhance people's loyalty to their *princeps* and cultivate Roman identity.

Amphitheaters became a symbol of the Roman Empire's glory. These arenas could host thousands of spectators who attended to see the performances of gladiators. They reenacted epic battles from Rome's storied history and hosted public executions. They had fights between gladiators and soldiers, among gladiators, or against exotic beasts. Later, during the Christian persecutions, the spectacle consisted of beasts hunting and killing Christians who refused to renounce their faith and worship Roman deities.

Among the most famous amphitheaters, we can name the theater in Aspendos, built under Marcus Aurelius' reign; the Theatre of Orange, built by Augustus in present-day France; the Arena of Nîmes, built during the 1st century; and the most renowned, the Colosseum (Montoya, 2022).

The Colosseum, or *Amphitheatrum Flavium*, was started under Vespasian's reign, around 70–72 C.E., but was inaugurated by Titus in 80. He organized 100 days of games and public spectacles to celebrate (Montoya, 2022). It was a masterpiece of Roman architecture and engineering. It could host 50,000 spectators who could attend the shows protected from the sunlight by a retractable shade called a *velarium* (Encyclopedia Britannica, 2023). It also had underground tunnels with gates that led to the arena, where gladiators and animals waited for their turn to fight.

Cultural and Artistic Advances

During the *Pax Romana*, arts and culture flourished, also promoted by the state as a way to enhance Roman identity. It is the period of the blossoming of Roman literature and history. Augustus didn't want to be considered a despot king, so he invested time and resources to develop popular support based on a common national history.

Augustus asked Virgil to write a poem to create an image of him as the father of the nation and the protector of the people. Virgil wrote the *Eclogues*, *Georgics*, and *Aeneid* in Latin, the empire's official language. These poems became an integral part of Western literature. The *Aeneid* tells the mythical story of how the Romans were linked to the people of Troy and glorified the figure of the emperor (*Roman Culture and the Aeneid*, n.d.). Augustus learned early on how to use cultural production as a means of political propaganda.

The Golden Age of Latin literature also witnessed the emergence of other influential poets: Horace and Ovid. Horace lived when the empire was being born. He was linked with Augustus and dedicated parts of his most famous poem, The Odes, to him. He also wrote charming poems about daily life in Rome.

Ovid's work also contributed to the creation of the Latin identity in the times of Augustus. He wrote the *Fasti*, an account of religious festivals recounting the early origins of Rome. In the poem, Ovid describes the royal family in a flattering way and with a great deal of patriotism. His greatest work was *The Metamorphoses*, a collection of stories from the creation of the universe to the death of Julius Caesar whose assassination and Civil War represent chaos. The Augustan Peace was the symbolic metamorphosis (Kenney, 2023).

Livy wrote the first official history of Rome. He wasn't the first historian to attempt to write the complete history of the nation, but unlike others, he didn't have a personal political interest. Instead, he had a moral approach to history. This was aligned with Augustus' project of installing moral ideas in imperial society (Ogilvie, 2023). Tacitus lived in the mature period of the Empire, during the rule of the Five Good Emperors. He contributed to building Roman history with a unique writing style and a sharp analysis of characters and events (McDonald, 20239).

The Golden Age of Rome also encompassed artistic achievements. Inspired and influenced by Greek artists, the Romans pursued all forms of artistic expression. Artistic production had many different purposes for the Romans: "Seal-cutting, jewelry, glassware, mosaics, pottery, frescoes, statues, monumental architecture, and even epigraphy and coins were all used to beautify the Roman world as well as convey meaning from military prowess to fashions in aesthetics" (Cartwright, 2017, para. 3).

The Romans created fascinating sculptures using different materials, including bronze and marble, for the most sophisticated pieces. The sculptures were characterized by detail and excessive realism. During the times of the *Pax Romana*, sculptures became bigger and dedicated to gods and emperors as a way to keep them alive forever.

Wall paintings and frescos were another distinguished form of art developed by the Romans. They used stucco to create real-life effects on the paintings in public buildings, private houses, temples, and walls all across the empire. One of the most famous is the House of Livia on the Palatine Hill, painted in the 1st century. It represents a 360° depiction of a garden. Another significant fresco was painted in the House of the Vettii in Pompeii before the eruption of the Vesuvius in 79 C.E., which destroyed the city. These paintings reveal how the ancient Romans lived and many of their values and beliefs (Becker, 2015).

Roman Stoicism

A philosophical school from Greece flourished in the Empire during the *Pax Romana*, and the last emperor of the period was one of the most important figures of the movement. The school of thought was called Stoicism and was founded by Zeno of Citium. The main idea was that our "ability to reason or consider action and consequence set humans apart from animals, and it could ultimately lead us to a better and more worthwhile existence. He (Zeno) also emphasized the importance of living in harmony with nature" (Lesso, 2022, para. 3).

In Rome, Stoicism had early philosophers who had worked with Cicero, although he wasn't a stoic himself. Later, this philosophical school gained importance with figures Like Lucius Annaeus Seneca, a statesman under Nero; Epictetus, a slave of one of Nero's freedmen; and Marcus Aurelius, the famous emperor. Stoicism was characterized as a philosophy of life suitable for people of every station. It taught individuals to deal with the vicissitudes of life by developing endurance and strength and always acting consciously. Stoics believed there was a natural order to the universe, and individuals should learn to accept and follow the natural flow of events (Saunders, 2023).

The philosophy, widespread in Rome, was important for many political leaders who found key guidelines for ethical behavior in the Stoic principles. Nonetheless, the influence of stoicism reached further than the political elite, and it was adopted by common people in daily life (*Did Stoicism Have Any Influence on Ancient Rome?* n.d.).

Essential Highlights

Augustus set the scene for the brightest period of Roman history: The largest expansion of the territory, the period of lasting peace, the safest moment for the Empire's boundaries, the greatest economic stability, and the flourishing of Roman culture. The first emperor started the reforms, and the following rulers continued to develop and ensure the empire's success.

While the sun shone brightly on Rome during the *Pax Romana*, no empire is immune to decay. The 3rd century brought crisis to Rome, and the challenges of a fading Golden Age.

Chapter 9: The Crisis of the Third Century and the Late Empire

How does a mighty empire like Rome, at the pinnacle of its glory, find itself spiraling into chaos in just a matter of decades?

During the 3rd century C.E., the Roman Empire entered an era of decline and uncertainty. The focus inevitably sets on the many problems that hampered social, economic, and political stability, leading to a crisis that put the state in danger after over two centuries of peace. Nonetheless, this period also reveals the tenacity and resilience that undergirded the Empire and enabled it to adapt and reshape itself.

The crisis of the 3rd century represents a turning point in the Western Empire and the beginning of its end; at the same time, the Byzantine Empire rose in the East, and it would carry Rome's legacy for another millennium.

Internal and External Threats to Roman Power

The Barbarians

The Barbarians were several Germanic tribes that lived beyond the limits of the Empire's boundaries, didn't speak Latin, and were considered savage by the Romans. The term was indistinctly used by the Romans to refer to any foreign people who didn't fall under the Roman concept of civilization. The term included the German, Celtic, Hunnic, and Slavic people from the northeast, among many others (*Barbarian Origin, Invasions and Kingdoms*, 2023).

From the Roman perspective, the presence of barbarian tribes had hampered the *Imperium Romanum* since the time of the Republic. Julius Caesar had fought against them during his campaigns against the Gauls, and Augustus consolidated the northeastern frontier at the Rhine and Danube Rivers (Britannica Encyclopedia, 2023). During the centuries of imperial splendor, Rome fought against foreign tribes and succeeded in pushing them away from Roman lands.

In 200 C.E., Germanic tribes coming from the Scandinavian Peninsula started a slow but massive and persistent migration into Central Europe. The Goths, Vandals, Burgundians, and the Gepidae left their lands in the north and headed southeast toward the Black Sea. These German tribes weren't nomadic; they migrated to settle in new lands where they could be established permanently. They settled in present-day Germany and the lands between the Weser and Vistula rivers. Later, they reached the Danube and settled near the Roman frontier (Britannica Encyclopedia, 2023).

As the Germanic tribes approached the Empire's boundaries, they pushed the local tribes into Roman territory. This was the mass migration's first impact on the Roman population and became a factor in destabilizing the frontiers, which were very far away from the capital by then (Kinder & Hilgemann, 1996).

From 150 on, the Barbarians spread across the Roman periphery, causing unrest among the local populations. The Romans fought and repelled the Marcomanni and the Alemanni in Italy under Marcus Aurelius. This was the first time a hostile force reached the peninsula since the German invasions repelled by Gaius Marius in 101 B.C.E. Nevertheless, the pressure continued, and many Germans established themselves inside the empire by 260 C.E. The Saxons and Franks violently ravaged the North and Britannia (Britannica Encyclopedia, 2023). By the middle of the 3rd century, the Goths and the Heruli pillaged the Black Sea and the Aegean.

The Goths entered and settled the Balkan Peninsula and Asia Minor and forced the Romans to abandon the northern Danube region. More tribes arrived: the Quadi, the Iazyges, the Sarmatians, and the Vandals, among others. Despite Roman attempts to defend their position, the army could not stem the tide of the invaders (Badian et al., 2023).

In the East, the Sassanid Persians replaced the Parthian empire, which had been weakening for centuries. By the middle of the 3rd century, the Romans had fought a long and exhausting campaign. Even though Emperor Aurelian reestablished unity through much of Roman territory in the 270s, the Empire lost all of its remaining land in Mesopotamia (Badian et al., 2023).

The external threat was an unbeatable problem for the Roman Empire due to its lack of satellite states to buffer the advance of enemy forces. This eventually led to the abandonment of the peripheral provinces or the foundation of foreign kingdoms (Kinder & Hilgemann, 1996). The legions' defeat in their attempt to repel the invasions proved the weakness of a widely extensive frontier that Rome couldn't defend properly.

Rome lost territories at the hands of the invaders and had to accept foreign tribes within its borders, which brought new issues threatening governability and weakened the central political apparatus in Rome.

Military Anarchy

The assassination of Emperor Alexander Severus in 235 C.E. triggered a crisis in political power and a shift in the Roman leadership paradigm. During this period, the Empire required more troops to control social unrest and repel external threats. This was a time of warrior emperors who were backed up by their troops. But in consequence, it was also a period of deep instability - any general who had military power could seize the throne.

The emperors raised by military means are called the "Barracks Emperors." Many emperors were installed by the army and remained on the throne for as long as they could retain the support of their troops (Mark, 2017). The empire had 24 emperors in less than 100 years. Before that, 26 emperors had ruled for 250 years (Bileta, 2023).

It was a time of anarchy because the rulers depended on violence to hold the throne. The unity of the Empire was torn, and it split into three parts, taking it close to collapse. In 260 C.E., the provinces of Gaul, Hispania, and Britain broke away to form the Gallic Empire. In the east, by 267, Egypt, Palestine, and Syria had also formed the independent Palmyrene Empire.

The Economic and Social Crisis

The Barbarian invasions coincided with a series of social and economic changes that led to new political struggles. On one hand, the regions neighboring the Empire in Asia and Africa developed an advanced agricultural system. It posed fierce competition for Roman production (Kinder & Hilgemann, 1996).

The *villae*, or country estates, of Rome's elite, became important political and cultural centers, and the differences between the cities and the rural areas deepened. The upper class of landlords became wealthier and monopolized political power, with growing influence in their lands far from the capital (Kinder & Hilgemann, 1996).

On the other hand, slavery withdrew due to the halt in territorial expansion. This impacted the workforce, which was then replaced by an increasing group of free peasants or *coloni* (*Crises of the Roman Empire*, n.d.). They settled on their own lands and worked for themselves, but were compelled to pay high taxes to the local authorities. Their properties and crops were constantly looted by the Barbarians. This group slowly resigned their rights as property owners to the elites in return for protection. This represents the first seeds of a system that would develop into Medieval peasant serfdom.

The production switched focus to subsistence goods, which caused a decline in trading, accompanied by the violent situation in several regions. Local economies became self-sufficient, and people moved from the cities to the countryside looking for the means to survive. It meant the decline of urban life and a decrease in cross-Empire trade (*Crises of the Roman Empire*, n.d.).

The Dominate: Diocletian and Constantine

The first emperor to introduce reforms to avoid the empire's collapse was Aurelian (270–275). He reunified the empire by defeating the emperors of the independent but short-lived Gallic and Palmyrene Empires. Then, he increased the security at the borders to reduce the impact of Barbarian pressure. Finally, he elevated the position of the emperor above the people and the military generals to reduce their power. However, there were many structural issues that needed further reform.

Diocletian's Tetrarchy

Diocletian ruled between 284 and 305 and is credited with putting the 3rd-century crisis to an end. He reorganized the administration and government of the Empire by establishing a "tetrarchy," or "rule of four," and settled the new administrative and political centers in Nicomedia (modern Turkey), Mediolanum (Milan), Sirmium (in modern Serbia), and Trier, Germany. These cities were closer to the borders of the Empire and needed closer oversight and stronger defense (Diocletian and the Tetrarchy, n.d.). Each of these four areas was further subdivided into *dioceses*, 12 in total.

The tetrarchy had two senior emperors, called *augusti,* and two junior emperors, called *caesares*. The *augusti* ruled from Mediolanum and Nicomedia, while the *caesares* administered Trier and Sirmium. Since each region was autonomous and self-sufficient, it led to conflicts between the four states (Woolf, 2012).

Diocletian continued Aurelian's trend of building the emperor's authority, fueling his imperial persona with ceremonies and building projects. This change in the fundamental role of the Emperor in Roman society represents the end of the Principate founded by Augustus. This later period became known to scholars as the Dominate. Diocletian promoted more military campaigns to control the frontiers and social unrest. All this increased the state's expenditures and led to taxation reform (*Diocletian and the Tetrarchy*, n.d.).

Constantine and the New Capital

The tetrarchy became a source of confusion. But in 306 C.E. Constantine I was pronounced *augustus* by his troops at Eboracum (modern York) in Britannia. He consolidated his power through civil war in the West, defeating his rival Maxentius in 312 at the Battle of the Milvian Bridge just outside Rome.

Legends surround the battle. Constantine's mother, Helena, was a Christian from Asia Minor. It is impossible to determine Constantine's thoughts about his mother's religion at the time of the battle, but tradition holds that he witnessed a radiant cross in the sky shortly before his forces met those of Maxentius, accompanied by the Greek words *en toutoi nika*. The Latin tradition has adopted the phrase *in hoc signo vinces* – "In this sign, you will conquer." Constantine adorned his troops' shields with a cross, and they carried the day, giving him control of the Western Empire.

In 313 C.E., Constantine enacted the Edict of Milan to establish religious tolerance within the Empire. During the past three centuries, Christianity had spread across the Roman world. Christians were persecuted because their beliefs clashed with Roman traditions. Constantine sought internal peace and new ways to bring cohesion to the collective Roman identity (*Constantine*, n.d.).

In 324, Constantine became sole emperor when he defeated Licinius I at the first Battle of Adrianople on the European side of the Bosporus. In an attempt to reinforce the empire's security and improve administration, he moved the capital to Byzantium (present-day Istanbul, Turkey). He changed the capital's name to Constantinople, bringing art and ornaments from Rome (History.com Editors, 2023).

Constantine expanded the administrative apparatus to 14 *dioceses*, built a wall to protect Constantinople, and provided lands to noblemen to ensure his position. To populate the city, he offered free food rations to new residents and built infrastructure, such as aqueducts, to improve the quality of life. Constantine made the new capital the heart of the empire, framed by Roman law and Christian beliefs, but adopted the Greek language in contrast to Latin. This reinforced the cultural division between the Western and Eastern Empires.

In 337, Constantine died. He had converted to Christianity and was baptized at some point before his death. It's impossible to determine the exact date of his conversion, as there are varying traditions. Nevertheless, he made important contributions to spreading Christianity throughout the Empire (Encyclopedia Britannica, 2023). His building program included the Church of the Holy Sepulchre in Jerusalem and the original Basilica of Saint Peter in Rome. In addition, he called the first Council of Nicaea in 215, which produced the original version of the Nicene Creed – a codified statement of belief meant to unite the diverse communities of Christians throughout the Roman Empire and beyond.

Constantine's dynasty would last for five generations until Julian the Apostate, the last pagan emperor, died in 363 C.E. Thereafter, the Valentinian and Theodosian Dynasties would rule from 364 to 457. However, there was a dizzying array of usurpers and intermarriages, and there were often several emperors ruling different parts of the Empire simultaneously. The final division of the old *Imperium Romanum* into the Western Empire and the Byzantine Empire came upon the death of Theodosius I in 395. His sons, Arcadius and Honorius, became rulers in the East and West, respectively (Phelan, 2022).

Essential Highlights

The 3rd century was marked by crisis and anarchy. The choice of emperor was often in the hands of the military, causing extreme instability and violence. This was fueled by the Barbarian invasions, which had started before but intensified. And the defenseless population living on the borders suffered from constant attacks and looting. Chaos was deepened by social unrest due to the economic crisis and a progressive loss of civil rights for peasants.

Emperors Diocletian and Constantine attempted to save the empire by reinforcing the imperial authority, improving the administration, enhancing the frontiers' defense, and keeping the political system intact. They enjoyed relative success since they avoided the collapse, and the Western Empire endured for almost 150 years after Constantine's death. However, the old *Imperium Romanum* was horrendously decayed. As reforms and religious transformations brought temporary relief to a beleaguered Empire, the relentless march of time and fate continued.

Chapter 10: The Fall of the Western Roman Empire

Every empire has its sunset, and for the mighty Western Roman Empire, dusk approached with a series of events that shook the ancient world. After the invasion of Hannibal over 600 years before, no Roman ruler or citizen could ever imagine that the Eternal City would ever fall. However, the moment arrived, and the glorious Empire collapsed under its own weight.

The year 476 C.E. became a milestone in Western civilization. That year, the Western Empire fell, and it meant the end of a monumental era. Moreover, it represented the end of Antiquity. The world, as it was known, would never be the same, with Rome as the epicenter of power and the lighthouse of culture. For almost a millennium, Rome set the pace for much of the progress of the West. After its collapse, everything had to be rebuilt.

Even though the Empire as a political unity collapsed in the West, it endured for another 1,000 years in the East, keeping the Roman flame alive and spreading its influence. Rome shaped subsequent civilizations and underscored lessons to glean from its rise and fall. Rome isn't a lost relic but the foundation stone of human progress.

Reasons for the Western Empire's Fall

Similar to the 3rd-century crisis, the fall of the Empire was the result of many factors. Many of them had their origins in the 3rd century or even earlier, and despite several emperors' attempts, the stress on the administrative, social, economic, and military infrastructure was too great. Political and economic instability deepened, and social unrest rose. The final blow was delivered by the Barbarians who had raided the Empire's borders since the 2nd century.

Political Instability

After Constantine established his capital at Byzantium, and renamed it Constantinople, Rome stopped being the center of political and economic power. The Eternal City quickly declined. Progressively, the eastern provinces became more powerful, and Constantinople surpassed Rome's influence. In the West, other cities such as Ravenna and Milan occupied the place of the old capital. The emperors moved out of Rome and hardly ever went to visit it, although it was still the largest and most populated city in Europe (*Roman Empire Politics*, n.d.).

Even though the decision to divide the Empire was made to improve border defense, streamline tax collection, and reduce local powers that could overshadow the emperor, it was only successful in the East. The division of the state brought religious and linguistic barriers that became obstacles instead of fostering cooperation to hold the Empire (*Roman Empire Politics*, n.d.).

Diocletian had organized a tetrarchy to avoid plots against the emperors by appointing two co-rulers (one for the West and one for the East), the *augusti*. Each of them was supported by a *caesar*. It was supposed to avoid weakness by having a successor in place before an emperor died or abdicated. However, Diocletian's experiment failed in the early 4th century, leading to constant civil wars (Bileta, 2023).

After the crisis of the 3rd century, the sources of legitimacy that had once kept the vast Empire cohesive were discredited. The emperor, who was in the past the embodiment of the res publica, and the Senate, the remaining symbol of Rome's ancient noble pedigree, were infected with corruption. The long process of economic evolution had contributed to concentrating impressive fortunes in the hands of the few who had the power to buy votes and seize power. An emperor could be easily overthrown if the opposition had enough support.

This internal instability hampered the ability to control local powers, social turmoil, and the more frequent attacks launched by the Barbarians.

Economic Decline

The economic decline is linked to the Empire's territorial fragmentation and the halt of outward expansion. The late Empire didn't obtain new lands or slaves to reward the legions and increase production. The slavery system had created a large gap between the rich and the poor, and that difference sharpened when the wealthy landowners charged the *coloni* with higher taxation (*The Fall of Rome*, n.d.).

As production capacity declined, the Empire's expenses continued to increase. Public funds were allocated to building public works such as aqueducts, bridges, and roads, which were key to supporting the expansion and better administration of a vast state. Grand public works like baths, amphitheaters, and monuments, had a symbolic purpose and were key to maintaining political cohesion and a strong centralized power. However, the bulk of the budget was used to pay the army.

The Roman legions had been the backbone of the state since the times of the Republic. At first, they were the means to conquer new lands, but after the 3rd century C.E., the legions were used mostly to repel the Barbarian invaders. Therefore, Rome faced higher expenses but won nothing. On the contrary, they slowly lost many important territories.

In the past, the main connection between the generals and the legionaries who spent years fighting for Rome far away from their homes was loyalty and a sense of belonging. Over time, that loyalty loosened, and the state had to continuously increase soldiers' salaries to avoid a rebellion or desertion.

Emperors faced a double problem: increasing costs and less income. On one hand, they attempted to increase the tax revenue, but most of the tax collection was concentrated in the provinces. The generals and other officers in the distant provinces collected taxes and used them at their own discretion. From their perspective, they were at the outer confines of the empire, dealing with the Barbarians. The bond with Rome as the core of the state was broken. This added to the increasing levels of corruption (Gill, 2019). Money from taxes didn't reach Rome.

On the other hand, emperors tried to increase their income by making more money. The denarius was a silver coin developed in the 3rd century B.C.E. and survived through the Empire. Under the early emperors, the *denarius* was made of 75% silver and 25% base. During the crisis of the 3rd century, the emperors reduced the amount of silver in the coins to double the production. This allowed them to manufacture more coing. But, far from solving the problem, it led to runaway inflation (Calvo & Quintana, 2022). The value of the currency fell, and prices rose, causing a sharp drop in trading, tax collection, and people's purchasing power.

As the external threats increased the tension, more military forces were needed, and this situation deepened. Meanwhile, internal cohesion and the common values that once held Roman society together had vanished.

Military Challenges

The importance of the legions for Rome in times of expansion and after the beginning of the Barbarian invasions has been explained. The civil wars triggered by the usurpers and emperors fighting for power had diverted the military to focus on internal issues. Meanwhile, the Barbarian attacks became more aggressive and frequent.

This chaotic situation witnessed a sharp decline in the Roman legions. In the past, becoming a soldier was considered a Roman citizen's right. After the 3rd century, it was harder to recruit legionaries.

Campaigns were longer, they had to remain for more years in the military service, and the rewards weren't attractive. Therefore, the generals began to admit non-Roman citizens to join the troops.

Many of those non-Roman inhabitants of the provinces were Barbarian people who had settled in Roman territory and blended with the local population. The blending process took place over centuries. Some historians have called it the "barbarization of the army." "In states of warfare of the third century, Emperors and their rivalries picked up soldiers from these tribes that stayed within the borders of the empire and these soldiers were given the commands of Roman commanders as mercenaries" (Gazioğlu, n.d., p. 2).

In Italy, men were more interested in achieving administrative positions and the recruitment rate continued to decrease (Vulic, 2023). The desperate need for more soldiers led the Romans to admit mercenaries. First, they were hired soldiers who didn't fight for their nation but for money.

In the times of the tetrarchy, emperors made drastic changes. They gave lands to Frankish tribes in Gaul in exchange for military cooperation to fight against the Huns. Emperor Constantine used the Vandals to defend the province of Pannonia in the northern Balkans, leaving the Vandal generals to carry out the recruitment. After a catastrophic loss at the second Battle of Adrianople, Theodosius admitted the Goths into the Balkans as *foederati*, allies, and paid them in exchange for peace and military support. In the East, the emperors admitted Arabic troops led by their generals to help the Romans hold their borders (Gazioğlu, n.d.).

In the long term, this had deleterious consequences for the army. The foreign generals and soldiers could never be effectively "Romanized," and the new troops lacked allegiance to the Empire. On the contrary, the Barbarians imposed many of their own customs. In the 4th century, thousands of Germans enlisted in the army and imposed their terms and practices, such as the *be*, an old Germanic battle cry (Frye, 2007).

This tendency resulted in the fragmentation of morale and cohesion that had made the legions nearly invincible for centuries. Moreover, it undermined the traditional military aristocracy since service was neither a privilege nor a profitable business. Even though there were new laws against the Barbarians, such as forbidding marriage between ethnic groups, the Germans had become predominant in many regions of the Empire (Frye, 2007).

In sum, the Barbarians weren't only an external threat; they were behind the Roman lines and even became a predominant cultural element in much of Europe.

Social Fragmentation

The transformation within the army also coincided with a shift in the connection between common people and the army. While many admired the Barbarians for their strength and military power and approved of their incorporation into the army, most of the population feared them. They had witnessed the violent raid against the villages on the frontiers. The provincial citizens had suffered through the devastation of their lands and had lost everything to the hands of those who were then received as Roman citizens in a privileged position. For common people, barbarians in the Roman army were mercenaries.

Besides the challenges faced by the army and the significant wealth disparity, there was another factor causing social dislocation: religious diversity. As mentioned, the Edict of Milan ended the formal persecution of Christians within the empire. However, it triggered a new cultural transformation that worked against Roman cohesion.

The law of religious tolerance and the increasing presence of Christianity undermined many ancient Roman traditions. Moreover, it became a political factor since Christians considered the god of Abraham the highest source of power and authority, above the emperor or homeland (*The Fall of the Roman Empire*, n.d.). It wasn't only a matter of individual faith but also a shift in the concept of citizenship. This contradiction between religious belief and citizenship at such a large scale was new within the Empire.

In the Eastern Empire, Christianity effectively served as a new moral background to hold political unity. However, it led the West into deeper fragmentation. The Church emerged as a parallel source of power. Historically, the chief priest of the Roman state was the Pontifex Maximus. Under the Empire, the emperors assumed the title. However, it is possible some Christian bishops of Rome may have used the title after the rule of Constantine. Even though Christianity blended with many Roman traditions, struggles emerged, adding to the conflicting relations with the pagan practices of Romans who refused to convert and the foreign Germanic tribes (*Did Christianity Cause the Fall of Rome?* n.d.).

The Scourge of God

The Barbarians, who had started a massive migration in the 3rd century, didn't stop moving across Europe. Wherever they reached, they caused problems by displacing the local population, attacking the communities and lands on the frontier, or settling inside the territory of the Roman Empire.

The Roman emperors employed many strategies to deal with the invaders. In the 4th century, German groups settled in the confines of the Empire, and to avoid war, the emperors allowed them to stay as *foederati,* allies. In exchange, Rome demanded their support to defend the frontier from other invaders that came from the Asian steppes.

In 376 C.E., a group coming from Central Asia challenged the integrity of the Empire. They were the

Huns, a nomadic people who had settled in the Hungarian plains. They had been displaced from their original lands and approached the Roman frontiers searching for the resources they needed to build their own Empire. The Huns attacked other Barbarian tribes like the Goths and the Burgundians in present-day France.

But the Huns weren't the Romans' only problem. They were simultaneously fighting the Vandals in Hispania and northern Africa. The Empire didn't have the powerful legions to move from one part to another, so taking the troops out of Italy left the old capital unprotected.

From 434 to 453, the Huns were led by Attila. He was called "the Scourge of God" because of the cruelty and violence he displayed toward the populations living in the Empire. Many considered his attacks on both the Eastern and Western Empires to be divine punishment. In 451, a Roman-Visigothic alliance defeated Attila at the Battle of the Catalaunian Plains in Gaul.

However, in 452, Attila and the Huns took advantage of Rome's weak defenses and launched an invasion of Italy that would have ended in Rome's destruction (Jarus, 2022). Emperor Valentinian III sent a delegation to meet Attila that included Pope Leo I (*What really stopped Atilla the Hun?* 2007).

It is uncertain what happened in that meeting. Some scholars suggest the Pope used Attila's superstitions against him. Alaric the Goth had sacked the city in 410 C.E. but had died shortly afterward.

Others believe that Rome was nothing but a pile of ruins and Attila searched for wealth in vain. Whatever happened between Attila and the Pope, the invasion stopped, and Attila turned his attention to the East. However, he could never accomplish his objective of attacking Byzantium because he died under mysterious circumstances on the night of his wedding in 453 (Jarus, 2022). The Hunnic coalition soon disintegrated.

Attila and the Huns didn't cause the Empire's collapse, but they exposed the fragility of its defenses. It was only a matter of time.

The Final Blow

By the time the Ostrogoths reached Rome in 476, the empire was barely a shadow of its former self. Besides the Huns, the Vandals and the Visigoths had also ravaged Italy, contributing to Rome's destruction.

The Visigoths under Alaric sacked Rome in 410 C.E. shortly after the emperor Honorius had moved the Western capital to Ravenna. However, they besieged Ravenna and compelled the emperor to pay tribute in exchange for an armistice. The Visigoths continued their migration and settled around Toulouse, France, where they founded their kingdom on the border of Italy.

The Vandals had crossed Europe from east to west, pushed by the Visigoths. The Romans attempted to keep them beyond their borders for decades, but they eventually crossed the Rhine and settled in Gaul, admitted as *foederati* in 405 C.E. However, the Vandals were again pushed by the Visigoths and crossed the Pyrenees to settle in Hispania in 409. Shortly after, they crossed to Africa, still under Roman power, and founded a kingdom in modern Tunisia.

At first, the Romans allowed the Vandal kingdom and split control of the coastline with them. But in 439, the Vandals surprisingly sacked Carthage. The Vandals' expansion wasn't over, and the Romans tried to ensure peace. The attempt failed and the

Vandals attacked Rome in 455. Just like when Attila had approached the gates of Rome three years before, Pope Leo I negotiated: The Vandals agreed not to kill the citizens, destroy buildings, or set the city on fire. In exchange, the gates of Rome were opened, and the invaders despoiled the Eternal City of treasures and carried off some of the citizens to slavery (Vulic, 2023).

Odoacer

During the 5th century, Rome was sacked on three occasions – first, by the Visigoths in 410, then by the Vandals in 455. In 476, Rome was ravaged again, but this time, the throne passed to a Barbarian king.

In 475, the Roman general Orestes was proclaimed *magister militum,* master of the army. Orestes wanted to control the throne, so he exiled emperor Julius Nepos and appointed his own young son, Romulus Augustulus, as the new emperor. Orestes lacked military support within Italy and the rest of the Western Empire; moreover, Constantinople refused to recognize Romulus as legitimate. Orestes only had his Barbarian *foederati* under Odoacer's command to rely on (*Odoacer and the Fall of Rome*, n.d.).

Scholars are unsure of Odoacer's origins, but he was likely Sciri (Mark, 2014). The Sciris (or Scirians) were a small Germanic tribe that had settled in present-day Poland and joined the Goths to fight the

Huns. Eventually, they were absorbed by the Ostrogoths, the tribe that moved into Italy as *foederati* and whom Odoacer now led (*Kingdoms of the Germanic Tribes*, n.d.).

In exchange for their support, the Barbarians demanded lands within Italy, but their request was denied because the area was already populated. Odoacer wasn't satisfied with Orestes' refusal to attend to their demands and raised his tribes against him. On August 23, 476, the Barbarians proclaimed Odoacer as their king and executed Orestes in Placentia (present-day Piacenza). Then they marched to Rome and deposed Romulus Agustulus, who was only a child. Odoacer seized power and named himself king, the first Barbarian king of Italy (Britannica Encyclopedia, 2023). The Western Empire was officially gone.

Essential Highlights

The Crisis of the 3rd Century dealt a death blow to the Roman Empire, but it took almost two more centuries to manifest its destructive effects. The emperors' attempts to save Rome were enough to hold the Eastern Empire, but the West couldn't resist the internal contradictions that undermined the traditional pillars of power. The thriving economy and a solid political authority no longer existed, and the army was more of a challenge to imperial integrity than the traditional backbone it had always been.

The Barbarians were already inside the empire. The series of successive Barbarian attacks on Rome wasn't the illness but the symptom. Odoacer only landed the final strike at what were already the ruins of the Roman Empire.

While the sun set on the Western Roman Empire, the embers of its civilization still burned brightly, influencing ages to come. As we journey toward the conclusion, let's reflect on Rome's enduring legacy and the indelible mark it left on all of human history. The spirit of Rome beckons you to delve deeper, to explore its enigmas and marvels, and to keep its memory alive.

Conclusion

Rome has grown since its humble beginnings, and it is now overwhelmed by its own greatness. –Titus Livius

The history of the Western world started thousands of years ago, in prehistoric times when people first learned to cultivate crops, organize themselves to build their houses and cities, and dominate nature. Ancient Italy was one of the epicenters where civilization as we know it took its first steps. The ancient Italic tribes are proof of the constant and uninterrupted progress of humankind. They built a long-lasting and flourishing culture that not only transcended the peninsula but also set the pace for the whole ancient world.

Romulus and Remus' mythical story was a precursor to what Rome was meant to be. Saved by the god Mars, they were destined to lead the kingdom that would rule the known world and expand it. Like most mythical stories of greatness, it required a touch of tragedy. Romulus assassinating his brother to be the only king was the prelude to the troubled history of Rome. It was the first stage of an alternation of splendor and crisis. For the ancient Romans, each moment of weakness became the perfect challenge to showcase resilience and emerge stronger and wiser.

Throughout these pages, we have seen Rome become a powerful kingdom and set the basis for most contemporary forms of political organization. We have witnessed how people fought for their rights to make law and justice the framework of social life during the Republic. The Romans didn't stop when they overcame their struggles and neither the rulers nor the common people settled for less. They sought glory and built the path to achieve it. It is a powerful lesson that still resonates whenever the name of the Eternal City is recalled.

The many centuries of the Roman Empire are a metaphor for human nature: How far ambition and conviction can take us, and how destructive both can be as well. Romans transformed the world and fell victim to their own changes. Despite the controversies that entailed their dominance of people and lands, it is unquestionable that they shaped the modern world, from Great Britain to the distant lands surrounding the Indus River in Asia. They had a vision and a purpose, and they triumphed, even after their collapse.

Ancient Rome's enduring legacy reaches us today. They remain one of the greatest empires in history for several reasons. Firstly, they covered vast territories at their peak. Additionally, they governed millions of people under their laws, who were categorized as subjects or citizens, a distinction created by the Empire and still relevant in contemporary societies. They imposed a Roman worldview but also embraced and blended with other cultures.

Extensive and multicultural, the Roman civilization lasted for almost 1,000 years in the West, and the Eastern Empire survived for another 1,000. Still, their legacy remains alive: "Roman inventions or innovations were so effective that they either continued in use or were later rediscovered to serve as models in virtually every aspect of human society, from the mundane to the sublime" (Mark, 2020). If we look around, we have inherited from the ancient Romans architectural and artistic styles, institutions, laws, and rights, a universal religion, and a language that is the root of many contemporary languages.

As the curtains draw on the grand narrative of Rome, remember: its legacy is not just in ruins and ancient texts but in the DNA of all the civilizations that followed. Don't let this be the end of your journey into Rome's majestic past. Dive deeper, explore more, and let the spirit of the Romans inspire you to greater understanding and wisdom. Let the history of Rome be a beacon, guiding you to uncharted territories of knowledge. Forge ahead, for many more tales are waiting to be discovered, and Rome's echoes call out to you!

The ancient Romans brought their culture and worldview with them wherever they went. They left their trace in every corner of the world where they settled their population or stationed their legions. They carried the light of civilization and spread the message of a thriving culture. Part of what we are today, wherever you are reading this, keeps the essence of the ancient Romans. We are compelled to continue with their mission and keep alive their legacy. *Valete*! (Farewell!)

Note to the Reader

Sharing sincere feedback is the best way to support (and improve) the work of independent publishers. If you enjoyed and found value in this book, please leave a review and invite others to learn about and reflect upon our common past to build a promising future.

References

10000 years of economy - Failure of the Gracchi's reforms. (n.d.). Citeco.fr. https://www.citeco.fr/10000-years-history-economics/antiquity-to-middle-ages/failure-of-the-gracchi-s-reforms#:~:text=He%20proposed%20an%20agricultural%20reform,charged%20with%20enacting%20the%20law

6.5: The Seven Kings. (2020, August 8). Chemistry LibreTexts. https://chem.libretexts.org/Courses/Lumen_Learning/Book%3A_Western_Civilization_(Lumen)/Ch._05_Early_Roman_Civilization_and_the_Roman_Republic/06.5%3A_The_Seven_Kings

Adam, B. (2023, November 27). *The Vandals, an infamous Germanic tribe that sacked Rome.* The Roman Empire. https://roman-empire.net/people/vandals/

Ancient Roman monarchy - (753 BC – 509 BC). (n.d.). Rome.net. https://www.rome.net/roman-monarchy#:~:text=Romulus%2C%20son%20of%20the%20god,Rome%20a%20body%20of%20laws

Ancient Roman monarchy: Timeline and overview. (2015, January 15). Study.com. https://study.com/academy/lesson/ancient-roman-monarchy-timeline-lesson-quiz.html.

Ancient Rome. Romulus and Remus. (2015, March 16). History Learning Site. https://www.historylearningsite.co.uk/ancient-rome/romulus-and-remus/#google_vignette

Ancient Rome—Early Republic. (n.d.). Heritage History. https://www.heritage-history.com/index.php?c=resources&s=study-qdiv&h=ancient_rome&f=republic

Ancos. (2018, June 11). *Italy 01: During Prehistory.* Life in Italy. https://lifeinitaly.com/italy-prehistoric/

Augustan army reforms. (n.d.). https://faculty.washington.edu/alain/CLAS.HSTAM330/ArmyReforms.html

Badian, E., Salmon, E.T., Forsythe, G.E., Ferguson, J., Hornblower, S., Vermeule, E.D. Townsend, P.P., MacMullen, Ramsay, S., Richard P., & Grummond, N.T. (n.d.). Ancient Rome. In *Encyclopedia Britannica*. Retrieved December 13, 2023 from https://www.britannica.com/place/ancient-Rome. Accessed 3 January 2024.

Barbarian origin, invasions and kingdoms. (2023, May 23). Study.com. https://study.com/academy/lesson/barbarians-history-invasions.html#:~:text=The%20term%20%22barbarian%22%20was%20used,downfall%20of%20the%20Roman%20Empire

Beard, M. (2018, October 7). *The collaborative and inclusive nature of the Roman Empire.* History Hit. https://www.historyhit.com/the-collaborative-and-inclusive-nature-of-the-roman-empire/

Becker, J. (n.d.). *Pompeii: House of the Vettii.* Smart History. https://smarthistory.org/pompeii-house-of-the-vettii/

Bellomo, M. (2022, June 12). *Dictator: The evolution of the Roman dictatorship.* BMCR. https://bmcr.brynmawr.edu/2022/2022.06.12/

Bennett, S. (n.d.). *The Iron Age.* Khan Academy. https://www.khanacademy.org/humanities/whp-origins/era-3-cities-societies-and-empires-6000-bce-to-700-c-e/32-long-distance-trade-betaa/a/read-the-iron-age-beta

Bileta, V. (2023, February 15). *What was the crisis of the Third Century?* The Collector. https://www.thecollector.com/what-was-the-crisis-of-the-third-century/

Bileta, V. (2023, February 20). *What was the Roman legion?* The Collector. https://www.thecollector.com/what-was-the-roman-legion/

Boissoneault, L. (2017, November 16). *Before the fall of the Roman Republic, income inequality and xenophobia*

threatened its foundations. Smithsonian Magazine.
https://www.smithsonianmag.com/history/fall-roman-republic-income-inequality-and-xenophobia-threatened-its-foundations-180967249/

Burks, A. M. (2008). *Roman Slavery: A Study of Roman Society and Its Dependence on slaves.* East Tennessee State University. Retrieved from https://dc.etsu.edu/cgi/viewcontent.cgi?article=3303&context=etd

Burns, R. (2022, May 19). *Cincinnatus: A Roman dictator's resounding impact.* Discentes. https://web.sas.upenn.edu/discentes/2022/05/19/cincinnatus-a-roman-dictators-resounding-impact/

Burns, R. (2023, November 21). *First Triumvirate | Definition, history and significance.* Study.com. https://study.com/learn/lesson/julius-caesar-the-first-triumvirate.html#:~:text=The%20First%20Triumvirate%20accomplished%20many,build%20his%20army%20in%20Gaul

Caesar's civil war: Ancient Rome destroys itself. (n.d.). History Skills. https://www.historyskills.com/classroom/ancient-history/anc-caesar-civil-war-reading/

Calvo, J. (2022, June 6). *La importancia de la inflación en la caída del Imperio romano.* El Economista. https://www.eleconomista.es/podcasts/noticias/1180105 5/06/22/La-importancia-de-la-inflacion-en-la-caida-del-Imperio-romano.html

Campbell, C.J. (2022, March 30). *Peace and prosperity: What was the Pax Romana?* The Collector. https://www.thecollector.com/what-was-pax-romana/

Carr, K. (2017, September 3). *Stone Age Italy – the history of Italy.* Quatr.us. https://quatr.us/history/stone-age-italy-history-italy.htm

Cartwright, M. (2017, September 1). Roman art. In *World History Encyclopedia.* https://www.worldhistory.org/Roman_Art/

Cartwright, M. (2018, April 12). Trade in the Roman world. In *World History Encyclopedia.*

https://www.worldhistory.org/article/638/trade-in-the-roman-world/

Chaliakopoulos, A. (2022, January 12). *Antiochus III the Great: The Seleucid king who took on Rome.* The Collector. https://www.thecollector.com/antiochus-iii-the-great-seleucid-king/

Chronology - Prehistory in Italy. (n.d.). Preistoria in Italia. https://www.preistoriainitalia.it/en/cronologia/

Comunale, J. (2023, November 21). *Etruscan religion, culture and influence.* Study.com. https://study.com/learn/lesson/etruscans-religion-culture.html

Crises of the Republic. (n.d.). Lumen Learning. https://courses.lumenlearning.com/atd-herkimer-westerncivilization/chapter/crises-of-the-republic/

Crises of the Roman Empire. (n.d.). Lumen Learning. https://courses.lumenlearning.com/atd-herkimer-westerncivilization/chapter/crises-of-the-roman-empire/#:~:text=Overview,%2C%20plague%2C%20and%20economic%20depression

Curiate Assembly (comitia curiata). (n.d.). Academic Dictionaries and Encyclopedias. https://en-academic.com/dic.nsf/enwiki/931745

David, J.L. (2013, March 25). The intervention of the Sabine women. In *World History Encyclopedia.* https://www.worldhistory.org/image/1125/the-intervention-of-the-sabine-women/#:~:text=by%20Jacques%2DLouis%20David&text=Fearing%20the%20emergence%20of%20a,the%20festival%20among%20Rome%27s%20neighbours

Did Christianity cause the fall of Rome? (n.d.). World Atlas. https://www.worldatlas.com/did-christianity-cause-the-fall-of-rome.html

Did stoicism have any influence on Ancient Rome? (n.d.). Stoic Simple. https://www.stoicsimple.com/did-stoicism-have-any-influence-on-ancient-rome/

Diocletian and the tetrarchy. (n.d.). Lumen Learning. https://courses.lumenlearning.com/atd-herkimer-westerncivilization/chapter/diocletian-and-the-tetrarchy/

Dyck, L.H. (n.d.). *The Gallic Wars: To northern Gaul*. Warfare History Network.
https://warfarehistorynetwork.com/the-gallic-wars-to-northern-gaul/

Etruscans: civilization, history and influence on Rome. (n.d.). TimeMaps.
https://timemaps.com/civilizations/etruscans/

Ferguson, J. & Balsdon, J. (n.d.). Cicero. In *Encyclopedia Britannica*. Retrieved November 25, 2023, from
https://www.britannica.com/biography/Cicero

Ferguson, J., Forsythe, G.E., Petit, P., Saller, R.P., Badian, E., MacMullen, R., Vermeule, E.D., Grummond, N., Hornblower, S., & Salmon, E.T. (n.d.). Ancient Rome. In *Encyclopedia Britannica*. Retrieved November 9, 2023, from https://www.britannica.com/place/ancient-Rome

Fernandes, F. (2022, March 14). *How to establish an empire: The Emperor Augustus transforms Rome*. The Collector.
https://www.thecollector.com/augustus-transforms-rome-empire/

Frye, D. (2007, March 5). *Rome's Barbarian mercenaries*. Historynet. https://www.historynet.com/romes-barbarian-mercenaries/

Fuhrmann, C. (2011, December). *"I brought peace to the provinces": Augustus and the Rhetoric of Imperial Peace*. doi.org/10.1093/acprof:oso/9780199737840.003.0004

Garcia, B. (2018, April 18). Romulus and Remus. In *World History Encyclopedia*.
https://www.worldhistory.org/Romulus_and_Remus/

Gazioğlu, H.H. (n.d.). *The "barbarization" of the Roman army*. Academia.edu.
https://www.academia.edu/36861074/_THE_BARBARIZATION_OF_THE_ROMAN_ARMY

Gill, N.S. (2019, February 17). *Who were the early kings of Rome?* ThoughtCo. https://www.thoughtco.com/the-early-kings-of-rome-119374

Gill, N.S. (2019, July 1). *Economic reasons for the fall of Rome*. ThoughtCo.
https://www.thoughtco.com/economic-reasons-for-fall-of-rome-118357

Gill, N.S. (2021, February 16). *Who were the Gracchi brothers of ancient Rome?* ThoughtCo. thoughtco.com/gracchi-brothers-tiberius-gaius-gracchus-112494.

Grant, M. (n.d.). Horace. In *Encyclopedia Britannica*. Retrieved November 27, 2023, from https://www.britannica.com/biography/Horace-Roman-poet

Harding, S.B. (n.d.). *City of the Seven Hills*. Heritage History. https://www.heritage-history.com/index.php?c=read&author=harding&book=seven&story=fabii

Hellie, R. (n.d.). Slavery. In *Encyclopedia Britannica*. Retrieved November 21, 2023, from https://www.britannica.com/topic/slavery-sociology

Henderson, M.M. (1968). Tiberius Gracchus and the failure of the Roman republic. *Theoria: A Journal of Social and Political Theory*, *31*, 51–64. http://www.jstor.org/stable/41801828

History.com Editors. (2023, June 16). *Constantinople*. History.com. https://www.history.com/topics/middle-east/constantinople

Hoffmann, J. (n.d.). Appius Claudius Caecus. Encyclopedia.com. https://www.encyclopedia.com/science/encyclopedias-almanacs-transcripts-and-maps/appius-claudius-caecus

How did the Etruscans shape Roman history and society. (n.d.). DailyHistory.org. https://www.dailyhistory.org/How_did_the_Etruscans_shape_Roman_history_and_society

How the First Triumvirate changed ancient Rome. (n.d.). History Skills. https://www.historyskills.com/classroom/ancient-history/anc-1st-triumvirate-reading/

Ides of March: The Death of Caesar. (n.d.). Penelope.uchicago.edu. https://penelope.uchicago.edu/~grout/encyclopaedia_romana/calendar/ides.html

Jarus, O. (2022, September 2). *Attila the Hun: Biography of the 'Scourge of God.'* Live Science. https://www.livescience.com/44417-attila-the-hun.html

Jasiński, J. (2019, February 18). *I found Rome a city of bricks and left it a city of marble.* Imperium Romanum. https://imperiumromanum.pl/en/curiosities/i-found-rome-a-city-of-bricks-and-left-it-a-city-of-marble/

Jasiński, J. (2020, April 18). *Values professed by Romans.* Imperium Romanum. https://imperiumromanum.pl/en/curiosities/values-professed-by-romans/#:~:text=Values%20%E2%80%8B%E2%80%8Bfor%20the,%2C%20meaning%20%E2%80%9Chusband%E2%80%9D

Kamash, Z. Shipley, L., Galaakis, Y. & Skaltsa, S. (2013). *Iron Age and Roman Italy.* In World Archeology at the Pitts Rivers Museum: A Characterization. Archaeopress, p. 336-357. http://archaeopress.com/Public/download.asp?id=%7B30DA1356-8CE5-467F-AD80-B67B30B82EA6%7D#:~:text=16.4%20Iron%20Age%20Italy&text=The%20Etruscan%20Iron%20Age%20material,and%20ceramics%20(43%20examples)

Kenney, E.J. (n.d.). Ovid. In *Encyclopedia Britannica.* Retrieved January 1, 2024, from https://www.britannica.com/biography/Ovid-Roman-poet

Kershaw, D. (2023, August 29). *The Twelve Tables: The foundation of Roman law.* History Cooperative. https://historycooperative.org/the-twelve-tables/

Kessler, P. & Dawson, E. (2019, January 11). *Iron Age Italy 800-400 BC.* The History Files. https://www.historyfiles.co.uk/FeaturesEurope/ItalyIronAge01.htm

Kessler, P. (n.d.). *Early Italy (Iron Age).* The History Files. https://www.historyfiles.co.uk/KingListsEurope/ItalyCulturesIronAge.htm

Kinder, H. & Hilgemann, W. (1996). World Historic Atlas. ISTMO

Kindy, D. (2021, September 29). *Where did the ancient Etruscans come from?* Smithsonian Magazine. https://www.smithsonianmag.com/smart-news/dna-analysis-shows-early-etruscans-were-homegrown-180978772/#:~:text=Before%20the%20glory%20of%20Rome,the%20known%20world%20for%20centuries

Kingdoms of the Germanic Tribes - Scirii. (n.d.). The History Files. https://www.historyfiles.co.uk/KingListsEurope/BarbarianScirii.htm

Lakha, S. (n.d.). *Overcoming ancient history challenges-Common problems and solutions.* Spires.co. https://spires.co/online-ancient-history-tutors/undergraduate/overcoming-ancient-history-challenges-common-problems-and-solutions

Latins. (n.d.). Oxford Reference. https://www.oxfordreference.com/display/10.1093/oi/authority.20110803100053207

Lecture 26: Fall of the Roman Republic, 133-27 BC. (n.d.). web.ics.purdue.edu. https://web.ics.purdue.edu/~rauhn/fall_of_republic.htm#:~:text=Internal%20turmoil%20provoked%20in%20133,Republic%2C%20133%2D27%20BC

Lendering, J. (2019, April 26). *Second Triumvirate.* Livius.org. https://www.livius.org/articles/concept/triumvir/second-triumvirate/

Lesso, R. (2022, July 1). *What Are the Origins of Stoicism?* The Collector. https://www.thecollector.com/what-are-the-origins-of-stoicism-history/

Lloyd, J. (2013, April 30). Roman army. In *World History Encyclopedia.* https://www.worldhistory.org/Roman_Army/

Malvasi, M. (2023, October 15). *A message from Rome.* The Imaginative Conservative. https://theimaginativeconservative.org/2023/10/message-rome-mark-malvasi.html

Mandal, D. (2023, June 19). *25 Incredible ancient Roman quotes you should know.* Realm of History.

https://www.realmofhistory.com/2023/06/19/25-ancient-roman-quotes/

Marcus Tullius Cicero. (n.d.). In times of war. Goodreads. https://www.goodreads.com/quotes/49233-in-times-of-war-the-law-falls-silent-silent-enim

Mark, J. (2014, September 20). Odoacer. In *World History Encyclopedia.* https://www.worldhistory.org/Odoacer/

Mark, J. (2017, November 9). The crisis of the Third Century. In *World History Encyclopedia.* https://www.worldhistory.org/Crisis_of_the_Third_Century/

McDonald, A.H. (n.d.). Tacitus. In Encyclopedia Britannica. Retrieved December 1, 2023, from https://www.britannica.com/biography/Tacitus-Roman-historian

Menenius. (n.d.). Heritage History. https://www.heritage-history.com/index.php?c=resources&s=char-dir&f=menenius

Montoya, R. (2022, May 3). *The 30 most important Roman structures that you can visit today.* The Tour Guy. https://thetourguy.com/travel-blog/italy/rome/most-important-roman-structures-that-you-can-visit-today/

Nuragic monuments of Sardinia. (n.d.). UNESCO World Heritage Centre. https://whc.unesco.org/en/tentativelists/6557/#:~:text=Nuragic%20cultural%20heritage%20of%20Bronze,extra%20classic%20constructions%20of%20any

Odoacer and the Fall of Rome. (n.d.). Lumen Learning. https://courses.lumenlearning.com/atd-herkimer-westerncivilization/chapter/odoacer-and-the-fall-of-rome/

Ogilvie, Robert Maxwell. "Livy". Encyclopedia Britannica, 1 Jan. 2023, https://www.britannica.com/biography/Livy. Accessed 6 December 2023.

Phelan, J. (2022, September 25). *Why did the Roman Empire split in two?* Live Science. https://www.livescience.com/why-roman-empire-split-in-two

Rocess, G. (2019, November 12). *History is filled with the sound of silken slippers*. Medium.com. https://glennrocess.medium.com/history-is-filled-with-the-sound-of-silken-slippers-going-downstairs-and-wooden-shoes-coming-up-a3bf57f544f3

Roman culture and the Aeneid. (n.d.). Faculty.gvsu.edu. https://faculty.gvsu.edu/websterm/Aeneid.htm

Roman Emperors during Pax Romana: 27BC to 180AD timeline. (n.d.). Timetoast. https://www.timetoast.com/timelines/roman-emperors-during-pax-romana-27bc-to-180ad

Roman Empire politics | Political reasons for the fall of Rome. (n.d.). Ancient Rome. https://mariamilani.com/ancient_rome/political-aspects-in-the-fall-of-the-roman-empire.htm

Roman Republic. (2023, October 19). National Geographic Society. https://education.nationalgeographic.org/resource/roman-republic/

Rome Geography. (n.d.). History Histories. http://www.historyshistories.com/rome-geography.html

Romulus and Remus: Story of the Founding of Rome. (2016, March 24). Retrieved from https://study.com/academy/lesson/romulus-and-remus-story-of-the-founding-of-rome.html.

Sal. (2020, November 14). *The rape of the Sabine women*. Medium.com. https://medium.com/lessons-from-history/the-rape-of-the-sabine-women-907950335319

Saunders, J.L. (n.d.). Stoicism. In *Encyclopedia Britannica*. Retrieved November 9, 2023, from https://www.britannica.com/topic/Stoicism

Schultz, C. E., Ward, A. M., Heichelheim, F. M., & Yeo, C. A. (2019). Early Roman Society, Religion, and Values. In *A History of the Roman People* (7th ed.). Routledge. Retrieved from https://pressbooks.claremont.edu/clas112pomonavalentine/chapter/94/

Servile Wars. (n.d.). Heritage History. https://www.heritage-history.com/index.php?c=resources&s=war-dir&f=wars_servile

Shaw, G. (2015, March 27). *Stone-age Italians defleshed their dead*. Science. https://www.science.org/content/article/stone-age-italians-defleshed-their-dead

Stanfield, J. (2023, October 19). *Julius Caesar*. National Geographic. https://education.nationalgeographic.org/resource/julius-caesar/

Sterling, D. (n.d.). *Julius Caesar versus Pompey: A civil war of subterfuge*. Warfare History Network. https://warfarehistorynetwork.com/julius-caesar-vs-pompey-a-civil-war-of-subterfuge/

Taylor, L. (n.d.). *The Etruscans, an introduction*. Khan Academy. https://www.khanacademy.org/humanities/ap-art-history/ancient-mediterranean-ap/ap-ancient-etruria/a/the-etruscans-an-introduction

Teach democracy. (n.d.). Constitutional Rights Foundation. https://www.crf-usa.org/bill-of-rights-in-action/bria-23-3-b-cicero-defender-of-the-roman-republic

The Cursus Publicus: The courier service of the Roman Empire. (n.d.). History of Information. https://www.historyofinformation.com/detail.php?id=1394

The Editors of Encyclopedia Britannica. (n.d.). Appius Claudius Caecus. In *Encyclopedia Britannica*. Retrieved January 2, 2024, from https://www.britannica.com/biography/Appius-Claudius-Caecus

The Editors of Encyclopedia Britannica. (n.d.). Barbarian. In *Encyclopedia Britannica*. Retrieved January 4, 2024, from https://www.britannica.com/topic/barbarian-invasions

The Editors of Encyclopedia Britannica. (n.d.). Battle of Actium. In *Encyclopedia Britannica*. Retrieved January

4, 2024, from https://www.britannica.com/event/Battle-of-Actium-ancient-Roman-history

The Editors of Encyclopedia Britannica. (n.d.). Colosseum. In *Encyclopedia Britannica*. Retrieved January 3, 2024, from https://www.britannica.com/topic/Colosseum

The Editors of Encyclopedia Britannica. (n.d.). Five Good Emperors. In *Encyclopedia Britannica*. Retrieved January 3, 2024, from https://www.britannica.com/topic/Five-Good-Emperors

The Editors of Encyclopedia Britannica. (n.d.). Gnaeus Marcius Coriolanus. In *Encyclopedia Britannica*. Retrieved January 2, 2024, from https://www.britannica.com/topic/Gnaeus-Marcius-Coriolanus

The Editors of Encyclopedia Britannica. (n.d.). Latifundium. In *Encyclopedia Britannica*. Retrieved January 2, 2024, from https://www.britannica.com/topic/latifundium

The Editors of Encyclopedia Britannica. (n.d.). Latin League. In *Encyclopedia Britannica*. Retrieved January 2, 2024, from https://www.britannica.com/topic/Latin-League

The Editors of Encyclopedia Britannica. (n.d.). Lucius Cornelius Cinna. In *Encyclopedia Britannica*. Retrieved January 2, 2024, from https://www.britannica.com/biography/Lucius-Cornelius-Cinna

The Editors of Encyclopedia Britannica. (n.d.). Macedonian wars. In *Encyclopedia Britannica*. Retrieved January 2, 2024, from https://www.britannica.com/event/Macedonian-Wars

The Editors of Encyclopedia Britannica. (n.d.). Odoacer. In *Encyclopedia Britannica*. Retrieved January 2, 2024, from https://www.britannica.com/biography/Odoacer

The Editors of Encyclopedia Britannica. (n.d.). Pompey the Great. In *Encyclopedia Britannica*. Retrieved January 2, 2024, from https://www.britannica.com/biography/Pompey-the-Great

The Editors of Encyclopedia Britannica. (n.d.). Province. In *Encyclopedia Britannica*. Retrieved January 2, 2024, from https://www.britannica.com/topic/province-ancient-Roman-government

The Editors of Encyclopedia Britannica. (n.d.). Punic Wars summary. In *Encyclopedia Britannica*. Retrieved January 2, 2024, from https://www.britannica.com/summary/Punic-Wars

The Editors of Encyclopedia Britannica. (n.d.). Punic Wars. In *Encyclopedia Britannica*. Retrieved January 2, 2024, from https://www.britannica.com/event/Punic-Wars/Campaigns-in-Sicily-and-Spain

The Editors of Encyclopedia Britannica. (n.d.). Roman Empire. In *Encyclopedia Britannica*. Retrieved January 3, 2024, from https://www.britannica.com/place/Roman-Empire

The Editors of Encyclopedia Britannica. (n.d.). Roman Republic. In *Encyclopedia Britannica*. Retrieved January 2, 2024, from https://www.britannica.com/place/Roman-Republic

The Editors of Encyclopedia Britannica. (n.d.). Romulus and Remus. In *Encyclopedia Britannica*. Retrieved January 2, 2024, from https://www.britannica.com/biography/Romulus-and-Remus

The Editors of Encyclopedia Britannica. (n.d.). Sabine. In *Encyclopedia Britannica*. Retrieved January 2, 2024, from https://www.britannica.com/topic/Sabine

The Editors of Encyclopedia Britannica. (n.d.). Senate. In *Encyclopedia Britannica*. Retrieved January 2, 2024, from https://www.britannica.com/topic/Senate-Roman-history

The Editors of Encyclopedia Britannica. (n.d.). Social wars. In *Encyclopedia Britannica*. Retrieved January 2, 2024, from https://www.britannica.com/event/Social-War-Roman-history

The Editors of Encyclopedia Britannica. (n.d.). Tanaquil. In *Encyclopedia Britannica*. Retrieved January 2, 2024, from https://www.britannica.com/biography/Tanaquil

The Editors of Encyclopedia Britannica. (n.d.). Titus Tatius. In *Encyclopedia Britannica*. Retrieved January 2, 2024, from https://www.britannica.com/topic/Titus-Tatius

The fall of Rome. (n.d.). Students of History. https://www.studentsofhistory.com/the-fall-of-rome#:~:text=Many%20of%20the%20issues%20that,poor%20struggled%20to%20find%20work

The geography of ancient Rome. (n.d.). Students of History. https://www.studentsofhistory.com/geography-of-the-roman-world

The Italian Bronze Age. (n.d.). Encyclopedia.com. https://www.encyclopedia.com/humanities/encyclopedias-almanacs-transcripts-and-maps/italian-bronze-age

The Punic Wars versus Carthage. (n.d.). Students of History. https://www.studentsofhistory.com/the-punic-wars#:~:text=The%20Third%20Punic%20War%20was,going%20to%20war%20with%20Numidia

The Roman Empire: A Brief History. (n.d.). Milwaukee Public Museum. https://www.mpm.edu/research-collections/anthropology/anthropology-collections-research/mediterranean-oil-lamps/roman-empire-brief-history#:~:text=The%20history%20of%20the%20Roman,31%20BC%20%E2%80%93%20AD%20476

The Roman kingdom (753–509 BC). (n.d.). Digital Maps of the Ancient World. https://digitalmapsoftheancientworld.com/ancient-history/history-ancient-rome/the-roman-kingdom-753-509-bc/#:~:text=Also%20referred%20to%20as%20the,Palatine%20hill%20in%20753%20BC

The Sabines: A glimpse into an ancient Italic tribe. (2023, March 19). Weird Italy. https://weirditaly.com/2023/03/19/the-sabines-a-glimpse-into-an-ancient-italic-tribe/

The Second Triumvirate: The ruthless alliance that finally brought the Roman Republic to its end. (n.d.). History Skills. https://www.historyskills.com/classroom/ancient-history/second-triumvirate-reading/

The Seven Kings. (n.d.). Lumen Learning. https://courses.lumenlearning.com/atd-herkimer-westerncivilization/chapter/the-seven-kings/

The Shift East. (n.d.). Lumen Learning.
https://courses.lumenlearning.com/atd-herkimer-westerncivilization/chapter/the-shift-east/

The Struggle of the Orders: Plebeians and patricians. (2016, November 2). Retrieved from https://study.com/academy/lesson/the-struggle-of-the-orders-plebeians-and-patricians.html.

The Struggle of the Orders: Plebeians unite to lift their shackles. (n.d.). Sites.psu.edu. https://sites.psu.edu/struggleoftheorders/

Traces of Ancient Rome in the Modern World. (n.d.). National Geographic. https://education.nationalgeographic.org/resource/traces-ancient-rome-modern-world/

Valgiglio, E. (n.d.). Sulla. In *Encyclopedia Britannica.* Retrieved December 14, 2023, from https://www.britannica.com/biography/Sulla

Vandiver, T. (n.d.). *Revelations of Rome in Virgil's Aeneid.* https://hilo.hawaii.edu/campuscenter/hohonu/volumes/documents/Vol06x16RevelationsofRomeinVirgilsAeneid.pdf

Vermeulen, M. (2020, August 1). *The Roman Senate: An in-depth understanding.* The Collector. https://www.thecollector.com/roman-senate/

Vernon, J. (2023, March 14). *The Ides of March—a day of murder that forever changed history.* National Geographic. https://www.nationalgeographic.com/history/article/julius-caesar-ides-of-march

Virginia. (n.d.). Heritage History. https://www.heritage-history.com/index.php?c=resources&s=char-dir&f=virginia

Vuckovic, A. (2023, June 25). *Numa Pompilius: The legendary second king of Rome.* Ancient Origins. https://www.ancient-origins.net/history-famous-people/numa-pompilius-0018697

Vulic, V. (2023, June 10). *Roman Empire map: Unveiling its vast territory.* The Roman Empire. https://roman-empire.net/maps/map-of-ancient-rome/

Vulic, V. (2023, November 27). *Uncovering the causes and legacy of the fall of Rome*. The Roman Empire. https://roman-empire.net/decline/uncovering-the-causes-and-legacy-of-the-fall-of-rome/

Wasson, D. (2016, April 18). Second Triumvirate. In *World History Encyclopedia*. https://www.worldhistory.org/Second_Triumvirate/

Whelan, E. (2020, July 8). *Romulus and Remus: Murder and the foundation of Rome*. Classical Wisdom. https://classicalwisdom.com/mythology/romulus-and-remus-murder-and-the-foundation-of-rome/

White, A. (2011). *The role of Marius's military reforms in the decline of the Roman Republic*. https://wou.edu/history/files/2015/08/andrewwhite.pdf

Williams, R. (2022, December 11). *The Sicilian slave revolts of ancient Rome*. Medium.com. https://medium.com/lessons-from-history/the-sicilian-slave-revolts-of-ancient-rome-22196981315e

Winters, R. (2019, January 14). *The seven kings of Rome: Tumultuous origins of the Roman Republic*. Ancient Origins. https://www.ancient-origins.net/history-famous-people/seven-kings-rome-tumultuous-origins-roman-republic-008821#google_vignette

Zhou, W. (2015). *The Roman Army: Strategy, Tactics, and Innovation*. Young Historians Conference. Portland State University. https://pdxscholar.library.pdx.edu/cgi/viewcontent.cgi?referer=&httpsredir=1&article=1075&context=younghistorians

Image References

Barskefranck. (2019, August 28). *Roman arena antique Coliseum*. [Image]. Pixabay. https://pixabay.com/photos/roman-arena-antique-coliseum-4436335/

Carlos Felipe Ramírez Mesa. (2022, September 10). *A statue of a bear and several baby bears.* [Image]. Unsplash. https://unsplash.com/photos/a-statue-of-a-bear-and-several-baby-bears-WwujhyrZH30

Dozemode. (2019, March 27). *Roman chariot race Rome Colloseum.* [Image]. Pixabay. https://pixabay.com/photos/-4086569/

Efrye. (2015, February 7). *Julius Caesar statue Italy.* [Image]. Pixabay. https://pixabay.com/photos/julius-caesar-caesar-statue-italy-626422/

Eugenio Barboza. (2020, November 4). *Art, Italy, statue.* [Image]. Pexels. https://www.pexels.com/es-es/foto/arte-italia-estatua-escultura-5793604/

Fabio Fistarol. (2021, January 13). *Aerial view of city buildings during daytime.* [Image]. Unsplash. https://unsplash.com/photos/aerial-view-of-city-buildings-during-daytime-t6BTXRe5BRc

Gioia Maurizi. (2022, February 26). *A very tall building with lots of columns.* [Image]. Unsplash. https://unsplash.com/photos/a-very-tall-building-with-lots-of-columns-4jQRmAUiffY

Gioele Fazzeri. (2021, April 30). *Man in gray and black suit holding brown wooden stick.* [Image]. Unsplash. https://unsplash.com/photos/man-in-gray-and-black-suit-holding-brown-wooden-stick-VPrcvxP9aUw

Ha110k. (2019, November 2). *Horse soldier warrior war battle.* [Image]. Pixabay. https://pixabay.com/photos/horse-soldier-warrior-war-battle-4596827/

JOE Planas. (2022, March 14). *A tall white tower with a clock on top of it.* [Image]. Unsplash. https://unsplash.com/photos/a-tall-white-tower-with-a-clock-on-top-of-it-kDiYOROr8vU

Maria Teneva. (2023, December 14). *A path going up a hill on a foggy day.* [Image] Unsplash. https://unsplash.com/photos/a-path-going-up-a-hill-on-a-foggy-day-TfeJqoie5dQ

Marina Gr. (2021, October 7). *Art architecture statue*. [Image]. Pexels. https://www.pexels.com/es-es/foto/arte-arquitectura-estatua-al-aire-libre-9818108/

Matteo del Piano. (2023, March 16). *The ruins of a Roman city lit up at night*. [Image]. Unsplash. https://unsplash.com/photos/the-ruins-of-a-roman-city-lit-up-at-night-Lfo7YMVHYA8

Photos_Marta. (2018, April 6). *Coins Roman coins money*. [Image]. Pixabay. https://pixabay.com/photos/-3298260/

PublicDomainPictures. (2012, February 27). *Ancient Roman Empire armor Caesar*. [Image]. Pixabay. https://pixabay.com/photos/ancient-roman-empire-armor-caesar-18496/

Richardprins. (2011). *Map of ancient Rome, showing the Servian wall with a blue line, and the Aurelian wall with a red line. Highlands are shown in pink (including the Seven Hills of Rome, with names) and lowlands are shown in white*. [Map]. Retrieved from https://commons.wikimedia.org/wiki/File:Map_of_ancient_Rome.svg

Ridoe. (2017, July 11). *Pont-Du-Gard Nimes*. [Image]. Pixabay. https://pixabay.com/photos/pont-du-gard-nimes-arles-ales-2493762/

Stephanie Klepacki. (2023, May 12). *A statue of a woman in a park*. [Image]. Unsplash. https://unsplash.com/photos/a-statue-of-a-woman-in-a-park-J7Jn2Vn1Xjs

Sweetaholic. (2020, January 23). *Hadrians' Wall Roman wall*. [Image]. Pixabay. https://pixabay.com/photos/hadrians-wall-roman-wall-4788570/

The_Double_A. (2017, January 31). *Colosseum Rome city Roman Coliseum*. [Image]. Pixabay. https://pixabay.com/photos/-2030643/

Travelspot. (2015, April 3). *Italy necropolis Etruscan dig*. [Image]. Pixabay. https://pixabay.com/photos/italy-necropolis-etruscan-dig-704870/

www.ingramcontent.com/pod-product-compliance
Lightning Source LLC
Chambersburg PA
CBHW070858120626
46546CB00001B/45